I'm Just Here For The Layovers

JOE THOMAS

Joe Thomas writes a blog called Flight Attendant Joe
www.flightattendantjoe.com

Also by Joe Thomas

Fasten Your Seat Belts
And Eat Your Fucking Nuts

Flight Attendant Joe

I dedicate this book to

_____

(Fill In Your Name)

List of Pairings

THE BOARDING ANNOUNCEMENT

You are about to enter a world of espionage, mystery, and suspense. Within the pages of this book, you will be drawn into a reality that few have experienced. Dive deep and immerse yourself into my adventures that will have you on the edge of your seat, clutching your pearls, and hanging on for dear life.

I am kidding. This book is filled with inappropriate language, humor, and anecdotes that will highly offend some people. In layman's terms, if you don't appreciate a decent dick joke or a downright offensive Catholic priest one-liner, I recommend passing this book along to your friend who does.

I won't be offended; I promise. In fact, I'll wait for a few seconds while you hand the book over.

Are we good? Excellent. Spoiler alert, this book is filled with more than tasteless tales from my life as a flight attendant, but if a reader frowns upon offensive language, they will never get through this entire book. I'm doing everyone a favor by giving them a quick out.

Yes, I'm thoughtful and kind. You're welcome.

Honestly, I'd hate for a reader to be repulsed by my words when I'm merely attempting to make light of the airline industry with humor and language most horny teenage boys use during a circle-jerk at summer camp.

A popular question asked by passengers who meet me in the galley while they finish up their mid-flight yoga pose, or wait for their turn for the lavatory tends to be, "Is this your usual route?" I hate to burst your fantasy bubble, but there is no usual route that flight attendants or pilots operate in 2019. That may have been the case in 1962 when you boarded a TWA flight from Idlewild to Orly Airport, but those days disappeared along with mini skirts and cockpit blow jobs.

In the golden age of air travel, a seasoned flight attendant may have answered, "I fly the Tokyo route." In this day and age, flight attendants and pilots have routes they prefer to fly, and they do their best to obtain those trips.

Let me contradict myself for a minute: I promise you there will be a flight attendant who reads this, throws her hands in the air, and dramatically exclaims, "He's full of shit. I do the Sydney flight five times a month. That's my route."

And she's right. There's a small percentage of fossilized flight attendants who spent time serving Howard Hughes on flights to Las Vegas who still work the same route, every week of every month of every year. And to those ladies I say, congratulations. You watched the Wright Brothers take flight on December 17, 1903, and stood in line applying to become stewardesses on December 18, 1903. You ladies— and a few men—have seen more pilot cock than the doctors who conduct the pilots' yearly flight physicals.

Being a flight attendant today isn't a lifestyle, it's a job. The airline industry is all about seniority, and we work whatever our seniority holds. I understand passengers ask this question to strike up a random conversation, but please stop. We don't have time to deal with alcoholics, medical emergencies, setting up beverage carts, and explaining the ins and outs of airline scheduling to you because you're killing time waiting for the lavatory.

From this point onward, all airline passengers need to remember is this: flight attendant and pilot trips change weekly and monthly. I can be in Seattle tonight, Las Vegas tomorrow night, and then Tampa the next night.

Make sense? Wonderful.

Writing is cathartic. It clears my head and gives me a sense of importance. In 1839, English author Edward Bulwer-Lytton coined the phrase "the pen is mightier than the sword," which meant, written language is more effective than direct violence. Although the idea of smacking stupid people around all day is enticing, it's easier to write down my frustrations and avoid jail time for bitch-slapping some asshole on Twitter who can't spell Kentucky. Writing, specifically, documenting my experiences in a journal, has evolved into an alternative for expensive therapy.

I keep separate journals for different aspects of my life. They're broken down into three areas: personal vacations, random experiences, and my life as a flight attendant. I encourage everyone to purchase a journal and start documenting their feelings. If you don't want to carry around a journal, use the note app on your cell phone. When I'm flying, and a situation occurs that I'll want to remember, but my cell phone is in my tote bag, I grab napkins and start jotting down details. When I'm on the jumpseat writing in my journal, I am often approached by co-workers and passengers who are intrigued that I journal.

A recent conversation went something like this, "You write in a journal? That's cool. I've thought about starting that, but I don't have time. Do you write a lot?"

I smirked, "I dabble."

This book was inspired by my journal entries between 2015 and 2017. I wrote this book to invite the reader to join me in my daily life as a flight attendant and follow along on my pairings. What are pairings? Pairings are the term the airline industry uses to describe the sequence of flights the flight attendants and pilots operate during a certain number of days that duty on and off at their base airport. I wanted readers to walk side by side with me on this journey. The early report times, the fatigue, the asshole passengers, the pleasant passengers, the bitchy flight attendants, the undercover dick pilots, the delayed flights, the amazing layovers, the shitty hotels, the questionable airline management, and the stumbling drunk adventures. All of it.

I guarantee there will he flight attendants who read this book and disagree with my description of life in the airline industry. There are flight attendants who love their job. Corner them, and they'll describe spending six hours at the airport on a delay with no hotel as an adventure. They believe waiting an hour for a hotel room on a short ten-hour layover allows them to appreciate when they are assigned a hotel room in five minutes. They smile when passengers order coffee on a thirty-minute flight and injure their backs lifting fifty-pound suitcases for someone half their age. They are enchanted by the idea of being a flight attendant.

You will quickly realize that I am not. I may not even like being a flight attendant anymore.

In fact, I may hate it, which makes sense because I'm just here for the layovers.

PAIRING 001: FLOPPY DISK

Sunday
SFO—LAX—MCO

I'm always surprised when I wake up at 4:30 A.M., and I'm not ready to commit murder. I guess the smoker who lives below us is lucky because if I'm going to kill someone, it's going to be the fucker who smokes on the patio downstairs.

Dreamt last night that I worked sweeping floors in a large warehouse. Maybe that's a foreshadowing of what's to come when I eventually get terminated. Perhaps it was a prison instead of a warehouse.

I should probably stop thinking about murder.

I always check to confirm my commute flight is on-time before I leave the house; I never have much faith. Nobody who flies on an airplane should depend on their plane to depart on time. Well, maybe billionaires who own their own jets, but for the 99% of the population who are not filthy rich, we shouldn't have high expectations. The rest of us should anticipate our flights will always be late, that way when the flight departs on time, we'll be pleasantly surprised.

At the house, the flight was scheduled to depart on time, but when I arrived at the airport, the flight was delayed. The same thing happened to me last week. Last week it was a weather delay. Today, they had to update the navigation system, and the pilot literally used the words "floppy disk" when he made a PA to all the passengers. I'm concerned that my cell phone has better navigation than the airplane.

Because of our two-hour floppy disk delay, I missed taking a nap and ultimately my day was as painful as an airplane television frozen on Fox News for the entire flight. When I walked into the lounge, it was buzzing with loud pilots complaining about something. I honestly couldn't tell you what they were talking about because they sounded like toddlers with full diapers at daycare. I've never heard people complain as much as pilots and I've seen gay guys accidentally spill their ecstasy tablets down the drain.

One of the flight attendants I'm working with, Coco, asked to switch positions with me and I immediately wanted to advise him I'm versatile and can handle any position. It was the first time I had met him, so I held that back. No need to scare co-workers before we're on the airplane. I like to ease people into my crazy like a thick girl eases into a bathing suit. We called Crew Scheduling, and I switched positions with him so he could be the lead flight attendant. To be honest, I didn't want to deal with boarding.

Our flight was delayed because—wait for it—one of the pilots overslept this morning and caused a delay which had a ripple effect for the rest of the day.

The gate agent asked, "What happens when pilots and flight attendants cause a delay?"

I sarcastically answered, "Pilots get a reminder to set their alarms, flight attendants get removed off their trip and get beat down so bad they need a wheelchair to get through the airport."

She laughed. I shook my head.

I stalked the guy in 9C the entire flight. His girlfriend was hanging all over him, and I wanted to strangle her with the oxygen mask from the demo kit, but going to jail because 9C was hot is not part of my plan.

Again with the murder.

I'm getting along with my crew, but that's because we're all gay and none of us are nasty queens. I dislike working with nasty queens, and my airline could have a sale on them.

When we got to the hotel, it was a quick poop, a rapid costume change, and then a few drinks in Coco's room before we walked over to a local bar. Flight attendants definitely know how to party. I only stayed out for an hour because another flight attendant—a friend of Coco's—joined us and all she did was bash the airline. I found that amusing seeing she's been out on disability for almost year. How bad can you hate a job that you haven't done in a year? I'd willingly work a flight to Ft. Myers than listen to this chick complain about work she hasn't done in the past twelve months. Her negativity overpowered my slight buzz, and I quickly made up an excuse to abandon them and head back to my hotel room. I'm cynical enough, I don't need someone else's negativity bringing me down.

Monday
MCO—LAX

I slept ten hours last night. I'm starting to think I'm either sleep deprived or fucking lazy. Probably a little of both. A sloth would get out of a burning hotel faster than me. Our flight from Orlando to San Antonio was uneventful. Except for the *Duck Dynasty* rejects that were camped out in steerage. Two of them were doable, and one of them refused a drink from me during beverage service. He's probably afraid of HIV. Even though I am HIV free, he obviously thinks every gay dude has HIV.

It was touch and go as we departed for Los Angeles. I'm being over-dramatic, but the bins shook back and forth like we were in an earthquake. To this day, I've never heard an airplane shutter that loud. I closed my eyes and counted the seconds until we were airborne. I didn't believe we would crash, but even though I work in the airline industry, what do I really know about airplanes? I pour cups of coffee, hand out sodas, and open the emergency slide once a year at recurrent training. I have no clue if that massive hunk of metal is moments away from crashing back to Earth in a fireball. I had this vision of sitting on the jumpseat, writing in my journal when suddenly the airplane explodes in mid-air. Among the body parts, burnt bags of nuts, and hair extensions, the NTSB finds my crispy fingers grasping my journal as I'm in mid-sentence. I'd be the Anne Frank of the flight attendant world.

While I'm on the subject of hair extensions, there was a young black girl in my section. The moment she climbed into her window seat, I started calling her Annie. One, because of the new movie, and two, because she came with all the accessories, including a white dad, He looked more like Daddy Welfarebucks instead of Daddy Warbucks. Daddy Welfarebucks needed a haircut, a shave, and judging by the way he let Annie talk to him, a set of balls. Who allows their child to speak to them like that? I bet you Jay Z and Beyoncé don't let Blue Ivy talk to them like that, and she's wealthier than everyone I know. Sure, Blue Ivy can't speak yet, but my money is on Beyoncé whooping her ass if she talked back. I don't know why, but Beyoncé looks like she can whoop some ass.

At one point during the flight, Annie spilled orange juice on herself and started screaming, "I need napkins."

As I said, if Beyoncé would have been one of the flight attendants, orange juice would have been the last thing that little girl was screaming about. Annie needed a beat down. Not the kind some random pimp gives his hoe when she's skimming money, but the beat down a bratty ass child needs when they act like a fool on an airplane. Not only was she abusing her dad, but she put the unfortunate passenger seated in the aisle through hell.

I thought it was essential to keep my distance, so I threw a handful of napkins at her to clean up the orange juice. There was no guarantee her head wasn't going to start spinning around, and I'm convinced that if you moved her weave slightly to the right, you'd see 666 tattooed on her scalp.

She stood up to use the lavatory, and as she climbed over Daddy Welfarebucks legs, she continued yelling at him like he threw the orange juice at her. The shocking part was, he sat there and took it. He never raised his voice or even broke a sweat. While I stood next to the lavatory watching this Lifetime movie play out, he barely acknowledged her. I realized I was watching a man who was dead inside. She sucked the life right out of him.

Daddy Welfarebucks may have been dead inside, but I was alive, and my temper was on fire. I felt it was my job to stand up for this man who lost his balls the day he signed the adoption papers.

I couldn't take it anymore. As Annie stepped past the man in the aisle, she continued yelling until she was standing in front of me. She went to reach for the lavatory door handle, and I bent down really close to her and whispered, "You need to stop yelling, now."

She looked like she was about to cry. I was ready to make an announcement requesting a Catholic priest to throw holy water on her and watch her melt through the floorboard, into the cargo bin, and out over Arizona.

I usually don't call upon a Catholic priest to help with a child—I mean, why tempt them?

When we landed in LAX, the captain called me in the back galley to inform me that my commute flight was boarding, and I still had a chance to get on the plane. This was great news because I didn't want to wait three hours for the next flight. As the passengers deplaned, I felt my anxiety rising as they meandered off the airplane without a care in the world.

In situations like that, I have to fight back the urge to pick up the interphone and scream into the PA, "Hurry the fuck up. Why are you so goddamn slow? This isn't a funeral procession."

Why can't people move faster? Boarding and deplaning an airplane seems to be more arduous than actually flying the metal tube through the sky. A family of five took their time getting off the aircraft. The mother talked to her preteen teenager like she was still a fetus. The daughter refused to take off her seat belt and deplane. To no surprise, these parents weren't parenting at all. Between Annie and this Italian preteen bitch, I had worked the flight of assholes. I was tapping my foot harder than a Republican in an airport restroom. Finally, she unbuckled her seatbelt and nearly crawled up the aisle. I was furious. Turtles move down the beach faster than these people. I followed behind them with my luggage biting my lip and trying not to seem pushy. The moment the five of them reached the front of the airplane, I saw my commute flight pulling away from the gate. Instead of tracking down that family at baggage claim, I decided to stay calm.

It's a new year, we'll see how long staying calm lasts. I'm guessing mid-February.

I changed out of my uniform into street clothes. Instead of lamenting, I sat at the airport bar and enjoyed three glasses of cheap red wine.

Maybe from now on, instead of stressing out about my commute, I'll drink wine.

PAIRING 002: THE OTHER BEAR FLIGHT ATTENDANT

Thursday
LAX—LAS—LAX—OAK

My morning started out horrible. While I was showering, I missed a call from Screw Scheduling. Usually, I would ignore these phone calls, but curiosity got the best of me, and I called back. Of course, they had no idea what I was calling about. I should have hung up the phone and brewed coffee, but I was quickly transferred to a child-sounding lady. She said, "We need to move up your showtime to work another trip. An earlier trip."

I didn't know how to respond. Did I tell this lady that she can't move up my report time without my permission? In the past, I've had Crew Scheduling contact me to come in twenty or thirty minutes early, but this bitch wanted me to go in almost three hours in advance. I didn't know schedulers did crack. If they don't, I believe this bitch does. I informed the helium-voiced person I still hadn't left my house, and I was a commuter. I didn't bring up the fact that it was eight A.M. and my report time was at one P.M. In all my years as a flight attendant, I've never had anyone talk to me in that tone. What about, we need your help. Can you help us? The airline will fall apart without you. I was furious and snapped my shoelace ten minutes before I was leaving to catch the train.

I tried something new with my commute this morning. I had no idea how it would play out, but I didn't want to wake up at four A.M. to take a six A.M. flight from San Francisco. I decided to fly out of San Jose on another airline. There were plenty of seats available, but I was extremely frustrated and disturbed from my earlier conversation with scheduling that I walked around the airport like a bumbling fool. It was a stressful situation. I commuted out of a different airport—on a different airline—and didn't land at my base airport.

When I fuck up, I fuck up big.

I planned on taking a car-sharing service to LAX, but I quickly realized Burbank didn't offer that service. I fell apart. Complete turmoil and mania, followed by an instant meltdown. That's how I get; I go from zero to losing my shit in less time than it takes a passenger to annoy me and trust me, that's a millisecond. As I paced around the airport contemplating leaving my job and going home, I remembered there was a shared van service that gave flight attendants a discount. My spirits lifted for a brief second as I walked back towards the pickup location while remembering that if there were many drop-offs scheduled, it could take hours to get to my base.

I did not have hours; I had forty-five minutes. After harassing the dispatcher to get me in a van—I didn't have a reservation—he waved one over that only had two stops scheduled after mine.

The van driver was older than Jesus Christ and drove like he had senior citizens in the backseat. There were no senior citizens, only me and three Asians who probably thought I was off my medication. Another flight attendant in the van delicately handed me a piece of chocolate with fear in her eyes like she was trying to remember her self defense training.

The chocolate calmed me down for three seconds. Trust me, I counted. There was a couple seated in front of me who probably thought I had Tourette's because I'd randomly yell, "Oh. This isn't good." My heart pounded so hard I hoped I'd have a heart attack so my suffering would end. Five seconds of pain and then darkness was better than being held captive in a slow ass senior citizen mover.

With all the tension and stress—and frightened Asians—I put myself through, the van driver dropped me off with fifteen minutes to spare. All that for nothing. Matt always tells me that nothing bad has happened, and he's usually correct. I explode before the dynamite has even been lit. I should practice meditation, but who has time to sit still for thirty minutes?

After arriving in the crew lounge, I asked my supervisor why we hired children who can't tell time to work in Crew Scheduling. There has to be some sort of law on the books that states all employees must reach puberty before trying to reschedule flight attendants.

I didn't know the lead flight attendant, and my first instinct was that I didn't like her. That's how I am with most people, I don't favor them. I warmed up to her later on because she expressed her passion for cats, and honestly, you get a free pass if you're a crazy cat lady.

The other flight attendant was one I had worked with once before. He's an older gay bear, Sam, and we have the best banter. Think *The Odd Couple*, if one was old and one was young. He's not bad looking either, but sadly for him, I don't do senior citizens. An AARP card only makes me lose my boner, not make me want to bend over.

Saying, "Daddy, do you get a discount on McDonald's coffee?" is not a pickup line. With all that said, I liked him. He keeps up with my jokes and doesn't act like an asshole on the airplane.

I'm sure you're curious, so I'll ask for you, what are gay bears? Gay bears are hot, hairy, built, butch—unless you're playing Madonna at a gay bar with glow sticks—muscular, and often chubby guys who will throw you down on the bed and eat your ass while telling you that Hillary Clinton should be the next president. Oddly, many of them like sleeping with twinks, but I've never understood that. To me, that's like sleeping with the enemy.

When we stepped on the airplane, Sam told me he had a six-pack of beer with him in his bag and asked if I wanted to hang out in his room after we were done for the day. I know what you're thinking—I thought it too—who the fuck brings their own alcohol on a layover? We have an entire liquor cart at our disposal. It's like having a key to a liquor store and bringing your own alcohol into the store. When a flight attendant brings their own alcohol on a flight with them, I immediately put them under the alcoholic umbrella. If there isn't enough alcohol in the liquor cart to satisfy their craving, they need twelve steps...and Jesus.

I rejected his invitation because I knew, hours in advance, that I'd be exhausted. I also declined because getting raped on an Oakland layover does not sound like something scheduling allows as an excuse for being late for report time.

I expect they'd say, "Raped? But can you walk? If he was black, we could schedule you a wheelchair down the jet bridge."

He asked a few more times, and I finally said, "Really? Stop trying to get into my pants. That beer was warm hours ago." After flying three legs, and the emotional rollercoaster ride that Crew Scheduling woman-child put me through, I needed a good jerk off session and my hotel bed, which is what I got.

Who offers a potential trick warm beer? That's fucking shameful.

Friday
OAK—LAX—SLC

Happy flight attendant anniversary to me. I've been doing this shit for seven years. I had no idea that I was a sadomasochist. Anyone who's a flight attendant must have a fantasy of being verbally abused and treated like shit daily. I think having a steel-toed boot pressed up against my balls is less painful than delivering a coach passenger their third Coke Zero. The way passengers treat flight attendants is an embarrassment to humanity. I need. I need. All you fucking need is for the airplane not to land in the ocean. That's all you really need.

In all seriousness, I do enjoy my job. If only my job consisted of layovers in fabulous destinations, and not dealing with demanding airline passengers who think I'm Viola Davis in *The Help*. I had a long layover in Oakland and decided to walk the Bay Trail on the Bay Bridge to take some pictures and enjoy the day. I wanted to invite Sam, but pushing an old man up a bridge in a wheelchair is not something on my bucket list. He told me he heard strange noises coming from my room last night. I corrected him and informed him it was most likely the Grim Reaper searching all the hotel rooms looking for him. He's really not that old, but I'm a dick.

We flew to Salt Lake City and only had seventy passengers on the flight. It should have been easy, but nothing ever is. I'm the cabin bitch on this trip, so I'm stuck in the middle of the cabin during boarding. I'd rather have a herpes outbreak and be out of Abreva than be the cabin bitch on a Salt Lake City flight.

While we boarded, I was standing in the exit row, and a heavyset guy and his almost equally heavyset wife walked past me and settled in the row directly behind me. She complained while walking down the aisle and when they maneuvered themselves into their row, she started talking even louder. She was obviously trying to get my attention, and it worked. I should have ignored her, but I love a good confrontation.

She stated, "I thought this was supposed to be more space."

I whirled around, "It's more leg space, not width space."

She continued annoying me after drink service. They both ordered a beer. Flight attendants keep beer on ice, but we only have a select number of each beer at any one given time. This isn't a 7-Eleven, it's a small galley on an airplane. It's a domestic flight in the United States, not an international trip on Emirates to Abu Dhabi. We don't have a walk-in freezer or the CEO of Anheuser Busch in the back galley. Sam had sold one of the beers these two passengers ordered, so of course, when I brought them their beers, one was ice cold, and the other was semi-cold.

While I collected trash, the wife stopped me and asked, "Can you bring us two more beers? And just so you know, one of those last beers was warm."

I put on my fake smile and apologized, but also educated them on how we keep beer cold. I finished with, "I'll try to find the coldest beers possible."

She sneered, "Hopefully, it's better than the last time."

They received the two warmest beers in the cart. With a smile, of course.

Saturday
SLC—LAX

It's raining cats and dogs in Los Angeles today. I can't stand it. I'm not commuting home tonight, and Sam was kind enough to drop me off at a hotel by the airport for the night. He didn't make an advance towards my ass, and that was disappointing. I wouldn't give it to him, but who doesn't want to be sexually harassed on a ten-minute drive to a hotel.

There's a local hotel that offers pilots and flight attendants a discounted overnight rate. The hotel looked sketchy as we pulled into the driveway. I don't want to be that guy, but it seems like the kind of place where a single mother tries getting you to give her cash for her WIC coupons when all your doing is filling up your ice bucket.

Seriously, from the outside, it looks like they host meth conventions.

Pairing 003: Orlando Hangover

It's still raining, and I left my brand new, never been worn, uniform jacket at home. It's not that I'm worried about my hair getting wet, I just hate the feeling of dampness. It reminds me of homelessness. That's my idea of being homeless, feeling damp. Not begging for food in the Tenderloin. Not sleeping in the Civic Center Bart Station, but feeling damp.

You'd think I was a Republican.

At the airport, the supervisor informed me that Sam, the bear from my last trip, had left me a care package. I expected this because Sam sent me a message advising me to stop by the office to pick it up. I said to the supervisor, "Sam tried giving me his package for three days. He's relentless. There's probably lube in the box."

When I opened the package, a tube of silicone hand cream fell out with magnetic collar stays I was promised. We both erupted into laughter. Thankfully, the supervisor found me amusing. I've been given gifts from co-workers before, but this was my first tube of lube.

Our pilots were in the lounge and after the five of us briefed, we walked to TSA to go through the Known Crewmember (KCM) line. KCM is the reason for living. Avoiding TSA and their searches are like walking away from a bareback orgy and not having to take medication for the rest of your life. I have no clue about that, I'm merely guessing. Breezing through TSA is a fantastic benefit. I'm waiting for some dumb asshole to ruin it by filling up their luggage with cocaine and trying to sneak through LAX.

When we arrived at the KCM door, it was locked. We followed the pilots into the TSA passenger area and the captain, some fat dude from JFK, yelled, "Hey, why is the door locked?"

A TSA agent, who looked extremely nasty, snapped her head around like a Lazy Susan and answered, "We're understaffed, KCM is closed."

Understaffed? Have you ever seen TSA without twenty people standing around sifting through the large plastic tubs filled with all the lotions, shampoos, and conditioners they're about to take home? If anything, they are overstaffed, and their bathrooms at home look like the beauty section at Big Lots.

The captain was not happy with that answer and demanded to see the TSA supervisor.

The supervisor walked over and apologized for KCM being closed and called someone over to scan us through. The TSA employee continued yelling out at us from her security post that KCM was closed, even as we were being processed through the line.

Our airplane was at a hard stand at a remote parking area not attached to a jet bridge. When we stepped on the aircraft, we were drenched from all the rain. When the sun is shining, boarding the airplane in this fashion is incredible, but when it starts pouring, they should shut the airport down and send everyone home. As we boarded, passengers dragged themselves onto the airplane with smiles and were pleased that it was raining.

One passenger said, "We need the rain," as liters of water poured off him and onto my jumpseat. I was surprised. I expected the worst from the passengers, but they proved me wrong. Before we were ready to close the door, I asked the gate agent for a mop to clean up the water on the galley floor, and she did not seem thrilled. There was enough water for a Labrador retriever to take a bath.

I guess safety isn't as important as closing the airplane door on time.

Did she think it was better for me to slip and break my neck? I'd have no problem causing that type of cancellation. Against her wishes, I mopped up a large amount of water I would have been ankle-deep in when we closed the door. I don't know why she was acting like it was a big deal, even after I mopped up the water, we closed the airplane done on time. I'm meeting friends out tonight in Orlando, but I need to eat before I drink. I can't get too crazy because I have to be up at eleven A.M. to fly back to California.

Monday
MCO—DFW—LAX

I felt like I was dying this morning. I'd rather Chris Pratt be gay and not want me than deal with a hangover. My insides were screaming. I should have called Alcoholics Anonymous and reported myself to Jesus. Never mind about AA's twelve-step program, I needed a twenty-step program straight to the lavatory to projectile vomit.

From memory, I had seven beers last night. And I woke up with my head feeling smashed in. Every movement felt like I was being slapped by Chris Brown on a continuous loop.

The only positive thing to come out of being alive was Laura, the flight attendant working the trip with me. Thoughtful, caring, and would pull my hair back when I retched in the toilet. I am sure death would've felt better than my hangover. If only I could have sipped on a Bloody Mary during beverage service, I'd probably have felt better. I think Italian flight attendants can drink wine while they work across the Atlantic Ocean.

When we took off from Orlando, I almost barfed all over the galley. It was notably turbulent and my brain slammed from one side of my skull to the other. A commuting captain gave me vitamin C powder to mix with water. I took sips of it with ginger ale, but each sip gagged me. I had a sandwich in my bag, but the thought of that crusty sourdough bread, brie, and turkey with an apricot glaze made me want to Linda Blair all over my jumpseat.

Laura made my mood better. Even though my balance was off, and I was beyond nauseous, we were able to laugh and joke.

She'd ask, "Are you feeling better?"

I'd laugh and answer, "No, I want to die."

For some reason, we both found that to be hilarious. We were telling jokes, and when Laura walked away, the captain said, "She seems like a dirty Catholic girl."

I agreed and responded, "Yeah. Laura's Italian, and I don't think she's wearing underwear."

His eyes bulged out of his head. I love watching pilots foam at the mouth.

The Orlando to Dallas flight pushed me to my limits. I can't drink anymore on layovers. It's too demanding on my body, and if anyone offers me a fireball shot again, I will stab them in the balls—or vagina—depending on their sex.

On the second leg of the trip, I started feeling better. I ate my sandwich and surprisingly it went down smoother than trying to stuff a cat in its carrier. The appearance of my skin went from ashy to a delicate pink. By the time we landed, I was back to normal.

I joked with Laura, "I think I'm ready for another drink," but as I said it, part of the brie sandwich I ate for lunch started to resurface, reminding me of the pain I had endured all day.

When I walked off the airplane, I gave my blog business cards to the two pilots standing in the galley and told them to check out my blog. One was the captain, and the other was the pilot who gave me the vitamin C mix and saved my life. The first officer who flew us all day was long gone. I think he actually departed the airplane before we even arrived at the gate. It was like he went down the emergency ladder in the flight deck to catch his commute. He was one of those pilots who literally—and I'm being fucking serious—pushes passengers out of the way to be off the airplane first.

Our captain asked me, "Are you giving me your number?

I laughed, "No, I don't do captains. I only do first officers."

He responded, "Well, maybe I should downgrade."

I ran to catch my commute home, and after receiving my boarding pass, I walked onto the airplane, and the lead flight attendant asked, "You're the blogger, right?"

Fame taste like a big slab of cheesecake.

Once I got secured in 4A, the gate agent strolled onto the airplane and sat next to me, inquiring if I stopped at the gate before boarding the flight. Was he being serious? How else did I get my boarding pass? I don't keep a company printer in my tote bag. After I reassured him that I was not a security risk, he left. I made eye contact with the female passenger seated across the aisle from me, and she glared at me like I was an illegal immigrant. That happens sometimes flying from one California city to another. I turned my head and ignored her because watching the ground operations guy outside on the tarmac, scratching his balls with the wand was extra entertaining.

When we landed, the lady across from me was still staring. I sensed her judging me for something that I was not privy to. I wanted to ask, "What the fuck are you staring at? Have you never seen this much hotness in a uniform before?" I refused to look her in the eye, but her daggers made me wish I was in civilian clothes so I could open the overhead bin and drop a bag on her head.

I took the train home. I hate taking the train after commuting, but by the grace of Madonna, tonight I made each connection and only had to wait a few minutes between trains. I was seated on the top level, and a sexy guy was sitting across from me. He must have recently left the gym: hairy legs, basketball shorts, cute face—he was the total package—until he stuck his finger into his left nostril, dug around for two stops, and then examined it like a juicy steak.

Everyone has issues, including hot guys on trains.

PAIRING 004: SAME-SEX ATTRACTION DISORDER

Friday
Home

My four days off went quickly. It was only three days ago that I found myself bored and missed flying. Now, I'm wishing a meteor would slam into the planet and destroy North America. That may sound extreme, but that's how badly I don't want to go to work. What about a missile hitting the apartment complex? And not my apartment building, but the neighbor across the alley who leaves his bathroom light on all fucking night long. With all the singing that goes on in his shower, he won't even know what hit him.

My trip tomorrow is another Orlando layover. I guess it's better than flying New Yorkers to Orlando. Those are the type of passengers you leave out on the tarmac for seven hours and then set the airplane on fire.

That's a joke. I would never destroy a perfectly good airplane.

I barely packed anything in my luggage. Last week, when I was in Orlando, I got so drunk I would have embarrassed a college frat house, so I'm keeping it low key.

I have to go to bed because 4:30 A.M. comes early. Matt's watching *Shark Tank* in the living room. I crave sex tonight, but sex seems like a lot of effort, and the additional ten minutes of sleep will do me right.

Saturday
LAX—PHX—MCO

I plan to retire at fifty years old. I can't see myself waking up before the Sun in my golden years to offer someone a bag of pretzels while getting yelled at because the seat belt sign is illuminated and the WiFi doesn't work. I crawled out of bed ready to fake-smile all day, but the second the hot water and soap hit my hairy chest, I wanted to call in dead and go back to sleep.

Where is that meteor when I need it?

I wish I loved my job, but I don't. Honestly, I tolerate it. It doesn't make my heart go pitter-patter like it once did. Now it makes my stomach churn like I ate tainted lettuce. I do my job, and I do it well, but oftentimes I'm as plastic as management when they act excited to see me, but only want to check me for uniform compliance. Most of these emotions occur at home. Once I'm at the airport, it's showtime, and I come alive. Fake Smiles. Fake waves. Fake comments. I'd say fake tits, but my tits are all real.

When I sat down on my commute flight, I tried napping, but three blonde chicks behind me forgot it was 5:45 A.M. Instead of quieting down, they chatted like they were on Hugh Hefner's jet.

Is anyone thrilled with their job? Matt seems to be content in his career. I wouldn't say content, I'd say ecstatic. He acts like he should pay them to show up each morning. He treats his job like a beautiful mistress, always complimenting and rarely complaining when he's caused heartache. I'm the complete opposite. If a passenger's seat is broken and doesn't recline on the airplane, I'm ready to call in sick for the rest of the year.

I had to get my new crew ID today. The picture looks good, but I'm getting old. I feel skinny, but from the neck down I resemble Jabba the Hutt right before Princess Leia strangled him with her chains. I still don't think that was realistic. He's Jabba The Hutt, and she's a princess dressed in a chandelier. Total bullshit, George Lucas.

My supervisor informed me that she'd have my ID activated before I landed in Orlando, but I don't have faith in it being done. I really don't have much confidence in this airline. The only thing I have faith in is that we will be delayed and that I will be in an eternally pissed-off mood when I have to come to work.

And that my ID will not be activated in time.

I'm working with a flight attendant who lives in Salt Lake City but insists she is not a Mormon. She's obviously lying and doesn't want me to poke fun at the ridiculous name, Deseret. A citizen of Salt Lake City who's not a Mormon, that's like a guy with a dick in his mouth in an airport restroom not being a politician. She asked me if I was watching the TLC show, *My Husband's Not Gay*, a Mormon show following men who say they aren't gay but have an attraction to men.

It's called S. S. A. D., same-sex attraction disorder. Call me a homosexual, but I think that means you're a cock loving, anal pounding, brunch eating closet case. Or you like to scissor for hours with your college roommate and tell her that you do this only because God told you to. It sounds fishy, and that's not a pun on cunnilingus. Do they actually believe this horseshit? I think I'll tell my doctor that I suffer from S. S. A. D. and see what type of medication is available for my late-night penis cravings. I hope it's Vicodin.

I didn't want to interact with anyone tonight. I was irritated by a mother on the airplane who refused to fasten her child in the seat belt. The kid flailed around like she was being attacked by bees. I didn't even argue. If that brat crashed into the overhead bin during turbulence, I refused to care. When the airplane arrives at the gate, and all the passengers have deplaned, my job is done, and I'm not responsible for cleaning up the baby blood over row seventeen.

Sunday
MCO—PHX—LAX

The airplane I worked on today was a complete and utter piece of elephant shit. Why does the airline even own this rust bucket? Thank the Pope we aren't on an Asian carrier or I'd have been saying my goodbyes instead of completing my security checks.

The day did not start out well. When I got to the airport before the flight, my ID wouldn't allow me access to the flight attendant crew lounge. Do I know this airline or what? They make the simplest of tasks difficult. All my supervisor needed to do was push a button—or make a phone call, I don't know how that shit works—to activate my ID. It's not like I asked the bitch to work the flight for me. When I finally arrived at the gate, our flight was delayed.

I'm starting to dislike this career.

PAIRING 005: TECH STOP IN ALBUQUERQUE

Saturday
LAX—LAS—LAX—LAS

I spoke with a friend on the phone today and expressed my disappointment in our management. I'm starting to believe the passengers don't make my job difficult; airline management does. Every time I turn around shady shit and favoritism is happening. Evan tells me to stop being like Elsa and let it go.

Fuck Elsa.

Nothing exciting happened today. I flew three Las Vegas flights and was overwhelmed by money-hungry prostitutes all day. I'm not trying to be rude; those flights are full of escorts, strippers, and ladies of the night.

I overheard one of the ladies say, "I'm getting tore up in Vegas," and I'm not 100% confident that she was talking about getting drunk. I hope she's one of them proactive type of prostitutes who carry around bungee cords to hold up her labia.

I went to the iconic Peppermill with my co-worker Carrie. She's a gem. Carrie is sweet and confessed that she likes boys and girls. I love bisexuals; I wish I knew more of them. Bisexuals are free-spirited and merely flip a coin for whichever genitals they want to snack on that night. It doesn't matter because they like both. That's the life right there.

Her male friend, Donnie, joined us for the evening. He's straight, and within five minutes of our meeting, I found out he hadn't had sex in over a year and a half. He was initially in Vegas to meet a potential hook up, but it fell through. His balls must be bluer than ripe blueberries. When Donnie went to use the restroom at the restaurant, I asked her if she was going to have a friend with benefits evening.

She responded, "No. We're only friends."

Sunday
LAS—LAX—JFK

I woke up early to get free breakfast at the hotel because I never say no to free food. On the way down to the van, I bumped into Carrie and Donnie. He looked pleased, so hopefully, she gave him at least a handjob. She's a great flight attendant, and probably a great friend.

Our flight from Las Vegas to Los Angeles experienced enough turbulence to prevent us from conducting a beverage service. Those short flights are like premature babies; you never know how they'll turn out. Winter storm Spartan spent the day attacking the Midwest and Northeast, which delayed our flight to JFK before we in the lounge due to our delayed flight. The flight was scheduled to depart at 3:45 P.M. but then the magicians who run operations changed the departure time to 3:15 P.M. The gate agents freaked out, and I wanted to tell them to relax. We found out the new flight time at the exact moment the gate agents did. Instead of being calm, they scrambled around, acting like they hadn't seen us all day. Or worse, that instead of us chilling out in the lounge, waiting for our departure time, we were at the Westfield Culver City mall shopping for Auntie Anne's pretzels.

The New Yorkers on the flight seemed friendly during boarding. I accidentally forgot where I was—which is a hazard for a flight attendant—and said out loud, "I do my best to avoid New York."

A male passenger heard me, "Hey, hey, now."

I guess I'll get a complaint letter for that comment.

The flight time to JFK from Los Angeles was a little over four hours. I've never experienced winds so strong in my entire career. I asked the first officer if a hurricane was pushing us to New York. A fast flight tonight means a lengthy trip back tomorrow, but I'll worry about that when the time comes. We landed in a winter wonderland. It's not snowing at JFK, but it's colder than an Anchorage tit.

A friendly passenger in 25F who had laryngitis tried conversing with me while it took the gate agent forever to move the jet bridge to the airplane. Alright, it wasn't forever, but it seemed like a few weeks. I can't blame the gate agent; the jet bridge was frozen. The annoying part of the entire experience was that we landed at eleven P.M. but didn't get to the hotel until after midnight.

I lost my patience waiting outside for the hotel van. It was 500 degrees below zero, and I yelled, "I flew across the fucking country faster than it's taking the van driver to drive three miles."

When we finally arrived in the hotel lobby, Carrie talked the front desk clerk into comping us free breakfast in the morning. Because I love the opportunity to overfill my plate at a free hotel breakfast buffet, I forgave the van driver for not owning a flying car that could fly over the tundra known to most people as Queens.

My friend, Adam, was on a New York layover at the same time. He sent me a frantic text message and called me twice while my flight was deplaning. I guess Adam doesn't know I can't answer the phone while there are passengers on the airplane. I thought he needed a place to stay because he helped out the airline, by flying one flight from somewhere in Hell (aka Florida) to LaGuardia, and when he landed, scheduling did not have a hotel room for him. That's typical and not a surprise. Now if they had done their jobs, I'd be shocked. That's why I rarely help the airline; they never seem to be able to return the favor. Lucky for him, they found him a hotel room, so he didn't have to stay with me. I'm having one of those moments where I dislike my job. It's a recurring theme.

Monday
JFK—LAX

I didn't want to get out of bed this morning. I was warm, comfortable, and still exhausted from yesterday, so I skipped my free breakfast and slept late. Madonna's Rebel Heart Tour presale tickets go on sale tomorrow, and I'm willing to pay $1,000 for floor seats. I know that sounds crazy, but it's my dream to see her up close, and I need to get cracking on that dream before she's being wheeled across the stage with an IV pole and attached to a portable oxygen tank. Although watching her swing oxygen tubing around a dancer's head while singing "Like A Virgin" seems incredibly satisfying, I'd prefer catching her on stage before that happens.

On second thought, I change my mind; I'd pay good money to see her pushed across the stage in a wheelchair. Matt once said that I'd sing along to a Madonna song if it were her burping into a microphone. I agreed. I'm sure with the correct auto-tune; it would be a huge hit.

In the hotel lobby, I asked the front desk clerk if I could redeem my free breakfast when I returned on my next layover.

In an unexpected tone, the employee snapped the free breakfast coupon out of my hand and said. "No. It was only good for today."

That's excellent customer service. Was she a flight attendant in her past life? Or last week? I decided not to throat punch her and will complain about her rudeness when I'm back on my next layover. I always get confused at what we can/can't complain about regarding hotels because we're technically not paying for the room. The airline is paying, so I guess I am a customer.

I'm getting that bitch fired.

When we arrived at the gate, I found out we had a fuel stop scheduled in Albuquerque. It's another old airplane—do they do this to me on purpose?—with no WiFi, no winglets, and we're flying against winds strong enough to pull off a South Side Chicago weave. The frustration lies in the fact that the airline has plenty of airplanes that could fly from JFK to LAX without stopping for additional fuel, but they use those airplanes on short flights. Why? To make me miserable.

Captain David came out from the flight deck after we were all boarded to inform passengers, reiterating the gate agent's announcement, that we would make a fuel stop in Albuquerque.

A passenger in 5E started making a scene. How do I know this when I was in the back of the airplane? Because Captain David began addressing the guy over the PA, "I'm sorry, sir, but I'm missing my commute, too."

I strolled up to row five to get involved in the action. I'm notorious for sticking my crooked nose in conversations on the airplane. There are countless things I could be doing—texting in the lavatory, flirting with the guy in 24F—but I always find myself at the head of the line for a nice passenger smackdown.

The passenger in 5E was arguing about the fuel stop, "This is bullshit. I'm going to miss my flight to Sacramento tonight."

Captain David kept apologizing, but I sensed he was annoyed.

That's when Super Joe came to the rescue. I swooped in like a vulture ready to feed on 5E's soul, or at least shut him down so Captain David could go back to his job of flying the fucking airplane.

I walked up to row four, smiled at Captain David, and turned to face 5E, "This is non-negotiable. If we don't stop for gas, we crash and die."

That shut him up for a moment, but his eyes were watery, and he continued to mumble under his breath like an angry teenager. I found out later that he had missed his flight yesterday due to weather. I understood he was upset, and I don't condemn him for being pissed off and ready to start tossing safety information cards at us, but you can't show your ass and be aggressive with the crew. Stay calm and write a nasty complaint letter to the airline or tweet about it like everyone else. Hopefully, they'll send you a few drink vouchers.

After addressing 5E, I stepped out onto the jet bridge to update the gate agents. They were huddled together texting on their cell phones and looked up at me like they were caught taking minis out of the liquor cart. Generally, gate agents are of no help. Some work their asses off, and I'm grateful for them, but many of them dislike confronting passengers. And you can always tell who those gate agents are when you watch passengers walk on the airplane carrying bags too big for the overhead bin—or boarding with five pieces of luggage. I don't think there is an airline on Earth that allows a passenger to carry five pieces of luggage on the plane. But in defense of the mighty gate agent, there is usually only one working each flight. I guess the airline hates all their employees equally.

For one flight, a solo gate agent is responsible for: making announcements, assigning seats to passengers who don't have one, dealing with standby passengers, scanning boarding passes, making more announcements, making sure there are no security breaches at the gate, running up and down the jet bridge with paperwork, and all the other shit they have to do for a flight to Buffalo. It's because of all that I try and cut them some slack, but when they are texting on their cell phones when I am doing their job, that turns me into an F4 tornado. The rule is, if the airplane is at the gate, the gate agent is responsible for handling these situations, but that's only when it benefits them. They could have turned 5E's mood around if they had put him on the later non-stop to Sacramento. It's difficult to be smart and work in the airline industry. It will eventually make you crazy.

Carrie, the lead flight attendant, didn't step up and get involved either, which made me curious. After I persuaded

35

the gate agents to do their job, one came on the airplane to talk to 5E, and I continued to the back galley to finish my duties. I know I can't technically complain, I was the one who walked up there and stuck my nose in their business, but if I don't, who will?

Halfway through the flight to Albuquerque, a passenger seated in 9F walked to the back galley and approached Karen, the mid-cabin flight attendant. He was sitting in her section and asked, "How much is the upgrade to sit in the exit row?"

She looked over and asked me and I responded, "It's a one hundred dollar upgrade fee, sir."

Without addressing me or acknowledging that I had spoken to him, he turned back to Karen and started rambling. I had no clue what the details of their conversation until he grumbled, "I'm sure you'd both have a different answer if my skin were a different color."

I responded, "I don't believe that has anything to do with the upgrade fee, sir, it's the same for everyone. "

Karen's eyes teared up while attempting to explain the upgrade policy. He steamrolled over her every time she tried opening her mouth to explain. His goal was to upset her, and he reached it the moment he stepped into the galley. I tried getting Karen to shut up and stop feeding this guy ammunition. Not that she said anything wrong, but he twisted each word that came out of her mouth.

I shouldn't have been surprised that the passenger brought up his race to argue about an upgrade fee, but I was. If anything, blame the airline for the policy, don't verbally attack us. During their conversation, he told Karen that he wanted a different seat because his seat did not recline. I understood that; I've sat in that same seat on a red-eye commute, and it sucked. She politely explained that seats in front of the exit row did not recline. He didn't want to hear it. His goal was to be abrasive.

While their conversation went back and forth like a heated tennis ball, I quietly questioned his motives. He had approached Karen and specifically asked her about the upgrade fee. He knew it wasn't a free upgrade, so why was he starting trouble? Did he think he could scare us into a free upgrade by bringing up race? That's what he was trying to do, bully his way into an upgraded seat. We have enough disagreements in the world, who wants to deal with some guy who's mad because he picked a seat that didn't recline? Had he ever heard of SeatGuru? There are more important things happening in the world than this fool starting trouble because we didn't tell him what he wanted to hear.

Finally, I exploded, "Karen, don't say another word. Sir, if you have an issue, you can discuss it with me or write to the airline."

Again, he didn't acknowledge me, and that was completely fine. He walked out of the galley and locked himself in the lavatory. Now it was recovery mode for Karen because this interaction had her shaking. She looked like she had run over a pregnant dog and her puppies.

We landed in Albuquerque for fuel, and my mood was unpleasant. I wanted to kick every last passenger off the airplane and tell him/her/they to eat a bag of shit. Not suck a bag of dicks, because that sounds like way too much fun, but eat shit.

A young male passenger seated in 18C was projectile vomiting in the lavatory during refueling. I couldn't tell if the loud gurgling and gagging sound was coming from his retching or the fueling truck. All I can say is that I've heard that sound countless times waiting to use the restroom at the Ramrod in Ft. Lauderdale.

He stepped out of the lavatory, looking pale and sickly. I asked him, "Have you been outside of the country?"

The young man answered, "No," and then sat himself down on one of the jump seats. I didn't remember inviting him to join us, but he looked like he was going to throw up his asshole, so I handed him a trash bag and put on a hazmat suit and smiled at him while he vomited into the trash bag.

There are two things flight attendants should always be prepared for when they come to work: (a) passengers possibly spreading Ebola all over the galley, and (b) making sure provisioning has stocked enough cans of Coke Zero for the Hasidic Jewish passengers flying from New York to Disney World.

Seriously, I don't know that much about Ebola, but I think that if you get it, you instantly turn into a zombie and eat your fellow flight attendant's face off. If it's a fellow pilot, the infected flight attendant will go directly to their genitals.

I'm merely stating a fact.

Between episodes of heaving, he quietly asked, "Can I sit here for the rest of the flight?"

I asked him if he'd lost his mind. I'm kidding; I did not ask that. I'm a retired nurse; I have a fantastic bedside manner. I informed him unless he was going to do beverage service on the next flight, he'd have to return to his seat. I handed him a bottle of water, some antacid tablets, another trash bag, patted him on the back and sent him down the aisle ala Grinch and Cindy Lou Who style. Once we refueled and Ebola Boy was back in his seat, infecting the rows around him, we closed the airplane door and departed for Los Angeles.

The only passenger I connected with all day was Sharon who was seated in 25F. Sharon was the first passenger to board the airplane in JFK, and we had a *Seinfeld* moment. She told me she hurt her calf at the gym and her father-in-law yelled at her, "Are you done with this gym shit now?

We both roared with laughter. I said, "You wouldn't get hurt if you sat down on your ass all day."

Again, we erupted with laughter. She said she wanted to push me Elaine style down the aisle. At first, I was open to it, but she was too enthusiastic, and something told me that this was more of a fetish than a one-time spontaneous request. I imagined her meeting customer service employees all over the country, making them fall for her fabulous humor, and then convincing the poor saps into letting her push them straight in the chest as Elaine did to her co-stars. The employee at the Genius Bar. Push. The employee at H&R Block. Push. The barista at Starbucks.

You got it, push.

My eight P.M. commute was delayed until ten P.M. I was irritated but tried not letting it upset me as much as say, ditching into Lake Tahoe. I sauntered into Hades Bottomless Pit of Fire and Brimstone—aka the supervisor's office—and spoke with my supervisor about a leave of absence. With a crooked smile that told me she had possibly/maybe/probably been sipping Fireball from a flask when nobody was looking, she said, "We're only allowed seven to eight employees to be on leave at one time, and we're already at fifteen for next month."

I responded with no emotion, "Well. What's one more?

That wasn't the correct response.

When I walked back into the lounge, the departure board read that the flight would depart at 10:30 P.M. By the time I came out of the restroom, it was delayed till almost eleven o'clock, Once that happened, I called Matt and had a complete meltdown.

Whenever I have any issues with commuting, I immediately want to blame my husband for moving us to California. I can't, though, because I agreed to move out here. Most often, I need to vent and have him receive all the data I'm sending. Sometimes nod his head. Sometimes hug me. But all the times tell me that everything will be alright. He excels at that, and I love him for it.

While Matt and I were on the phone, I paced outside the lounge like a standby passenger waiting for a seat. I confessed that I'm not happy with my job anymore. I don't know if it's because I'm tired and frustrated or if it's how I genuinely feel. This is the first time I've admitted it out loud to someone, so now I have to deal with it.

Matt told me to forget commuting home and instead, get a hotel, get a shower, a good night's rest, and fly home in the morning. I agreed, but when I pushed the button to end our call, a few questions shot across my brain. Do I hate my job? Yes. Which parts? All of it except layovers. Am I feeling this way because I am burnt out? Highly likely so my lousy attitude will change once I get a nap. What else would I do if I quit? I hear Target is hiring. Target Joe, it has a ring to it. I should purchase the domain name to be safe.

Back in the crew lounge, the flight board showed a new departure time after eleven. Even though I planned on getting a hotel room for the night, I'm not going to lie; I became unhinged. I wasn't the only one in the lounge at that exact moment, so there's a high probability that a video exists on YouTube somewhere called: *Flight Attendant Loses His Shit.*

I haven't had the nerve to type that into the YouTube search box and I never will.

I called the local hotel that gives discounted rates for airline employees and booked a room for the night. Once I booked the room, it felt like the pressure of a full 747 was lifted off my shoulders. As I pulled up Uber on my phone for a ride to the hotel, a flight attendant preparing to work a Miami red-eye flight—who had watched me have a total bitch fit in the lounge—offered to lend me her car overnight. That was too much for me to handle, and I almost started crying. When you think nothing ever goes right and all you want to do is rip your flight attendant wings off, grab a few minis from the liquor cart, and give management the middle finger, someone restores your faith in humanity.

Tuesday
LAX—SFO

I took the eight A.M. flight home, and my friend, Darlene, was working. It was great to see her. Full confession, if I were into female genitals, and not married to my husband, I'd marry her in a heartbeat. I'd most likely still have a boyfriend on the side, but I'm a man who likes sex with other men.

What I'm saying is…I'd be Mormon.

Matt picked me up from the airport so I could rush home to purchase Madonna tickets. I know that asking

JOE THOMAS

your husband to leave work so you'll have a better chance of buying Madonna concert tickets is selfish, but it's Madonna. And that's almost like rushing home for a blood transfusion. Those tickets were going to bring my attitude back. I needed something positive to happen after my lounge breakdown last night in front of my co-workers. I'm sure that embarrassing episode has already been retold to gate agents, pilots, Jesus Christ, and that Ebola Kid.

If he's still alive.

Matt raced home in time for me to log on and purchase one ticket for $533.00 in the lower level. I planned to buy floor seats, but they were too expensive. I originally said I'd pay $1,000 for Madonna tickets, but when they were actually $1,000 fucking dollars, I decided against it. And let's face it, I'm not paying $1,000 unless I get to hang out with her after the show and ask questions about what it was like on the set of *A League of their Own*.

I spent most of the day depressed because I have to work tomorrow. I also cuddled with Tucker. He loves to cuddle, and I could lay with him in bed all day. I should be a professional cat cuddler.

PAIRING 006: POSITIVE KARMA

Wednesday
SFO—LAX—LAS—JFK

I had gout pain in my wrist during the middle of the night but I took medicine, and that curbed the gout demons coursing through my veins.

Tucker vomited in the middle of the night. That cat is a handful; he'd turn a crazy cat lady into a dog lover. I don't want him to die, but when he does, I hope he's fifteen years old so I can throw him a catceañera. I'll be the only one in attendance, and it will be me drinking wine, crying that I miss him, but also celebrating that I won't have to clean up hairballs and undigested food every fifteen minutes.

I won't be home for the next six days. Whenever I go to work for more than five minutes, it seems like I'm moving out. I wonder if other flight attendants ever think that. Do they walk out the door saying, "It's been a lot of fun. Hopefully, I'll be back. And hopefully, my spouse has vacuumed the carpet and picked their clothes up off the floor before I return."

I took the 10:22 A.M. train today to catch my one P.M. flight. Such a waste of time but my husband hates me and can't leave his important job to transport me to the airport like a princess. He doesn't hate me, but when he refuses to pick me up and drop me off at the airport—it feels like hatred. The shitty part of the entire day is that I don't report until six P.M., so I'm leaving my house almost eight hours before I even start my day of flying.

Why don't I work as a train conductor for Caltrain?

I got to the train station at 10:18 A.M. because I read the schedule wrong. My train wasn't coming until 10:32 A.M.

I texted Matt: *I could have stayed home 10 more minutes.*

He replied: *Better to be early than late.*

I change my mind, he hates me. I wanted to call Crew Scheduling and tell them I wouldn't make my report time because I had to go back home and stab my husband for always being right.

They'd only have been worried about the flight departing on time. "Hi, Joseph, can you stab him and still make your report time?"

When I walked up to the gate, the gate agent informed me that the flight was full. I've said this a million times, I really don't know how that fucking happens. One minute there are twenty seats, the next there are zero. I believe the available seat numbers are a lie, like vegans who say they are happy eating soy curd and people who think Republicans care about poor Americans.

I sat there worried about commuting on the jumpseat until the gate agent called me up and handed me a boarding pass. A few flight attendants were non-revving on the flight this morning, and I don't understand why. Why do we choose to go to work when it's easier to stay at home and watch *Live with Kelly & Michael Ryan*?

As I grabbed the handle of my luggage and walked towards the boarding door, I saw another airline flight attendant standing by the gate.

I raised my brow, "Are you trying to commute on this flight?"

"Yes," she answered with a sad, pathetic look, "but it's full and doesn't look good."

That was an understatement. That flight attendant had a better chance of being attacked by a bull shark—INSIDE THE AIRPORT—than making the flight.

"Well," I replied, having my boarding pass scanned, "Good luck."

When I stepped into the front galley, I had a terrible feeling of guilt. The hard, painful guilt, the kind you feel after your unconditional loving dog jumps up on the sofa to cuddle, but you push her away because you are too busy juggling Pornhub and a white tube sock to pay her any attention.

I'm not saying that happens to me. I have cats.

As I inched closer to my seat, I began convincing myself that it wasn't a big deal if I had to sit on the jumpseat for a one hour flight.

If no one else was willing to help this pitiful looking human being who was attempting to get to work, I'd have to. I put my luggage in the overhead bin, walked back up to the gate, and told the gate agent I'd sit on the jumpseat so the other airline flight attendant could take my seat. Putting positive karma out into the world is essential. There's so much hatred, anger, and cruelty (yes, people on Twitter, I'm talking about you) that doing spontaneous random acts of kindness for another person is refreshing. It's also a sure way to bet someone will eventually let you cut them in the ten items or less line at the grocery store.

My positive karma came back to me faster than I had expected.

A passenger who purchased two seats overheard the conversation I had with the gate agent and offered to let me take one of their seats. I helped a stranger, and a stranger helped me. It felt great. Typically, a passenger who purchases two seats together needs them because of weight issues, but that wasn't the case. I think the guy hated sitting next to strangers. I could relate, I feel the same way.

I worked two flights to the east coast today. The trip to Las Vegas only had sixty-eight passengers. That's a great way to start a long night. The JFK red eye was a different story. It was completely full, and we had two flight attendants on the jumpseat. Sitting on a jumpseat to commute is dreadful, but having to do it on a red eye—I'll be straightforward—I'd call in sick. I'm sorry, but if I arrived at the gate and the agent told me I had to take the jumpseat, I'd laugh my crazy laugh and call Uber to pick me up at the terminal.

Not only were these two flight attendants on the jumpseat, but one of them had to work at seven A.M. We were scheduled to land at five, so I don't know how she planned to pull that off. I decided not to ask any questions.

I was the lead flight attendant and decided to board the flight five minutes early in Las Vegas. One of the flight attendants gave me lip about it, but I acted like she was a fly and swatted her attitude away. I also reminded her I was in charge. I hate pulling the I'm-in-charge card, but she got sarcastic first. I simply ended it.

The boarding went well for the two hundred New Yorkers on their way home. A few airlines canceled flights bound for JFK, so some of our passengers paid $1,000 to fly on us. One way. And that's after emptying their wallets out at the poker tables in Las Vegas.

Working a red-eye flight is smoother than morning or afternoon flights because passengers sleep. The hardest part for me is staying conscious. It was easier to stay alert working nights as a nurse than it is trying to keep your eyes open on the airplane. I'm sure it has to do with the rocking of the aircraft and the humming of the engines, although I distinctly remember the humming of oxygen concentrators never made me want to curl up at the nurse's station for a quick nap.

As we landed in JFK, the snow was coming down in blankets. Not sheets, but thick down comforters. I haven't seen snow in over a year, and it was nice, but the second I stepped outside through the terminal glass doors and my snot instantly froze inside my nose, I was ready to fly back to California.

At the hotel, I asked the night manager about my free breakfast voucher. He handed me a new one and apologized for the rude front desk clerk that they clearly hired by mistake. As much as I don't believe she deserves working with the public, I hope they don't terminate her. I'm pretty confident that my airline would hire her as a customer service agent without any references.

PAIRING 007: THE PILLOW THIEF

Saturday
LAX—FLL

Belinda, the older flight attendant I'm working with, is entertaining. She has some great stories, and she's writing a book. Everyone seems to be writing a book. Her husband came on the layover with her, but because our flight from Los Angeles to Fort Lauderdale was full, he's flying out of San Francisco. He's seventy-two years old and spending hours on a cross country flight to rest for twenty-five hours in Fort Lauderdale.

I think she's trying to kill him.

When we arrived in Fort Lauderdale, Belinda asked me to find out if the hotel van would come back to the airport to pick her and her husband up after his flight landed. Do I get paid extra for that? I was cranky and tired, but I told her I'd find out.

The van ride to the hotel was not as long as I expected. Many flight attendants dislike the hotel because it's in the middle of nowhere. Our last hotel was two feet from the beach, so I understand why my co-workers are complaining about the new hotel. At the beach hotel, you could practically jump from your hotel window into the ocean, now, because we are close to the Everglades, I wouldn't plunge into any water for fear of losing an arm to an alligator.

At first look, I liked the property. It reminded me of being in San Juan or a nice hotel in Haiti. Is there such a thing as a nice hotel in Haiti? I'm sure there are, but I can't think of any right now. After checking in, I took my room key and meandered through the confusing corridors at seven A.M. The humidity was already as thick as cake batter. I found my room, but the worst possible thing happened. No, someone wasn't having an orgy in the room, but the key didn't work.

I hate dragging my tired ass back to the lobby after working all night. I hate walking back to the front desk even if I didn't work all night. I asked for another key, but that key didn't work either. That triggered my temper. I found a hotel phone outside the elevator; it didn't work. I looked up the hotel phone number and called the front desk from outside my hotel room to ask them what kind of fuckery was going on. That's a lot of bullshit for one person to deal with after spending the entire night awake on an airplane. The maintenance man showed up ten minutes later to let me in.

I asked, "What's the deal? Two different room keys didn't work."

He didn't respond. I took it that as my key, his English didn't work, either. He smiled and let me in the room without uttering a single word. I was too tired to pull up the Google Translator app on my phone and type in: *What the fuck is wrong with your hotel?*

I threw my tie on the desk, placed my bags against the wall, and called the front desk to ask whether I would be locked out of my room again if I ventured out to the ice machine. The front desk clerk was irritated with me, but fuck her. If anyone was allowed to be bothered in this diabolical scheme to keep me from sleeping, it was her and this key mishap. The front desk clerk told me to come back after the shift change, and they'd issue me a key that would work for my entire stay. She made it sound like receiving a key YOU CAN ACTUALLY USE was a bonus to staying at their hotel, like a warm chocolate chip cookie or a maid who ignores the Do Not Disturb sign on the door.

I got undressed, walked into the bathroom, and came face to face with the biggest cockroach I have ever seen. And I lived in Florida for twenty-three years. I've seen flying cockroaches. I've seen a cockroach use my laptop to plan a Disney vacation for his 10,000 kids. I've seen cockroaches tanning on a bathroom sink after using up all the SPF 50.

Side note, I may have been dreaming with those last two.

But this was different. This cockroach wasn't any cockroach, it probably had a social security number and received benefits. It could moonlight as an airport tug carrying bags to the airplane. This hotel refused to let me have a moment of peace. There was no way I could allow that future man-eater to live while I was staying at the hotel. There was no way I could let that monster live while I was 1,000 miles from Florida. All I thought about was Mr. Roach finding his way into my ear and making me do unthinkable things, like booking myself a personal week-long stay at this abysmal hotel.

As big as this dude was, he was no match for a face cloth and my 220 lbs of weight crushing him to death. The sound of a cockroach being crushed to death will stick with you forever. Falling down a flight of stairs and breaking both legs sounds better than the sound of crunching a live insect to death.

And to think, some citizens of this planet eat cockroaches. Gobble them up like almonds on a charcuterie board. Apparently, right before they molt (that made me vomit a little) they have soft, juicy bodies that when fried, sauteed, roasted, or boiled (okay, vomited a little more) taste like chicken. I refuse to believe cockroaches taste like chicken, but I won't be eating any, so I'll take the country of Thailand's word for it.

I didn't know if it was my exhaustion or not, but as I relieved Florida of this future Godzilla, I swore Jesus whispered in my ear, "Don't kill one of God's creatures,"

I said out loud as I pushed down on that hard exoskeleton, "Settle down, Jesus. You never had to stay in a hotel room with an insect that could easily fold you up and eat you like a fucking taco. You don't know how to suffer, you barely sat in that tomb for three days."

While I took my shower (by the way, the soap was divine), I thought about Mr. Roach's cousins coming back for me while I slept. I stuffed toilet paper into my ears and hoped for the best.

I set my alarm for eleven A.M. A three-hour nap should be plenty.

Sunday
Ft. Lauderdale

I must have shut off my alarm because I woke up at noon. I'm pretty sure I'm sleep deprived because who else believes Jesus whispers to them in a hotel room. Who do I think I am? Mike Pence?

I have a long day tomorrow, so I took it easy today. Also noticed my neck and back were stiff when I crawled out of bed, which tells me I need to start stretching and exercising more. I'm getting fat again. I say again like I was a skinny twink six months ago and that I woke up this morning with Oreo gut. Seriously though, I need to do some stretching because my muscles are probably tighter than a freshly anointed altar boy who's visiting The Vatican for the first time.

I'm obsessed with these Catholic jokes. I look at it this way, as long as those creepy priests keep fucking children, I'll keep running their religion through the mud. I think it's only fair.

After getting dressed, I stormed down to the front desk. I didn't have to storm down dramatically, a calm saunter would have worked fine. The young latino behind the counter provided me with a new key that actually worked. I haven't been that shocked since Jennifer Hudson was sent home on *American Idol*.

The front desk clerk updated me in his broken-just-got-here-English, "The key creator was down last night, and nobody figured out the problem until this morning."

I responded while walking away, "No shit. This is my third key." I wondered if he'd report that to the airline. You know what, sometimes I don't care, and that was one of those times.

It's hot, humid, and disgusting, but I walked a mile to a sport's bar. I definitely don't miss Florida weather. There are only three days in Florida when the weather isn't like taking an escalator down to Hell; I think those dates are: January 14, 15, and 16th.

Ordered a beer at the bar when some random guy came in and sat between a middle-aged lady and me. Now that I think about it, that lady seemed to be there looking for a new boyfriend. And she had come to the right place because the entire bar was packed with golfers. Golf was on every television, and although golf wasn't my first choice to watch, it was tolerable.

The chick next to me needed attention because she randomly yelled, "Golf is stupid. Why would anyone watch this?"

The entire bar quieted down. The bartender stopped pouring, and every mouth gaped open. Tiger Woods on the television even fucked up his shot. I turned and looked at her, expecting beer bottles to be tossed in her direction.

The guy next to me whispered to her, "Be careful. Everyone here plays golf."

They became instant best friends. I tried not eavesdropping on their conversation, but that lasted a mere few seconds. I heard him randomly say, "Yeah. A manatee is just a speed bump in the water."

I wished I had a car with me because I'd have waited until he walked outside and repaid the gesture. Who says that? Even if I were hornier than a ship full of Navy sailors, the moment—

Sorry, I lost track of what I was narrating the second I wrote out "hornier than a ship full of Navy sailors."

Alright, even if I were hornier than a ship full of Navy sailors, the moment some stranger referred to an animal near extinction as a speed bump, I'd have poured my beer down his pants and stormed out.

Sometimes I'm amazed by the lack of decent humans running amok on this planet, and I genuinely believe we're well past our expiration date. When the meteor comes to take us out like the dinosaurs, we will deserve it. Maybe after the ashes settle and the clouds clear, something else will have a chance to survive and do better.

Something tells me this time it will be the fucking cockroaches.

My chicken wings arrived, I ordered my next beer, and I was surprised that the loudmouth chick next to me hadn't been sexually assaulted by these golfers on a pinball machine in the back of the bar.

What would make me even say such a thing? I'm obviously still upset about the manatee comment.

While I drank my beer and snacked on my chicken wings, I didn't want to give them any more of my attention, but Manatee Man added, "I almost died. They had to reattach my legs."

She snapped at him, "No fucking way."

He proceeded to pull his shorts up higher, throw his legs up on the bar,—I'm gay, and I can't even work that fast—and show her the scars on his legs. I stand corrected, it looked like someone had already used him as a speed bump. I gave a quick glance over while sucking the blue cheese dressing off my greasy chicken wings. His right leg looked like someone made an origami butterfly out of it, showed it around the room, and then unfolded it to display a hideous, deformed leg. The hobbling scene in *Misery* looked more pleasant than what that leg went through. With that leg, he'd handle a hobbling and still be able to play eighteen holes of golf in the Florida heat. I had had enough with the right leg, I didn't even bother giving the left any attention. I needed a good night sleep, and shit like that will keep you up for weeks.

After he downed his third whiskey shot, he said for no reason, "I'm good at putting my foot in my mouth."

Again, I can't do that, and I've been putting my feet up for decades.

But with how manicured his fingernails were, I'd say he's good at putting a lot of things in his mouth. My wings could barely go down my throat with all that strange conversation, but when she finally brought up a rock and roll church she attends—I was out.

After paying the bill, I headed back to the hotel, stopped by the pool for an hour to read, and then went up to my room to relax. Thankfully, the key worked. That's good, I would have hated to burn the hotel down before my report time.

I can't shake the feeling of fatigue and exhaustion that hangs over me like a rain cloud. I really want to be home with Matt, the cats, and the Ikea pillow I sleep with between my legs.

That pillow and I are incredibly close.

I had spoken with Adam, and he said he'd stop by the hotel for a quick visit on his ride home from the airport, but at the last moment, I canceled. I was not in the mood to chat and entertain.

Monday
FLL—SFO—LAX

Let me be completely fucking honest, I do not like Fort Lauderdale. I don't like the airport. I don't like the food options inside the airport. I don't like the walls, the ceilings, the restrooms, the service animals, or the hum of all the oxygen concentrators used by people seated in wheelchairs who should already be dead. I absolutely 100% don't like the people living in South Florida. The heat and humidity at seven A.M. were horrific, and we were inside a building in the 21st century. Is this the Amish International Airport of South Florida? The air conditioning should be on full blast to mask the decaying flesh smell from the spinster seated by the gate who hasn't showered since Nixon was in office. The only good thing about Fort Lauderdale is that when global warming melts all the ice caps, it will be the new Atlantis. I'm sure I'll still hate the airport even when it's underwater. Everyone in the airport looked miserable and unhappy; they should all be ecstatic that their social security hasn't run out.

Maybe I'm projecting because I really think I hate my job. What should I do? Quit? Can I quit? It sounds fantastic. When I say the words out loud, "I want to quit," I feel immediate pressure off my chest. I'm not sure, but that could be my tits adjusting under my t-shirt.

Anyway, my friend Dee once told me that being a flight attendant, and working for this airline, should not define me as a person. I'm more than this job, and if I didn't work here, I'd be fine.

Sound advice from a smart woman.

I either need to stop complaining about this every second of the day or quit. Where is that bright, exciting spark that I always carried around with me like my flight attendant manual? Did I ever have one? Do I hate the job or the commute? That is what I need to figure out.

Boarding in Fort Lauderdale was chaotic, and passengers were pushing and rushing onto the airplane like a tornado was headed directly down the runway towards us.

The flight was completely full, and we ran out of overhead bin space with over ten passengers still left to board.

The gate agent was on the jet bridge staring down at the floor, and I yelled out to him, "We're all out of bin space. We have to start checking bags." He glared at me as if he had never heard of that happening before.

A Latin woman walked into the galley with her suitcase, and I informed her there was no overhead bin space, and we would have to check her bag. Daggers came out in place of her fingernails, "I have many important things in my bag."

I smiled, "I understand, but there's no space."

That was definitely not good enough for her, "But you don't understand, my work is in this bag."

While she complained about the airline, I continued moving bags to the jet bridge that had collected around my feet in the front galley.

Without making eye contact, I responded, "I apologize, it's not my fault your bag has to be checked."

She yelled, "Am I blaming you?"

I lost my composure and waved for the gate agent, "I can't do this with you right now, ma'am. Your bag needs to be checked."

When the gate agent grabbed her bag, I realized I needed to turn the situation around with this passenger. The checked bag lady and I were stressed, but the gate agent was calm because he wasn't doing anything. I yelled to him to hold her bag, but as the words flew out of my mouth, he dropped the bag into the slide, and it glided down to the tarmac. I turned to her and told her that I would have her bag tagged so that it was brought up to the jet bridge in San Francisco.

When I told her that, she failed to remember how much she hated me—and how snippy I was to her—and started blowing me kisses as she walked down the aisle towards her seat. I ran over to the jet bridge door and yelled down to the ground operations guy to tag her bag. Once he acknowledged me, I felt better and confident that this crazy Dominican lady wouldn't stick her long fingernails into my neck while I poured hot coffee on the flight to San Francisco.

Halfway through the flight, during a lavatory break for the pilots, I stood in the front galley looking towards the rear of the airplane. With my arms folded, I watched the passenger in 4C step out of the back lavatory, grab himself a for-purchase pillow from behind the last row, and then walk up to his seat.

Did he steal that pillow? No. It couldn't be, I thought. We made eye contact the entire time he walked towards me. I picked up the interphone and called the back galley, "Hey, did someone buy a pillow?"

The answer was as I expected, "No."

"I think the dude in 4C stole a pillow behind row thirty."

I hung up the interphone and mentally prepared myself for the confrontation that would happen the moment the pilots were back in the flight deck.

Usually, I love confrontation, but I was apprehensive. After the other flight attendant stepped out of the flight deck and closed the door, I moved the trash cart out of the way, walked up to 4C, bent down, and asked, "Would you like to purchase that pillow now?"

He looked straight at me and in a deadpan voice, "Pillow? I didn't take a pillow."

I tried processing the lie, but it made no sense, "You didn't take a pillow from the back of the airplane?"

"No."

"Are you sure?" He looked directly into my eyes without responding. I continued, "What you're saying is that you didn't take a pillow from behind row thirty and then walk up here with it?"

"No. If I want a pillow, I'll pay for one."

I started questioning myself. Did I actually see this guy take the pillow? Was the stench of all the old Floridians affecting me? Then I thought, *No, bitch! You saw him steal that pillow.*

"Again, sir, you didn't take a pillow from behind the last row of the airplane?"

"No. I only have a seat cushion that I travel with." He sat up and pulled a black u-shaped cushion out from under him. I smirked, stood up, and walked away. What else could I do? Wrestle him into the aisle and injure my back for a $7.00 pillow? Not with all the old people standing around who might go into cardiac arrest once I pinned him to the carpet. And you never want to wrestle an insane person on the airplane. Anyone who stares you directly in the eye, without blinking and lies to your face is someone you should be extremely cautious around.

Twenty minutes later, I walked by 4C's row when the passenger in 5C grabbed my attention, pointed to the floor, and asked, "Does that belong to you?"

Under the middle seat, between rows four and five, there it was…the fucking pillow. I smiled and answered, "Yes. That belongs to me."

That motherfucker was a psychopath. Even though he was dressed in slacks and a handsome button-down blue dress shirt, he probably had stolen jewels stuffed into his checked luggage. I left the entire situation alone and didn't question him. To be honest, I was slightly worried he'd write a complaint to the airline telling them I called him a thief. Sadly, airline management rarely sides with the flight attendant, even when dealing with criminals.

There was a friendly passenger from Menlo Park on the flight traveling standby with her husband who works for FedEx. During boarding, the gate agent assigned Mrs. Menlo Park to seat 3C, but the moment she sat down the passenger in 3B rang the call bell to inform me that nobody could occupy 3C because she purchased the entire row for her and her incredibly handsome son (I added that last part). The mother and son duo were on their way to San Francisco so that the remarkably good-looking son could have a procedure done. I wonder if it was for a penis reduction? No. Who does that when you are THAT hot?

Mrs. Menlo Park was reseated in 4E, but after we closed the airplane door, the captain called to inform me that I had to move three passengers from the front of the airplane to the back for weight and balance.

It would be easier to pull the airplane across the tarmac with my teeth.

Asking passengers to move to the back of the airplane can be tricky, especially when the only seats left are middle seats. I skipped over all the black passengers. Thank goodness I wasn't working a flight from Fort Lauderdale to Oakland or I'd have nobody to move. I asked Mrs. Menlo Park and her husband, Mr. FedEx if they'd move to the back and they happily obliged. I needed one more person to move, and I did something we are never supposed to do when re-assigning passengers on a flight—I made an announcement. I even went one-more-step further and added, "I'll buy you some drinks." As fast as I put the interphone back on the receiver, an older black lady raised her hand.

If only that stupid racist white bus driver had offered Rosa Parks lunch, she might not have made such a big deal about moving seats.

When the three passengers were reseated and happy, I sat down in my jumpseat, and the husky passenger in 1D looked over at me and asked, "Why did you have to move people?"

Was that a joke? Was the airline setting me up to finally terminate my employment? I'm smarter than most of our management so instead of answering with, "Because of you, chunkalicious," I smiled and said, "Because of weight and balance."

I really hate Ft. Lauderdale.

When we landed in San Francisco, I walked up to the gate and typed in a note under the Pillow Thief's ticket number with a full description of what I witnessed during the flight. Instead of using the word *stolen*, I used the word *took*; like when I use the word *asshole* instead of the word *passenger*.

I flew one more flight and then I commuted home. My five days off in a row were so close I almost felt my sofa under my ass.

On my commute home, a flight attendant I've known for years was the lead. He's also a writer. He shared a recent crazy experience with our management. During a recent storm, he was informed by management that there were no hotel rooms and he had to find his own place to sleep. That same thing happened to me in Orlando, but I made sure they found me a hotel room. If we have to do our jobs, find our own hotels and transportation, then who the fuck needs a scheduling department? We might as well get their pay.

I rode the train home, and as I was arriving at my stop, I stood up from my seat, reached forward to assist myself up, slipped, and literally punched an old Asian lady in the back of the head. I tried making eye contact with her, but she wouldn't look up. I gay gasped, "Oh my God, I'm so sorry."

She smiled and nodded, "Okay. Okay," and then went right back to reading her book. This woman was too comfortable with being assaulted; that was unsettling.

PAIRING 008: EXCRUCIATING BACK SPASM

Thursday
SJC—LAX—AUS

The flight attendants working my commute this morning were fucking terrible. They conducted the wrong beverage service and the mid-cabin flight attendant yelled at a passenger about his bag during boarding. I hid in the seatback pocket so that nobody noticed me.

I don't know if you've noticed, but it's tight as fuck in a seatback pocket.

It was a two-leg commute, so in Las Vegas, I stepped off the airplane to get lunch at Pei Wei and then ran back to the gate to get my new seat assignment. When I walked onto the aircraft, the flight attendant said, "I've never been to Pei Wei, but people talk about how good it is."

I agreed, "It's amazing," and then added, "It's like PF Chang's."

Her attitude changed, "Well, I live in New York City, I don't do chain restaurants."

I better never see her dumb ass in a McDonald's at two in the morning scarfing down french fries and a twenty-piece Chicken McNugget because I'll shove her to the ground and steal her food.

I've been annoyed all day. I'm sure this feeling will pass.

I devoured most of my lunch before we were airborne. I even ate the sticky rice with chopsticks, which is something, because I have an issue eating rice with a fork. I expect eating rice with chopsticks is challenging for most people, but when you're hungrier than an overworked gate agent, you'll figure out how to eat with wooden sticks. I felt terrible eating a hot meal on the airplane. While I inhaled my food like a cast member from *Survivor*, the passengers seated around me starved. Well, maybe they weren't famished, but I'm sure a bag of nuts only goes so far before the urge to rip the flesh away from the lady next to you kicks in. I sat in the window seat, the middle seat was empty, and some young dude in the aisle continued staring at my bowl.

He licked his lips and smiled, "That smells good."

I smiled back, "Yes. It does," but then dropped the smile and pursed my lips delivering a warning stink eye. The kind of stink eye that basically says, stop thinking about how great my food tastes before you find yourself walking off the airplane with a chopstick sticking out of your left eyeball.

A robust flight attendant started collecting trash and stopped at my row, "Oooooooooh. It must be nice to have something to eat."

Yes, it was. It was extremely nice. I figured this flight attendant barely went thirty seconds without a snack, but I didn't want to fat shame someone on such a short flight. Then she fixated on me like I was required to apologize for eating. That irritated me. I fantasized stabbing her in the eye with a chopstick as well, but I held back that impulse. Gouging someone's eye out with chopsticks is not how you handle conflict. Or at least that's what my therapist taught me.

Can you imagine that conversation with a supervisor:

Supervisor, "Why did you stab her in the eye?"

Me, "She got snippy with me, and I was trying to eat and watch the last five minutes of *House Hunters International.*

Supervisor, "Okay, then why did you stab the passenger in the eye with a chopstick?"

Me, "Oh, well, that bitch had it coming. He was eyeing my food like he hadn't eaten since 2005. I was scared."

I'd definitely get called into the office for something that egregious.

When I landed at LAX, my attempt at purchasing a cup of coffee became futile. The line at the coffee shop next to the gate twisted around the entire terminal. I became dizzy trying to locate the end of it. I'm not confident that a few lines became intertwined and some lady not paying attention ended up on a flight to Tucson instead of picking up an iced mocha. You'd have thought it was three A.M. outside an Apple store the day a new iPhone was released. Instead of waiting—because time is money—I walked across the terminal to another coffee shop that never has a wait. I don't believe in God, but this coffee shop is about the closest a Catholic can get to Heaven without being baptized by a pedophile. This coffee shop is a secret well kept.

My patience for standing in any line for any reason decreases daily. I'll probably never visit another theme park. I once waited five hours in line for *Harry Potter and the Half-Blood Prince*, and I was thirty-two years old.

Never again.

I sauntered up to the secluded coffee shop counter, "Hi. Can I get a large coffee?"

The young lady behind the counter looked up from her phone, "We don't got no coffee."

That wasn't proper English, but I was too annoyed to correct her. I was standing in front of a coffee shop that had no coffee to serve. It's situations like this that make me question humanity. If you don't have coffee, why not close up and go home? Why are you teasing patrons when you're out of the main item? That's the type of bullshit that makes people like Michael Douglas's character in *Falling Down* start breaking shit. Was the cafe owners paying her to stand around delivering a message that a $0.03 sign could convey? Do they realize that extra time off for her would be better spent taking an online remedial English class?

I'm working with Karen, who was called a racist the last time I flew with her, and a guy who looks like Benjamin Franklin. It's uncanny how much he looks like Benjamin Franklin. I wonder who I look like? I guess I'll figure that out when I'm not so tired.

Friday
Austin

I have a massive zit on the right side of my neck, and now I know who I look like, Frankenstein's homosexual cousin, Fagenstein. It's disgusting and in the worst location. Is any place a good zit location? I had a zit on my back once, and I thought it would never be seen until someone took a picture of me and the zit made it in the image. I still don't know how that happened.

It was drizzling today, but I dodged the raindrops to check out the replica of the house from *Bates Motel* that A & E built for SXSW. When I walked up to the mock lobby, I was greeted outside by a young woman with the name Norma on her badge. I didn't believe for one second that her name was Norma. It was probably Kayla or some other millennial sounding name. I snapped a few photos and then went inside to find another female employee—where was the mock Norman?—working at the counter.

I moved around, checking out the artifacts from the television show hanging on the walls. When I arrived at the counter, the girl robotically handed me a keychain, "Thank you." I said, "This is incredible how much work they put into this motel."

She seemed to be in pain like she was being kept there against her will. "I guess. It's alright."

I put the keychain in my pocket, "Do you watch *Bates Motel*?"

She answered disinterested, "I think I've seen a few episodes. It's scary, right?"

That's why I dislike people under the age of thirty.

While I meandered around the lobby, some twenty-something douchebag walked in with his friend. Douchebags are standard for Austin—it's a college town—but it's what he said that left me baffled, "You know about this show, right?" He chatted with his friend, "From *Psycho*. The movie with Vince Vaughn."

I wanted to take the keychain out of my pocket and Norman Bates him in the temple.

Did I use Norman Bates as a verb? I need to mark that down on my writing resume.

Who the hell references the movie *Psycho* and credits Vince Vaughn instead Anthony Perkins? I'm going to be upset about this for months.

Again, another reason why I dislike people under the age of twenty-five.

Even after dealing with those incredibly annoying childlike adults, my day in Austin was fantastic. After I had lunch, the sky started rumbling, so I raced back to the hotel to chill out for a while. That's a lie, the sky wasn't rumbling, it was the sausage and peppers in my stomach. Suffice to say, I had to shit.

After my shitcapade, I intended to venture back outside, but the rain began coming down in sheets, so I ordered dinner from the hotel bar. I sat at the bar and, Santiago, the fat adorable Mexican bartender walked over and asked, "May I serve you with something?"

I had to remind myself that I was a married man.

Two pilots were sitting at the bar next to me, and I wasn't snooping, but I overheard one of them say, "Obama," and "monkey," in the same sentence. I grabbed my beer and slid a few seats away from their ignorance.

After they finished their drinks, the two Grand Wizards walked out. I assumed they were heading to the local Walmart to pick up who-knows-what kinda groceries racist white people buy for a KKK rally? I'm thinking mayonnaise with white bread and a gallon of white milk to wash it all down. I started thinking about what would happen if one of the cult followers got distracted by a Walmart employee who happens to have all their teeth still. Picture it: there he is—dumb and young—trying to do right by David Duke, but in his confusion that someone uses their dental benefits at Walmart, carelessly grabs the wrong color milk. I almost feel bad for that foolish skinhead walking up to the burning cross-section of the rally with a gallon of chocolate milk in his hand.

That's probably worse than bringing a transgender date.

I'm not saying those pilots were white supremacists, what I'm saying is, I wouldn't be surprised if housekeeping is down a few white sheets when they check out.

After I received my second beer, a skinny blond woman sat down next to me and ordered a salad with the dressing on the side. That's really no big deal, but when it arrived, she exclaimed, "Oh my God, that's so big."

I looked up from my phone to see if Santiago pulled out his foreskin burrito and slapped it down on a tapas plate. He didn't. And what was I thinking tapas plate? That beast would need a serving platter. I eyed her pecking at her salad like a baby dinosaur and concluded that if she started choking on an olive, I'd let Santiago give her the Heimlich maneuver. Or would it be the Santiagolich maneuver?

Oh Santiago, you cute Mexican, show me your tamale.

Do you think that would have been too direct to leave as a note on my bill?

Saturday
AUS—LAX—SJC

I don't know what I did, but I woke up at four A.M. with excruciating back spasms. Maybe I dreamt of being a pro wrestler and twisted my back in the middle of the night. Leave it to me to get pinned down in my dreams and then spend the rest of the day bent over in pain. The alarm went off at five A.M., and I rolled out of bed—screaming—and crawled to the bathroom to climb into the shower. The words rolled, crawled, and climb are not exaggerations. I was in complete denial of my predicament and figured I'd be mended up after I took a hot shower.

Because as we all know, hot water cures back pain.

That's sarcasm. The only thing the hot water did was trigger an anxiety attack because as I dragged myself onto the cold, dirty bathroom floor, I realized that when I eventually slithered to my phone, I'd have to call scheduling.

For once in my entire career, the scheduler was empathetic.

I barely got four words out without gasping in pain, "Hi. This is Joe...Thomas. Employee number 019...72. I've pulled my back...and can barely move."

The female voice answered, "That sounds terrible. Do you need an ambulance?"

Did she work at the same airline? Did I call the wrong number? I checked the phone number. Nope, I had the right place.

She must have been new. I responded, "No. I'm gonna work...the one flight to LAX, and then I...need someone to replace me for the rest of the day."

After confirming my request, the scheduler wished me well and hung up the call. To be honest, I should have never worked that one flight. Walking was challenging, how the hell would I open the airplane door if we crashed tits-up in the parking lot of the In & Out next to LAX? I put the phone down and attempted to get dressed. It was tragic. I looked more pathetic than a one-eyed cat being squeezed too hard by Sarah McLachlan. At least those animals were able to walk. Well, most of them anyway. To prevent myself from crumbling to the floor in agony, I kept my lower back as straight as possible. With one hand on the dresser, and the other pulling one polyester pant leg up at a time, I'd involuntarily scream at the top of my lungs. No doubt the people in the next room thought I found a family of bed bugs living in my pajamas. Bed bugs would have been easier to handle than my body fighting against itself. All that to get my pants on, I thought I'd never make it through the airport. My left hip pushed out from my spine while my right hip sank five inches below my belt line. I stood in front of the mirror resembling someone who failed their elementary school scoliosis check.

Miraculously, I made it down to the hotel lobby. I take that back, I wouldn't say it was a miracle, I'd say it was luck. If I had walked without screaming every few steps, then yes—a miracle—but I pulled my luggage behind me yelping while my body jerked to and fro like I was on *Dancing With Scoliosis*.

I briefed Karen and Benjamin Franklin on my situation. Karen seemed to care, Benjamin Franklin gave zero fucks. I'll remember that if he's ever struck by lightning. While we waited for the hotel shuttle van, Karen handed me some ibuprofen which never helped. The shuttle was supposed to leave the hotel at 5:30 A.M. but we stood outside waiting past our departure time with another airline crew.

I tried not moving. I stood in one spot while Karen continued asking. "Are you ok? Can I help you? What do you need?"

I needed Percocet with a vodka chaser, but that's not easily accessible so early in the morning.

The hotel van pulled into the porte-cochère, and the other airline pilots and flight attendants pushed past my injured body like I was invisible. Do they do that on the jet bridge when a wheelchair passenger is waiting?

They probably do.

Before the van driver grabbed any bags, he addressed the other airline crew, "You guys are scheduled for the next van. This is the 5:30 A.M. for them," he pointed at Karen, Mr. Franklin, and me, Mr. Scoliosis.

The ride to the airport was barbaric. Christians fed to hungry lions at the Colosseum were in less distress. There was no way in hell the van had shocks, and that was confirmed whenever we hit a crack in the pavement. Not a pothole, but a tiny crack. My entire body shook as we sped down the highway. I wanted to cry, but when you're in that much pain, your tear ducts cease up.

My body said, "You got yourself into this mess, Joseph, you'll have to deal."

I wanted to yell back, "Listen, body, I woke up like this; it's not my fault. I love you. I treat you well. I fill you up with cake and wine and cheese. WHY DO YOU HATE ME?"

But you try arguing with your body when all it wants to do is run to the emergency room and ingest morphine. Each time the driver hit the brakes, my body jerked forward, and I howled like the van seat was trying to penetrate me. Then the driver would hit the gas, I'd fling backward, and I'd roar like the van seat finally got its way.

Because we left the hotel late, there was no time to get food at the airport before the flight. I'd been craving brisket tacos, but in my state, I didn't know if I'd even be able to lift them satisfying blankets of love up to my mouth.

I baby-stepped onto the airplane and was pleased when the gate agent alerted me that my section was empty.

Now that's a miracle.

Karen completed my security checks while I stood in the front galley shrieking in pain. Without me asking, Benjamin Franklin placed my bags in the overhead bin. I take back that comment about him getting struck by lightning. I'm thankful for my friendly co-workers and founding fathers.

The pilots didn't care, but do they ever?

After takeoff, we sat in our jump seats for almost forty minutes due to extreme turbulence. No position was comfortable. Karen tried distracting me with a conversation, but I barely paid attention and interrupted her with my wailing. The two old ladies in 1A and 1B watched as my back spasmed and my body jolted forward. I smiled at them, then my smile transformed into a grimace. The jump seat felt like a concrete block that was attached to my spine. It was the worst pain I'd ever experienced, and I suffer from gout.

When the turbulence finally ended, we stood up to conduct service, but the pain made me anxious, which resulted in my muscles tightening with each step. I couldn't relax, and I barely finished my duties. Thankfully, Karen saved the day. She completed my beverage service, and Mr. Franklin collected trash. Karen encouraged me not to move, but that was impossible. My body jerked unintentionally. I had no control over the spasms. The pressure from the airplane made it a painful three hours.

I bid farewell to Karen and Benjamin Franklin and dragged myself to another terminal for my flight home. Thankfully, I didn't have to rush because the flight wasn't departing for three hours. I found a quiet little nook to camp out in and tried listing for a flight home by calling the airline's standby passenger number, but I was placed on hold for over forty minutes. I hung up, called back, and after waiting another twenty minutes, I hung up again. Being ignored on the phone distracted me for a moment from my back spasms. Well, that and the ten ibuprofen I ingested within five minutes. I don't recommend taking that much ibuprofen at once, but I also don't recommend flying when your nerve endings think they are dancing The Macarena. I shuffled slowly towards the gate to ask the gate agent to list me, but she quickly dismissed me.

I wanted to shout, "Is this how your airline treats the disabled?" But because I fly for free, I left without making a scene. My back continued to spasm, which forced me to move around like a cat with clothes on. I'd take a few steps, stop, yell out in pain, and then pop a few more ibuprofen.

I called the airline's toll-free number again, and after spending another thirty minutes on hold, I was angry. I mustered up all the energy left in my body, and with my ibuprofen-overdosed self, I stormed back over to a different gate agent. Never go to the same person who wouldn't help you the first time.

Holding myself together, I pleaded that she list me on the flight to San Jose. I explained that I had been placed on hold longer than it takes two airlines to merge. Without blinking, she listed me.

It took her about three minutes.

On the airplane, I sat next to an older Canadian couple. The husband was talkative, and before we took off, he informed me that he and his wife had spent forty-nine days on a cruise that sailed around South America from Fort

Lauderdale to Los Angeles. I was impressed. They had to be in their early seventies. On our way to San Jose, the gentleman shared that in 2013, he and his wife visited almost fifty countries and spent three and a half months cruising around the world. I hope I live a life like that when I'm that age. If I'm able, and not bedridden with back spasms.

I tried napping, but it was only a one-hour flight, and the flight attendant barely put down the interphone. At one point I thought he was auditioning for *Last Comic Standing*. He had more jokes than the *Comedy Central Roast of Joan Rivers*. The anecdotes continued rolling off his tongue, and as annoying as that sounds, the passengers applauded him. That shows how ridiculous people are when they walk on an airplane.

He lost me when he said, "Alright, people, I need you off this airplane, I haven't had lunch." I shook my head, but all the passengers laughed.

I know that sounds gruff coming from a guy who writes a comedy blog, but I don't believe the interphone should be used as a microphone to tell jokes on the airplane. I find that to be rude. When a flight attendant does that, they are holding the passenger's hostage, forcing them to listen to a questionable comedy routine. Airline passengers didn't pay to hear your set, they paid for you to give them safety information, hand them a drink, a bag of nuts, and get them to Reno without slamming into the Sierra Nevada Mountains. If a flight attendant wants to be a stand-up comedian, then they should sign up at an open mic night and perform.

When I walked into the house, I downed more ibuprofen and carefully laid down on the heating pad. I have recurrent training tomorrow in LAX, so I need to rest and heal my back. The heating pad gave me enough relief to fall asleep, and I napped for three hours. Matt came home with Chinese food for dinner, and I spent the rest of the night in bed watching *Sex in the City.*

I'm lucky to have him.

PAIRING 009: RECURRENT TRAINING DAY

Sunday
SFO—LAX

Matt woke me up at nine A.M. Thankfully, the pain in my back decreased from sleeping on the heating pad all night. Instead of causing my body to contort like a circus performer, the pain left me walking stiff. I handled that better than screaming each time I moved. The heating pad shut off during the night after a few hours, which was good, the last thing I wanted to do was bake myself to death while sleeping.

Getting old is a big bitch.

I emailed my doctor yesterday for some pain management. When she hadn't responded within the appropriate time—thirty seconds—I almost called 911 and reported her missing. She finally replied and called in a prescription to the pharmacy for a muscle relaxer. It was twenty-four hours later, but that's better than never. Honestly, I don't know if I need it now, but I'll fill the prescription and have it on hand for the next time my body decides to give out. Muscle relaxers and vodka? That's my type of afternoon. Makes me sound like Karen Walker from *Will & Grace*.

Spent the morning cuddling with Tucker on the sofa, which left me feeling content. He's been on Prozac for a month, and it seems to be working. My cat's on Prozac. It's ridiculous, but I'm crossing my fingers that it curbs his depression, obsessive behavior, and panic attacks. I'm not sure that he suffers from panic attacks, but his actions trigger me to have panic attacks, so one of us needed medication. We did a vote, and because he's not a registered voter with a valid ID, I won by a landslide. Now that he's on medication, he's more independent and doesn't gravitate to us as much, which makes me slightly sad. I'm never happy, I grumble when he's too dependent, and I groan when he's too independent. My kids would be fucked up.

I packed my backpack for my overnight trip to LAX for recurrent training. Recurrent training is the annual training class we must attend for a refresher on how to save lives if the airplane crashes into the Gulf of Mexico. That and how to manage passengers mental outrage when we run out of Dr. Pepper. I thought about taking the flight tomorrow morning, but that's cutting it way too close. If one cloud appears in San Francisco, the airport goes into a delay program, and I can't miss training.

Matt dropped me off at the airport, and while walking towards security, I started panicking that I left a required training item at home. Do I need Tucker's Prozac? Probably. I believe most flight attendants fear they are not prepared for recurrent training. I also think most flight attendants are on Prozac. If a flight attendant forgets only one of their required items (flight attendant manual, passport, watch, our patience), we get sent home for the day and have to follow up with our supervisor. I've never had that happen, but I imagine it sucks. Getting kicked out of recurrent training can result in the flight attendant's disqualification and not being able to work until they take additional unnecessary training classes.

My friend Derek is teaching the class, and it would be awkward if he had to kick me out because I left something behind. Interestingly, he's teaching my training class because I sort of got him the job at my airline. I shouldn't say that; nobody gets someone a job. I only provided him with a recommendation, and his personality and charm did the rest. Derek flew to Los Angeles to teach this one day class, and he was kind enough to let me stay in his hotel room tonight so that I don't have to pay for one. Management doesn't book hotel rooms for flight attendants when we have recurrent training in our base. They expect us to have accommodations, even if we don't live in the city. Most of us commute in and out of LAX, and rarely spend the night. Sadly, that doesn't mean anything to the airline industry.

I arrived at the airport and waited thirty minutes for the hotel shuttle van. My luck with hotels in the past three weeks has been subpar. Who did I piss off? Is there a hotel shuttle van God? If so, I'm sure I pissed her off. No doubt I'm being punished by the Universe for all those dollars I've saved not tipping shoddy van drivers. Listen, if you are an unsatisfactory van driver, you shouldn't get rewarded with a tip. Why is that so hard for people to understand? Once, in El Paso, our van driver was forty minutes late. He talked on his cell phone the entire drive, and when we asked him to turn down his music, he ignored us. The flight attendant sitting next to me complained the whole ride. When he finally pulled up to the hotel, she pulled out a dollar bill and handed it to him after she grabbed her luggage. I was astounded. I hauled my bag up onto the curb and walked away.

Inside at the check-in counter, I asked, "Why did you tip him?"

She frowned, "I don't know. I'd feel bad if I didn't"

Mediocre service does not deserve a tip. An employee like that will forever undoubtedly believe he deserves a tip for being an asshole to his customers.

I should apply to the hotel van work ethics committee, but the way some of these drivers act, there is no such committee.

Derek and I met in the lobby and had dinner and a beer at the hotel bar. It was nice to catch up. Derek's married to one of my ex-boyfriends, and I'm curious about their relationship. Not in a negative way, but I find it fascinating that I can be friends with my ex and his husband and not have any animosity towards them. I think that's a gift. I know too many people who hold grudges for the rest of their lives.

After dinner, we went back to his room, settled into our respective beds, and immediately shut off the lights.

Derek was asleep in three seconds, and that's not an exaggeration. There may be a shut off switch behind one of his ears. I think he's a robot. If so, I hope he's one of those cute robots, like *WALL-E*, and not all angry like *The Terminator*. I rolled over, comfortably placed my earbuds into my ear canals, and was pleased I downloaded the noise maker app. Not only does Derek fall asleep in record time, but he snores and inhales enough air to drag Mars closer to Earth.

Monday
LAX Recurrent

Recurrent training is soul-crushing. Passing kidney stones sounds better than spending ten hours in a classroom watching mindless PowerPoints, performing CPR on a baby mannequin, and rehearsing through mind-numbing emergency scenarios. Do you want to fight the war on terror? Put down the hoses and stop waterboarding. Waterboarding is for amateurs. If your goal is to torture terrorists to make them talk, send them to a flight attendant recurrent class. They'd tell you everything you want to know.

There were a total of three flight attendants in my class today, which made the day long and drawn-out. I told funny stories to make training more tolerable, but it was still painful. The reason being, even though Derek was teaching, I disliked a classmate. One of the guys I had never met but seemed friendly. The other flight attendant, the one I loathed, is a pile of buffalo scat.

Let's talk about him. Let's talk about Freddy. I may be crossing the line, but I personally think Freddy is an abomination to all flight attendants on the planet. He's vile enough to have 666 tattooed on his body. I'm guilty of not fancying many people, but I have a reason for not liking Freddy; he was friends with Evan. Unlike me getting the job for Derek, Evan helped Freddy get hired as a flight attendant. Evan went above and beyond by contacting the right people at the airline, briefing Freddy on the interview process, and then wrapped it all up in a perfect job recommendation bow. In return, Freddy did what anyone born from Satan would do—he used Evan. Evan gave him a free place to stay. Evan let Freddy use his apartment as a storage shed. Evan lent him money, which Freddy never paid back. The list is endless, and all Freddy did was take advantage of Evan. I'll admit, Evan keeps his emotions in check far better than me. Can you imagine bumping into someone on the jet bridge who owes you money and used you for months? I'd be terminated for verbal and physical abuse. Sadly, it took Evan a while to put this trash to the curb, and when he did, even the trash collectors didn't want to touch him.

Recurrent wasn't the first time I had met Freddy. We operated a flight together when I first transferred to LAX. I learned during that flight that he was not only a terrible human being, but he was also a terrible flight attendant. Those two qualities usually go together.

I was working the back galley position, and while the airplane taxied to the runway, Freddy walked to the back galley for reasons unknown to me. A mother seated in the last row stopped him, and politely asked, "May I get some water for my son?"

Freddy turned, "Is he dying?"

I stood with my arms folded in the back galley staring at him in disbelief. He never gave the passenger a chance to respond to his surly tongue, he quickly spun around and stomped back to the front of the airplane. I fought off my instinct to run after him, snatch him by his neck, drag him back to the last row, and force him to apologize while letting her thirsty kid kick him in the balls.

And that's me being polite about it.

I grabbed a small bottle of water and walked up to the passenger, "Here you go. I'm sorry about his tone. I'm Joe, your flight attendant. If you need anything else, please let me know."

I smiled. The passenger smiled. I turned and headed back to my galley pleased that I had covered my ass for when she wrote in a complaint letter. Sometimes protecting your own ass while working with a shitty flight attendant is all you can do.

I committed to not interacting with Freddy during recurrent, but it was challenging sitting in a classroom with only two other people.

During a classroom conversation, Derek asked, "So, you're trying to get a hold of the pilots. You call them twice, and they don't answer. You knock, and there's no answer. What could be happening?"

I yelled out, "Sex. The pilots are having sex."

All three of them laughed, which delighted me to have produced the funniest comment of the day. Too bad management doesn't hand out a pin for the most comic flight attendant at recurrent. If that were the case, I'd have no room left on my uniform. Freddy attempted to be funny and followed my lead by telling a few zingers, but like everything else in his life, he failed.

On the flight home, I sat next to a sexy muscle guy. I was seated in 11F, the window seat, and he was in 11D, the aisle seat, and the only thing between us was the steam coming off his hot body. He was so muscular he could have snapped me in half and then put me back together straight. And I don't mean straight like an arrow, I mean straight like I'd have to sleep with women. He had that type of body. The kind that turns a gay man straight because after he was done with you, you wouldn't need to sleep with another man ever again. I took a few stalker pictures. When I looked at the photos later, I noticed he was picking his nose.

I landed in San Francisco, and Matt called me while I walked through the terminal. Matt lost his house keys and hadn't left to pick me up from the airport. I suggested not worrying about the house key because I had mine. All he needed was the car key to drive me home. He asked, stressed, "Are you sure you have your house keys?"

I answered, "Yeah, I've been carrying them around for two days. And why are you worried? If you don't have keys, you can't lock the door."

Matt spent forty-five minutes looking for his keys. Apparently, while I was flying home sitting next to a hot guy digging deep inside his right nostril, my husband was at home having a nervous breakdown. He said he retraced his steps throughout the entire apartment to no avail. I informed him that I'd take the train home and then help him locate find his keys.

When I walked into the apartment, I found his keys within five minutes. I take that back—it was more like three minutes.

This is how it happened: I walked inside, placed my luggage against the wall in the dining room, walked into the bedroom to check his pants pockets, looked inside the desk drawers, swept through the bathroom, opened up the trash can—jiggled the trash bag—and heard the keys in the bottom of the trash bag. That's really two minutes. Once I found the elusive keys, I yelled, "I found them."

He stared at me in amazement, "How did you know to look in the trash can?"

I stepped past him and into the bedroom. As I began undressing, I answered, "Keys are always lost where you'd never think to look."

He walked over to me while wrapping his arms around me, "What would I do without you?"

"You'd be stuck inside the house for eternity, that's what you'd do without me."

I poured myself a glass of wine, sat on the sofa, and began complaining about Freddy. Merely talking about Freddy turned my neck crimson. When I brought up how infuriated I was at Freddy, Matt told me that I need to concentrate my energy on controlling my temper. He says I have too much hostility towards people who haven't done anything terrible to me. He questions if I'm annoyed with someone like Freddy—for wronging Evan—or truly angry.

I don't think my brain knows the difference.

He told me that when I get angry for no reason, I sound like a crazy person with a hair-trigger for rage.

I don't think my brain knows any other way to process information. I'm hardwired to bypass humiliation, rejection, disappointment, and jump headfirst into anger. I'm not playing the victim card, but this is a trait I acquired from being raised by alcoholic parents.

Thanks, Mom.

Matt doesn't jump directly into anger when someone irritates him. Since we've been together, he's never expressed feeling slighted by another person. On numerous occasions, when I believe that someone disrespected Matt, I'm the one who's gotten angry. When this happens, I rant and rave about how he should be furious, but he's not. He looks at me, "Why are you mad? Nobody did anything to you."

It makes sense at the moment, but my head is clear, and I'm not angry. I'm jealous that Matt can stay calm during challenging moments. I'm the complete opposite,

I'm ready to throw knives at our neighbors who bring their dog to the pool when the sign clearly reads: NO DOGS.

Anger feels great. It's powerful. It's an internal fissure letting out the steam of my volcanic temper. It's a long process, but I'm working on handling my anger. If I could get to a place where I don't throw my shoes across the room when my shoelaces are tied in a knot, I'll consider that winning.

PAIRING 010: JOE'S FIRST DRUG TEST

Tuesday
Home

Germanwings flight 9525 crashed in the French Alps, killing everyone on board today. I'd never heard of that airline, but it's a sad day whenever there's an airline disaster in the world. I often think that I could be in an airplane crash one day, which makes me want to quit my job and never leave the sofa. I can't do that, so if I died in an airplane incident, it was my time. When it's our time to go, it doesn't matter where we are. We're all on borrowed time; doomed to die eventually. Some peaceful, some burnt to a crisp on the side of a mountain.

Jesus Christ. I'm morbid.

Wednesday
SFO—LAX

I flew into base tonight, and I'm sleeping in the flight attendant crew lounge. Thankfully, I have the entire room to myself. I'm a little disappointed with my friend Chris. He is in Los Angeles for business and offered to let me stay in his hotel room tonight. First I had a free room with Derek, and now I was planning on rooming with Chris. That's two free rooms this week. I know I'm a mooch, but I report at 5:50 A.M. tomorrow and spending money to sleep for eight hours in a hotel is not acceptable. While I waited for Chris to respond to my text, I set up camp on one of the recliners. It would be a long wait.

He never acknowledged my text.

Thursday
LAX—PHX—DEN—PDX

I slept fine. Not good. Not terrible. No coffee and no breakfast before my first flight. If I murder someone, I shouldn't be held accountable.

Chris finally texted me back this morning: *Why didn't you call me? I saw your text this morning. I was back in my room.*

I didn't respond; I probably won't. I call total bullshit on Chris not receiving my text until this morning. Why the fuck can't people text you back? There should be a texting guideline for people to follow. It's completely ridiculous. It's a fact that he keeps his cell phone next to him at all times—like everyone else in the world—so I know he received the text. Whether he didn't want me to stay with him was another story. Why are people so unreliable? If you don't want me to stay with you, say it.

The first fight of the day was rough, but I managed even with all the trashy passengers pushing my buttons. When we were landing, a few passengers voiced their displeasure because while I picked up trash and conducted a compliance check, I requested their half-empty coffee cups that they didn't have time to drink on the short flight. My solution is: don't order coffee on a short trip. Problem solved.

We landed in Portland, and I was crankier than a toddler with a shitty diaper. I took a short nap and then showered. Refreshed, I met the entire crew for drinks at Portland City Grill, which is my favorite happy hour in Portland. After four beers and some light food, we all headed back to the hotel. On the walk back, I had to pee; I quickened my step and relieved myself in a bush a few blocks ahead of the other flight attendants. Nothing feels better than urinating outside. I feel bad for women who can't whip it out and pee on the side of the road. That's not the case in San Francisco. I once watched a woman pissing at a bus stop, mid-morning, without a care in the world. If I were straight, single, and into homeless women who don't wipe after they've used the bus stop as a toilet, I'd have brought her home.

Word on the street is that the first officer took down that Germanwings A320. The captain came out to use the lavatory, and the first officer put the flight deck on lockdown and did a nose dive into the mountains. How fucked up is that? When you buy an airplane ticket, you don't expect the airline to kill you. This is different than an unfortunate accident, this guy suffered from depression and had a note from his doctor telling him not to fly on that day.

Why the hell was he on that airplane?

Friday
PDX—SAN—LAS—SFO

Flying three legs again today, but I'm rested and have coffee with a delicious sausage quiche to inhale. Our first flight was an early morning flight, and most passengers slept. That's the best way to start a long day.

The second flight, from San Diego to Las Vegas, was full so the gate agent made a gate announcement asking passengers to check their bags. A straightforward request that happens daily. A few seconds later, a middle-aged woman brought her luggage up and was handed a ticket to collect her bag at baggage claim in Las Vegas. Simple, right? Not for this lady. When Mrs. Checked Bag Lady stepped on the airplane, she asked the lead flight attendant, "What bin did you put my bag in?"

The lead flight attendant was confused, "Your bag is in the cargo bin."

Mrs. Checked Bag Lady lost her mind. Honestly, the jury is still out on exactly how much of her mind was actually lost before she arrived at the gate. We quickly found out that her goal was to have her bag inside the airplane the entire time. She checked it at the gate assuming the gate agent would personally carry it to the aircraft for her. Mrs. Checked Bag Lady was delusional. When the lead flight attendant informed me of these shenanigans at the front of the airplane, I suggested having the passenger drug tested to determine if she was high or utterly ignorant to procedures at the airport. That sounds like a great idea, drug testing passengers at the airport. Sounds cumbersome, but let the TSA handle it. They don't do anything except stand around all day and take half-empty bottles of perfume home.

During boarding, a male passenger walked to the back of the airplane and stuffed his bag in a bin that read: CREW ONLY. The sign was self-explanatory, but not to this dude. I stepped over to the row and fished the backpack out, "Sir, you can't place your bag in there."

As I began moving his bag to the next available space, he challenged, "Why?"

Without saying a word, I hoisted his bag into the bin directly next to the one he was attempting to use, and with a pleasant fake smile, I pointed at the placard explaining it was crew only.

He planned on making our encounter as painful as possible. He pointed at the overhead bin we were discussing, "But I want my bag in that bin."

My smile had faded into a grimace. I reminded the man for the third time, "Sir, that's for crew only. If you don't like the bin I placed it in, we can move it to another one. Or you can put it under the seat in front of you, or we can do the easy thing and check it."

None of these were options he accepted. "I don't think you hear me. I want it in that bin."

Before I could respond, a white guy behind him jumped up and caught me off guard. With a voice presumably obtained from twenty years in the military, he announced, "The flight attendant told you now three times. That's it. Drop it. You can't put your bag in that bin." He glanced over at me and with a deep tone, added, "I've got your back."

I liked this guy. Someone wanted free drinks on the flight and that someone was my new bodyguard. I felt like Whitney Houston without having to deal with Kevin Costner. Although I was thrilled this brute stood up for me in a crisis, I worried our standstill might become disorderly. All I needed was to be on Fox & Friends after my new bodyguard beat up a Middle Eastern guy on my flight.

I offered to find another overhead bin for his bag—spoiler, there was nothing wrong with the overhead bin where I moved his backpack—but he waved me off with a flick of the wrist and sat down. My first instinct was to get the attention of my bodyguard to rough this guy up for being rude, but then I remembered Fox & Friends.

While performing the safety demonstration in the middle of the airplane, I stopped what I was doing, turned around, and waved to the lead flight attendant to pause for a moment while I politely asked a large group in the exit row to quiet down. And to clarify, I mean large like three people who bring Krispy Kreme doughnuts on the airplane as their carry on. These three passengers talked loud enough to drown out the lead flight attendant making the safety information announcement. And mind you, I stood four rows away from them. It was extremely distracting. As I placed the life vest over my head, I heard the words "Animal Style," "Double Double," and "The Flying Dutchman" echo through the cabin. I figured they had passed on hotel accommodations in San Francisco and decided to sleep under the drive-through window at In-N-Out Burger.

These passengers quieted down without me having to take their doughnuts away. Wonder how that would have turned out for me? Probably a few broken teeth and a few empty Krispy Kreme boxes shoved up my ass. Certainly not as easy as taking candy away from a five-year-old. We continued with the safety demonstration and almost finished without incident when a disruptive family in the front row kept talking loudly and sitting on their knees to face the seats behind them. It took longer to complete the safety demonstration than it did to fly to Las Vegas.

I'm starting to think that today is National Asshole Day.

During our quick beverage service, I had two older white Republican-looking ladies in 17A and 17B who each ordered a seltzer with lemon, cranberry juice, and decaf coffee on the fifty-five-minute flight to Las Vegas. I hate profiling, but they looked like their idea of a good time was watching Oprah Winfrey go to jail in *The Color Purple*. You know the type, they kneel by their bed wrapped in an American flag housecoat saying their nightly prayers while holding an autographed copy of *The Art of The Deal* by Donald Trump's ghostwriter. I expected after drinking all those fluids, these two white devils walked off the airplane with a heavy Depend Silhouette undergarment.

I wonder if pilots take full adult diapers into consideration when calculating weight and balance before departure? Most likely not. If they did, flights to West Palm Beach would only have four passengers on them.

At the short stay hotel by San Francisco International Airport, I attempted a nap, but the moment I closed the curtains, Matt called and invited me to dinner. My alarm is set for four A.M tomorrow, instead of going home and having Matt drive me to the airport that early, I opted to stay at the hotel. That also gave Matt a reason to hang out with me on my layover. Honestly, it's like meeting a secret lover in a different city. We have to keep our relationship spicy after all these years.

After dinner, we stopped in Williams-Sonoma to browse all the gadgets Ina Garten buys to make her kitchen look fabulous. That's what I do on my layovers, purchase kitchen gadgets. I stand corrected, I don't buy them, Matt does. If you want to see a gay six-foot-five man queen out over an All-Clad Belgian Waffle Maker—go shopping with my husband. I question whether we are buying items or he's auditioning for *RuPaul's Drag Race*. Matt really loves anything to do with having an elaborate Food Network-style kitchen. I, on the other hand, only care about eating food from a Food Network-style kitchen.

Earlier today, I received a disturbing email from a fan who lives in Ireland. Well, I don't think he's a fan anymore. Let's call him, Mr. Groceries because he's a bagger in a grocery store. Mr. Groceries is gay and informed me that his co-workers bully him about wanting to become a flight attendant. He also stated that the human resource department at his current job knows other human resource employees who work for the airline industry, and his company threatened to sabotage him becoming a flight attendant.

My first thought was, *this guy must be one hell of a grocery bagger.*

Why would he want to leave if he's that important to the success of this grocery store? I'd be asking for a raise and stock options. My second thought was, *how do they know human resource employees at all the airlines?* That seems like a lot of people, but what do I know. There could be an entire underground human resource ring that prevents grocery store employees from becoming flight attendants. My third thought was, *why do they care that he wants to be a flight attendant?*

I don't know what the deal is with this Mr. Groceries, but after our email exchange today, I'm glad I don't live in the same country as him or shop at his market. I'd ask for paper, and he'd give me plastic. It would be a travesty. This was the third email he sent, and in it, he worried about the Germanwings Airlines disaster and how it would impact his chances of working as a flight attendant. He also added that with this recent airplane crash, his co-workers will have another reason to discourage him from becoming a flight attendant.

Who the fuck are these co-workers? They sound extremely nosey. After reading his emails, I've concluded that Mr. Groceries shouldn't be stuck in an airplane at 38,000 feet with no escape.

I question if he should even bag groceries.

All joking aside, I do feel bad for him. I don't know if he's looking for an ear to chew on or wants a United States husband. Sadly for him—and happily for me—I'm off the market. I responded back to him with a short five sentences and encouraged him to stop letting people bully him and to live his life for himself.

Sweet and to the point.

He emailed me back almost immediately. As if he had the response in the draft folder of his Gmail account. Like the previous ones, it was long and drawn out. Six paragraphs long to be exact, making my email look uncaring. Mr. Groceries laid into me hard and told me I'm not the person he thought I was, which made perfect sense because we've never met. He added that I don't care about him (another true statement) and that he is barking up the wrong tree (again, this guy gets it when he's upset) when he emailed me about his co-workers bullying him for being a gay Irish guy whose dream it was to become a flight attendant.

I'm a tough-love kind of guy; I don't beat around the bush, and if that's too much for this stranger, then fuck him.

Mr. Groceries ended his email rant with: *...please don't respond because I don't want to hear from you.*

He missed the part where he emailed me first.

I think Mr. Groceries is a ticking time bomb. I can't think of this anymore tonight, I'm going to bed. I'm grateful he lives on the other side of the pond.

Saturday
SFO—BOI—PHX—LAX

I woke up in a great mood. At the airport, I stopped at the small coffee shop next to the gate for my caffeine fix. While waiting for my coffee order, "Easy Lover" by Phil Collins started playing inside the airport. I began humming along and noticed an older gentleman standing next to me, nodding his head to the music. In unison, we started singing along to the song. It was five A.M., and here I was singing a duet with a complete stranger. Typically, at that hour of the morning, I don't make eye contact with people. My duet partner swayed from side to side while we harmonized, and I noticed his wife giving him the side-eye while she grabbed their drinks off the counter.

When the song ended, I looked over at him, "We should go on the road as a duet."

He grabbed his drink and laughed, "That sounds like a great idea."

I enjoy unexpected life moments. These experiences lessen my disappointment for humanity. I believe that positive interactions with fellow humans are important, specifically ones where I find myself singing along to Phil Collins with a stranger.

I walked on the airplane and met our friendly pilots. What a great start to the day. I was in a positive mood, I'd sung a duet with a complete stranger, and our pilots were not assholes.

On that note, the flight attendants were a different story, their attitudes sucked. They bitched nonstop on the shuttle ride to the airport. I totally understood it was early and that roosters hadn't started crowing yet, but I needed them to relax their negativity. Their mood was bringing me down until I recognized my duet partner boarding the airplane. He walked to the back of the aircraft and camped out in the last row with his wife and two sons.

I stepped over to him and leaned into his ear, "You were the one singing with me at the coffee shop to Phil Collins."

He smiled, "I sure was."

We both laughed. I responded, "I got my eye on you." Then I realize that may sound odd because I'm white and he's the color of roasted coffee beans. I worried that he was insulted, so during beverage service, I handed him two cans of orange juice. During boarding for the flight to Phoenix, a boisterous lady walked to the back of the airplane and yelled, "Can you turn some air on or something? It's hot in here."

I thought about asking her to sing a duet with me to lighten her mood, but she didn't seem like the duet type. I picked up the interphone and made a call to the flight deck, asking the pilots to lower the temperature in the cabin.

Here's a confession, it was a fake call. While the passenger leaned against the lavatory door gawking at me, I picked up the handset, created a made-up one-way conversation, and then hung up the interphone. I deserve a Golden Globe for this job, or at least a People's Choice Award.

"They're gonna cool off the airplane," I informed her.

"Good. How can you handle this heat? I didn't pay to sweat on an airplane."

I smirked. When the lady turned around to stomp back to her seat, I may have flipped her the bird while ducking behind my jumpseat. I'll give her this, it was slightly warm inside the airplane, but because she acted like an asshole when she walked to the back galley, I decided to suffer so she'd be miserable.

Now I understand how Republican voters feel when they vote against their own interest.

The general public is making me act like a bigger dick than I portray on my blog. A few minutes later, I noticed a different female passenger step out of her row and head towards the lavatory. While I stood in the back galley watching people herd to their seats, she opened the lavatory door and disappeared inside.

When she finally opened the door, she barked, "The water isn't working. Is it broken?"

"They're servicing the water during boarding," and to be kind, I immediately opened the service bin and produced a few hand sanitary napkins for her to use.

She rolled her eyes, "Oh, that looks sanitary."

I had no idea people flying out of Boise were such assholes. We were on our way to Phoenix, so I'll assume that's where she resides. Makes sense she's an asshole, I'd be an asshole too if I lived in a city where the temperature reached 500 degrees in July. As she wiped her hands clean and placed the soiled napkins in the lavatory trash bin, I thought, *Maybe you should use the fucking restroom in the airport and not rush on the goddamn airplane to take a piss.*

I may need a sabbatical.

Before the front airplane door closed, I called the flight deck and asked the pilots to cool off the cabin. I had suffered enough.

After landed in LAX and opening the airplane door, the lead flight attendant called the back galley to alert me that an employee from the Drug and Alcohol department was there to administer a drug test on me. I thanked her for warning me but thought, *what the hell can I do about it now?* If I had cocaine or a liter of vodka coursing through my veins—I'd be fucked.

Mr. Drug Tester was humorless. I wanted to ask him if his dog died five minutes before my flight landed, but decided against it. Drug testing is slightly unnerving. I don't do drugs, so I have nothing to worry about, but as I stepped onto the jet bridge, my brain convinced me that I had shot myself up with enough smack to take down a herd of elephants. A flight attendant once told me, "Don't worry. If you aren't doing drugs, you have nothing to fear."

That's complete bullshit. My tension had my heart racing and sweat dripping down my forehead. I imagined as we walked by the gate heading towards the hallway leading to the drug testing center, the gate monitor read: JOE DOES CRACK.

Mr. Drug Tester was silent as he escorted me to his office. The silence was maddening. Who walks down a dark hallway in complete silence? This must be how inmates feel as they walk the green mile. My hysteria almost led me to confess a drug addiction that at no time has ever existed. I've never once put a joint to my mouth.

Okay, that's a lie. A long time ago, I tried smoking marijuana outside a gay bar; it did not go well. I tried impressing a guy I was into by playing cool in his car. He pulled out a joint, took a hit, and then passed it over to me. I took one puff and yelled, "That tastes like a forest fire," and never tried it again.

He left me at the bar that night. And this was decades before Uber.

For me, drug testing is time wasted when I could be doing something productive, like getting coffee or fighting off the advances of horny pilots in the crew lounge.

What? It's possible.

Lucky for Mr. Drug Tester, I had five hours to kill before my commute home. I'd guess that's why I wasn't angry about this inconvenience. If I'd been running to catch my flight home, I'd have been arrested.

Mr. Drug Tester walked me around a corner and into a nondescript door right into his minimal office. There was a small desk, one chair, and a door leading to a bathroom.

He finally spoke and pointed at the paper, "Please read and sign here." Once I signed the form agreeing that if I had even smelled whiskey that morning, I'd be terminated, he watched me wash and dry my hands. Then, to my surprise, he walked me into the restroom. I immediately thought, *Oh shit, these people are fucking serious. This is a visual drug test.*

He squirted blue dye into the toilet and asked me to pull out my pockets. It felt like the end scene in the movie, *Clue*, when Leslie Ann Warren surprised the audience as she pulled the gun from her purse, except the only thing I was pulling out of my pocket was lint. In my seven years at the airline, this was my first drug test. Did he think I was carrying around stale urine for the past seven years waiting for this moment?

Now that we were standing on top of each other in a restroom smaller than the airplane lavatory, I figured a joke would ease the tension, "I dumped out all my extra pocket urine this morning."

Do not joke while getting drug tested. Mr. Drug Tester glared at me as I imagine Kim Jong Un looks at one of his uncles before they are decapitated. Instantly, I was pleased my filter held back me saying, "I hope crack doesn't show up on these things."

He barked out all the rules again and added, "I need forty-five cc's of the yellow stuff or you'll have to wait around and give me more." The last time I heard someone asking for more urine was in the backroom of the Dallas Eagle in 2009.

After I completed my task, I stepped out of the restroom and handed him the cup. He grabbed it without wearing a glove, and my lip curled up in disgust. I rewashed my hands as he tested the temperature. Curious, I asked, "Why do you check the temperature?"

He answered, "To make sure it came out of your body. People carry other people's urine around."

Shocking. People really do that sort of thing. To think, I can barely drag my luggage and tote bag through the airport, and there's some dude out there with his neighbor's urine strapped to his leg waiting for this exact moment. "Do people cry while doing this?"

Without looking at me, he continued to fill out paperwork and answered, "Yes."

I signed more paperwork—again—and said, "If that thing comes back positive, your system is broken. I barely eat the poppy seeds off a muffin." He nodded, which left me feeling like I walk Hollywood Blvd at night.

When Mr. Drug Tester finally released me from his office, I headed over to my supervisor Barbara's office to complain about how I had been violated. Mr. Drug Tester hadn't touched me inappropriately, but having someone demand your urine is off-putting. Barbara agreed, and we began a lovely chat about being violated, but then our conversation turned south quickly.

We started talking about flight attendant work rule policies, and our debate overheated rapidly. The topic: the flight attendant sick policy. More specifically, calling in sick during a holiday period.

I understand that the airline needs to protect itself from sick calls. Flight attendants are notorious for calling in sick. In fact, I am one of those flight attendants. But I don't agree with our new policy. The new policy is based on a point system. We receive a certain number of points for each sick call, for being late, for not showing up for our report time, and so on. If we get too many points within a rolling twelve-month period, we go on disciplinary action. Fair enough. But my issue with the policy is that management doesn't make an exception for a flight attendant who brings in a doctor's note. A point is a point, no matter if you bring in a doctor's note or not. I think policies like this punish the people who might honestly be sick during a holiday. Not all flight attendants who call in sick during a holiday are trying to play the system. Not everyone who calls in sick over a holiday is a liar. I don't care what day it is if I'm sick, I'm calling in. If I've taken the time to go to the doctor to prove that I am in fact, dying of something, the airline should forgo the point.

Barbara disagreed with me, and my neck turned fire engine red. While we bickered, her voice shook, and my hands flared around like I was swatting bees. Anyone looking into the office through the glass window would think we were playing charades. What annoyed me the most about Barbara was all the airline propaganda she tossed at me.

North Korea uses less propaganda than my airline.

We left the conversation on a good note. We agreed to disagree. And honestly, there was no need to trigger Barbara's angina discussing flight attendants who call in sick during Easter weekend.

When I got to the gate, the gate agent asked, "Are you willing and able to sit in the exit row?" while staring at me in full uniform.

Was she joking? Does she understand what the flight attendant does on the airplane? Why am I getting drug tested when employees are running around the terminal higher than a 737 at cruising altitude?

I looked down at my ID with the word CREW printed on it, and I said, "I hope so."

She looked back down at her computer, "I'll call you back to the gate in twenty minutes to give you your seat assignment. Stay close to the gate."

At first, I thought she was a new employee, but that wasn't the case—this bitch was crazy. There were twelve open seats, and I was the first one checked in on the standby list. Why wait? Did she expect twelve people to purchase $500 tickets in the next twenty minutes? The day that happens, I'm applying with the cruise lines.

I should reevaluate my employment at this airline. I need some wine, or better yet, drugs. I had my first drug test, and now, my answer to a stressful afternoon is getting high. What's wrong with me? Honestly, the perfect time to start popping some edibles is five minutes after your first drug test; and if I'm getting high, I'm definitely an edible kind of guy. This is LAX, it should be easier scoring a pot brownie in one of the restrooms than it is sneaking a bottle of mouthwash through security.

What if the FAA allowed flight attendants the opportunity to get high when we fly? I'm not talking about being stoned to the point that we think the actors on the television are plotting against us, but maybe right in the middle—the high sweet spot—where we believe the actors on the television are merely talking to our pets.

Imagine how happy flight attendants—and passengers—would be throughout the entire flight. A passenger might inquire, "May I get one more bag of nuts?"

And we'd respond with giggles and glazed over eyes, "One? Nonsense. You deserve ten bags."

We'd probably laugh to death opening the aircraft door during an emergency evacuation, but at least we'd be having fun.

PAIRING 011: DRAMA QUEENS

Monday
LAX—JFK—BOS

My stomach was in knots regarding the two flight attendants on this pairing. I'd never met them before, but word on the street was that they were a train derailment. Generally, I like making my own conclusions about people, but after hearing horror stories about these two since transferring to LAX, I had little faith.

I walked past Freddy at the airport this morning, and I addressed him with a soft, "Hello." He ignored me. That's refreshing; I can officially stop acting fake towards him. Acting fake is exhausting.

I stopped into the supervisor's office, and when they heard who I was flying with, one of the supervisors broke out into a deep laugh for five minutes.

I wanted to run.

When I met Marlie, the one I've heard the most rumors about, she seemed tolerable. A complete relief. She had received fantastic news—I have no clue what it was about—putting her in a pleasant mood. A few minutes later, the other flight attendant, Stan, sauntered into the lounge and it became quite clear that he's scatterbrained and sloppy. While the two of them stood in front of the row of computers chatting, I watched the hands on the clock inch closer to our gate report time. I'm the mid-cabin flight attendant, which means I'm at the bottom of the barrel of importance, but I require things done in a certain way. And I do not like arriving at the gate late, not even one minute. My goal is to always be at the gate as early as possible. Without speaking a word to me, the two of them grabbed the handles on their luggage and marched out of the room without conducting a safety briefing.

That was a strike against Marlie. Not so much that we didn't conduct a thorough safety brief, but that she didn't ask a security question. I didn't remind her, either. I know that's bad, but I'm not in charge, and it's not my responsibility to tell a flight attendant—who's been here over ten years—the most fundamental aspects of her job. During the safety briefing, the lead flight attendant is required to ask a security question to the other flight attendants. It's not imperative that we have the correct answer, but it's essential that we ask a safety question. If one of us doesn't know the answer, we all work together to answer it as a team. It's the same as a group classroom quiz. I figured that if we crashed into the side of a mountain and the FAA found my charred body among the rubble with my vocal cords still attached, I'd tell them Marlie never asked us a safety question. To make matters even worse, she didn't have a watch with her, which is a mandatory flight attendant item. How are you supposed to tell how much time you have before the airplane crashes into Lake Mead without a watch? Don't quote me on this, but I'm pretty sure that not having a watch is a terminable offense. If not terminable, definitely execution by an airplane engine.

When the three of us stepped onto the airplane, we found out the WiFi was inoperative. I decided a little instigating was in order, so while standing in the front galley with Marlie, I kept whispering under my breath, "This is bullshit. Someone should do something about this."

What Marlie overheard was, "Marlie, do something about this."

Once the ignition is lit, there's no stopping Marlie from transforming into the drama queen. She complains to anyone whose ear she has the privilege of bending, and most often it's one of the pilots.

That's the gossip I heard about Marlie. She loves drama. I mean, LOVES drama. And if there is none, she'll create it. Stan is so laid back; you have to check his pulse. He's a cool dude, but I think it's time for him to retire.

Hell, it's time for me to retire.

In regards to Stan, I think it's perfectly acceptable to relax at your job, but you should still follow some guidelines. The airline has volumes of policies and procedures to follow. Do I agree with them all? No. Do I support them all? No. But Stan does whatever he wants from the moment he steps on the airplane until he steps off. That's fine if you own the airline, but the last time I checked, Stan wasn't the CEO.

Our flight to JFK was extremely demanding. The passengers weren't demanding; Marlie and her dramatic personality were. Each time I stepped in her galley, her emotions were bunched up in a knot. Every situation or interaction with a passenger was a grand production. Something as uncomplicated as a passenger needing an extra napkin sent her into a frenzy. To me and you, it's a simple napkin, but to Marlie, it's the airplane nose-diving into Mt. Rainier. As annoying as her dramatic outbursts were (she asked if we should divert because a passenger had a headache) I'll confess, it's fun to watch. I'm a horrible person for finding joy in her dramatic personality, and I don't apologize for it.

After service, Stan and I sat in the back galley while he told inappropriate jokes.

He asked, "How do you make a gay guy cry twice?"

"I don't know. How?"

"Fuck him in the ass and then wipe your dick on his new drapes."

I let out a weak giggle and responded, "I'd be way more upset if a guy fucked me in the ass and then let the cats out when he left."

I did not hold back that his joke sucked and that I don't even have drapes. Okay, I have drapes, but he doesn't need to know that.

Halfway through the flight, the pilots came out for a lavatory break. When I walked out of the flight deck into the front galley, the smell of the captain's rectum permeated my nasal passage. It was horrendous, and the scent is hard to describe. He didn't only take a shit; he dropped a shit bomb in the front lavatory. He's a shit bomber. If Osama Bin Laden were alive, he'd crawl out of a cave in Pakistan to award this guy's ass a metal of terrorist honor. If you ask me the airplane needs to be taken to the airplane graveyard in the Mojave desert and destroyed. Seriously, it's the nastiest odor I've ever experienced on a plane, and I've smelled some nasty airplane lavatory shits. I've even dropped a few off myself.

After service, I spent the flight writing. Marlie wanted to know my backstory so I gave her the edited version, which honestly, I can't even begin to remember what I said. There was probably some truths thrown in with a few fabrications. Stan commented that he recognized me from being on the cover of our departmental flight attendant magazine and at that point, Marlie looked confused and asked, "How have you only been here eight months, and you're already on the cover of a magazine?"

"Eight months?" I asked, "I've been here for seven years." She jumped up from sitting on one of the service bins and pointed at me as if her amnesia had cleared up in an instant. She recanted a story, from 2009, when she and I had dinner together in New York City with a group of flight attendants. I do not remember that at all. I nodded along with her in consensus.

She smiled, "Do you remember?"

While shaking my head in agreement, I smiled and answered, "Nope."

The second time the pilots required a lavatory break, Stan decided to go up to the flight deck because he wanted to speak with the first officer. In the states, there have to be two people in the flight deck at all times. If that were the case in other countries, maybe that first officer wouldn't have been able to fly that airplane into the side of a mountain so effortlessly.

Too soon?

But imagine if while the captain is out of the flight deck, the first officer has a heart attack. I think the flight attendant is expected to fly the airplane until the captain returns from destroying the plastic airplane toilet seat with his shit bombs. Honestly, I haven't a clue of what to do if a pilot has a heart attack while I'm in the flight deck. Management states they trained us on these procedures in flight attendant training, but they've also stated they wouldn't give us any trouble if we ever called in fatigued, and that was a lie. Maybe I was searching online for a crash pad the day they discussed the—*How To Fly The Airplane When Your Pilot Dies*—module because I don't remember shit about flying an airplane. What I do know is that if a pilot has a heart attack, or passes out in the flight deck, we are required to ~~unzip their pants~~ undo their tie and pull their feet off the pedals. After that, I have no clue. Does it even matter? I'm sure by the time I've finished screaming; we'd be hitting the Pacific Ocean head first.

The pilot's lavatory break went on for thirty minutes. While Marlie stood guard in the front galley, and Stan hibernated in the flight deck telling the first officer his boring gay-guy-cry-twice joke, I ran around answering call bells and running drinks to passengers like a waitress at a strip club. It became hard to manage, especially while countless passengers were using the back galley lavatories forcing me to dance around them while carrying Chardonnays and Diet Cokes to passengers that weren't seated in my area. Technically, we share all the sections but screw that when I'm doing all the work.

Once they finished, Stan sauntered to the back galley. I threw out a bitchy, "I'm starting the second service."

With a playful grin, he responded, "Thanks."

Did he think I was conducting a drink service in his section? I think he did too many drugs in the 70s. Before we landed at JFK, I jotted more down in my journal. Marlie noticed and asked, "Are you writing about how beautiful and wonderful I am?"

I smile, "Something like that."

We landed at JFK and made our way to a different airplane because we had an airplane swap. An airplane swap is when the crew lands on one aircraft and has to fly to another city on a different one. Airplane swaps suck. After flying across the country for six hours, we're expected to deplane, drag our luggage through the airport, board another airplane, redo our security checks, and then put on our happy smiles for a new set of passengers. I used the restroom, and when I got to the gate, the agent handed me the paperwork.

"I'm not the lead flight attendant. Are the other flight attendants down there?"

The gate agent answered, "Yes. They walked by me and didn't say a word."

That did not surprise me. When I walked on the airplane our new captain—hopefully not a shitter like our last one—addressed me as if I was the lead flight attendant.

I politely said, "The female flight attendant is in charge." and pointed to row six where Marlie sat chatting on her cell phone. Stan stood in the back galley throwing peace signs up in the air as I walked down the aisle to place my luggage in the overhead bin. You need a lot of alcohol to work with Marlie and Stan...or some decent meditation skills.

We had a short flight scheduled to Boston. After departure, Marlie and I heard a bell ringing while we sat in our jump seats. It chimed every few seconds. Marlie said, "I think it's coming from the engine when the blades go around."

I turned my head and leaned in closer to her, "You think you can hear a bell on the engine at this speed?"

When we reached 10,000 feet, she called the captain, and he confirmed that we had an engine issue after take-off, but they resolved it quickly. I apologized for questioning her hearing and decided not to talk about her behind her back within a hundred-mile radius.

I wonder how frequent engine problems occur that we aren't aware of on the airplane. It probably happens more often than I want to admit. Passengers would never fly on planes if they knew this kind of shit happened.

The van ride to the hotel was quiet. We checked in, and as I walked to my room, I passed room 1048, and some lady was moaning loud enough to wake up a homeless person sleeping in Boston Common. She wasn't holding back, it sounded like she was getting pounded harder than a nail into a concrete wall. Whoever was banging her hit her G, H, I, and J spot, and she wanted everyone in the hotel to know about it. At least someone's getting worked out tonight.

Tuesday
BOS—SFO

My hotel room was small enough to brush your teeth in the sink while taking your morning shit. That's not a joke. At one point, I farted, and the person in the next room called the front desk to complain about the smell.

Okay, that's a joke.

I woke up and texted Evan, and he met me for breakfast. I've only seen Evan twice in the past nine months, which is a record. We met at a local cafe and caught up on life and work-related gossip. After breakfast, we stopped for coffee at a small cafe, and a handsome security guard winked at me on the street. One thing about Boston, they may sound like they're talking with a mouthful of marbles, but they are hot.

When we arrived at the airport, I was randomly selected to go through regular screening instead of through Known Crewmember. As I walked back down the corridor away from the KCM access area, I passed a pilot walking towards me and said in a slightly bitchy tone, "You're lucky you weren't thirty seconds earlier."

I tried keeping a positive attitude about the flight. My attempts at having a better outlook about my job are mentally exhausting. One minute I like coming to work, the next minute I consider working at the Valero gas station down the street from our house. How bad could that be? Do you think they have a 401K match? Anyway, if I have a positive attitude about work, positive things will happen at work. If I'm a negative bitch, bad shit will happen at work, like a passenger yelling at me for running out of Sprite, or the airplane crashing into another aircraft on the runway.

What's with me and always talking about airplanes crashing into something?

During boarding, the passengers seemed pleasant, which was excellent—positive thinking in action. Then the captain came over the intercom, "Ladies and gentlemen, the winds aren't our friend today. We'll be fighting some powerful winds today, so we may have to make a fuel stop on our way to LAX."

I'm officially tossing that positive thinking bullshit right out onto the tarmac.

As we boarded the flight, I asked a lady to put her small dog inside the carrier. She looked at me with the saddest eyes—the lady, not the dog—and responded, "But she's my baby and keeps barking."

"I'm sorry, ma'am, but all pets must be inside their carriers throughout the entire flight." After that, the lady refused to look at me.

Then an overweight male passenger, who was in the middle seat next to the lady and her dog, complained that he couldn't possibly sit there because he was allergic to dogs. I'm guessing furry dogs you pet and not hot dogs you shove in your mouth. His gut suggested he ran a hot dog shelter inside his stomach.

I moved the big guy to another middle seat, and before I had a chance to walk away, the skinny passenger seated in the aisle demanded that I do something for him because he was uncomfortable and not happy. I didn't give a damn. I was hoping the chubby passenger would eat him to shut him up. My level of irritation was palpable. I despise boarding, and the mid-flight attendant position is the airplane bitch. When you are the mid-flight attendant, you deal with ALL the bullshit. The pet bullshit. The overweight bullshit. The everything bullshit. Stan didn't help my mood by sitting on the back galley jump seat working on his recurrent modules while ignoring his job. We ended up moving the skinny aisle passenger to another seat because the overweight guy oozed into his space. I can't blame the thin passenger for being pissed off; I'd have been furious. If this story were all over social media, people would be defending the overweight passenger, until they had to sit next to him and then they'd be as outraged as the skinny aisle guy. I hate to say this, but if you are big enough to take up two seats, your ass should purchase two seats. If you're obese enough that your body parts hangover into the next seat, we have a problem. Maybe we should weigh people at the gate instead of carry-on bags? Let's replace the carry-on bag sizer with a scale and measuring tape. It's an idea. Listen, you must think outside the box, that's how we have Facebook.

Halfway through the flight, Marlie walked to the back galley and asked me to talk to the overweight passenger because while standing in the front galley he told her, "I want to confront that asshole."

I looked over at Stan to suggest that he talk to the guy, but he was preoccupied working out with a hefty rubber band on the airplane door. He created a Bowflex in the back galley. I'm telling you, that guy is a piece of work.

When I walked up to the front galley, I hadn't realized how big this passenger was. He could easily squash the skinny aisle passenger with his big toe. I asked him if he was alright; I could tell he was heated. He got upset, but not at me, "That fucking asshole isn't brave enough to tell me to my face that he was uncomfortable. I know I'm a big dude. I asked him if he was comfortable, and he ignored me."

I tried to diffuse the situation, "I understand you're frustrated. Don't let some stranger get the best of you. I'm verbally abused by strangers on the airplane every day. If I let them get to me, I'd never be able to do this job."

"That's messed up. I want to confront that guy so bad."

"Well, if there is an altercation on the airplane and we have to divert, you will most likely get arrested, and we don't want that."

"You're right. Thanks, Joe."

That was easier than I had envisioned. I walked passed the skinny passenger and wanted to lean in and say, "I just saved your fucking life. Can you write in a compliment letter for me?"

Once things seemed to settle down, a kid in row eighteen vomited everywhere. Stan had to help the parents clean up the area while I sat in the back galley and didn't give two shits. Marlie helped them too, but I played the two-many-hands-in-the-kitchen clusterfuck card. The vomit smelled about as bad as Captain Shitner's shit bomb yesterday. What food causes your vomit to stink like the inside of a pilot's asshole?

I do not want to know. The father was embarrassed and stared at his kid like the first thing he was doing when we landed was send him to boarding school. I felt shame for the dad because even after his son retched all over the row, he continued walking around the airplane in his socks.

The captain made of PA informing all the passengers, and flight attendants, that we had enough fuel to make it all the way to San Francisco. It made me happy, and I checked in for my commute flight home for tomorrow, which means I'm only twenty-four hours away from being on vacation.

Wednesday
SFO—LAX

I've learned a valuable lesson on this trip, don't believe all the gossip you hear about other people. Marlie and Stan are entertaining and growing on me. I still don't know if I'm compatible with the two of them on the airplane, but they are entertaining characters. If I was working with each one of them separately, it might be easier to manage their personalities. Together, they'd push Mother Teresa's buttons.

When I'm in the front galley, Marlie says, "Stan is a mess."

When I'm in the back galley with Stan, he says, "Marlie wants me so bad." They act like high school sweethearts. I wished they'd screw and get it out of their system.

At some point, I asked Stan, "On a scale of one to ten—ten being John Belushi and one being a toddler—how many drugs did you do in the 70s?"

Before he had a chance to respond, I answered my own question, "I'm thinking a solid six."

He agreed.

On our flight today, he set up his homemade Bowflex again and began exercising in the back alley. I laughed and said, "People told me that you'd work out during the flight."

Marlie chimed in, "What have people said about me?"

I laughed, "We don't have enough time today for that."

She stared blankly at me, but I played it off with a chuckle. If Marlie only knew how many stories I've heard about her, she'd probably have a breakdown and need therapy. She probably needs mental health treatment whether she's heard those things or not. Marlie's tolerable, but I don't think I'd ever want to work with her again. Maybe if I were the lead flight attendant, I'd be happier.

As we taxied to the gate, a lady in 3A stood up and stepped into the aisle. Marlie yelled, "Return to your seat."

The passenger responded, "Bathroom."

She sat back down, but a few seconds later, she stood up again and pulled her son into the aisle. She yelled at us, "He can't hold it."

Marlie began to warn the woman to return to her seat, but I put my hand on Marlie's leg and reminded her about the flight attendant who refused to let a child use the lavatory, and the kid pissed herself. I don't want that happening on my flight. Some flight attendants abuse their power. All flight attendants are required to do is inform. Yes, we sometimes must enforce, but when the seatbelt sign is illuminated, and I tell you to sit down—and you don't— I don't care. I'm covered if you get hurt in the lavatory because I've informed you that it's not safe to be out of your seat. I often remind passengers that if the flight attendant is seated in their jump seat, it's probably a good idea for you to be seated.

I walked into the crew lounge and bumped into Maggie who advised me the schedules were out and that she was back on reserve. Maggie's only five flight attendants below me, so panic took over. My palms started sweating, and my neck turned bright red. I sat down at a table and pulled up the scheduling app on my cell phone. At that exact moment, a younger flight attendant—who I don't know—walked by me heading to a recliner and exclaimed, "Oh, you're on reserve."

I don't even think I looked at her, "I am?"

She giggled, "I don't know."

I destroyed that poor girl, "Don't say that. What's wrong with you? You don't tell someone who has been here for over seven years that they're back on reserve if they aren't. That's not even funny."

She quietly stared at me. I waited for her to start crying, thankfully no tears appeared. Who jokes about being back on reserve? I felt terrible for raising my voice, but you don't do that shit. Does a doctor walk in and say,

"Mr. Thomas, you have cancer." Pause for dramatics, "No. I don't know if you have cancer."

I frantically pulled up my schedule, and I am not on reserve. With that confirmed, I turned to the flight attendant that I had berated, "Hi. I'm Joe. I'm sure you were joking, but that's not even remotely funny."

She nodded and went back to texting on her cell phone.

Now if she said, "You have a line filled with all red-eye turns," that might be possibly funny. I take that back, that shit is not funny, either. I have a schedule, but it sucks, and I'm hoping I can swap out of a few trips. I have a couple Ft. Lauderdale layovers, and you know how I feel about the passengers in Ft. Lauderdale.

I waited for almost four hours for my commute flight home. I finished flying at one P.M. and walked into my house at nine P.M. Why am I forgoing better seniority for this shit base? I'm thinking about transferring to JFK. The deciding factor will be if I go back on reserve in LAX. If that happens, I'll be out of there faster than a flight attendant who tested positive for drugs.

Speaking of drugs, I haven't heard about my drug test so I assume everything must be okay.

PAIRING 012: THE GREAT CHEESE DEBACLE

Tuesday
LAX—TUS—LAX—OAK

I think it's easier to call in sick if you're going to be late to work. I've been a flight attendant for years, and I'm still confused with the different tardy levels that management has in place. It's exhausting. I arrived at the gate in San Francisco for my commute, and because of the low cloud ceiling the incoming airplane was delayed landing, and now we are delayed departing. I should have taken the earlier flight, but I didn't want to wake up at four A.M. All the passengers were boarded, including me, and while I sat in my seat I thought about grabbing my suitcase and going home. I give up way too easy, but I'm having one of those—I HATE MY JOB—moments which is terrible because I've been off of work for three weeks. I think the running theme for this year is how much I despise my job. I tell myself daily how lucky I am to have the opportunity to be a flight attendant. There are millions—that may be an exaggeration—of young hopeful college graduates out there pining for this job, and here I am, bitching about it at every turn.

I am stressed about marriage equality. It's all anyone talks about right now, and I honestly don't understand why straight people are worried about gay people getting married. Why is it any of their fucking business? Two gay people getting married has no effect on straight marriage. Thinking that it does is absurd and ignorant. The Christian rights argument is that gay people and their straight allies are redefining marriage. The laws of marriage have been modified for centuries. At one point in time, kings married off their daughters to obtain land and power. Women were once considered property with no say in who they married. Can you imagine if that were the case in America today? How many conservative women against marriage equality would allow their daughters to be traded like property? Possibly for land, or perhaps so their husband might maintain his position as HOA president. What about a girl from Florida coming home from work and finding out that her daddy married her off to the mechanic down the street without her knowledge?

Wait a minute, I think that actually happens.

Adapting to the times, and treating women like human beings and not property was a positive change to marriage. In my opinion, marriage is a contract between two adults. Some Christians argue that marriage between a man and women is sacred because a man and a woman can produce offspring. That's bullshit. If that's the fucking case, then why are straight people who don't plan to have children allowed to marry?

And what about heterosexuals who are on their second and third marriages? How's that helping the sanctity of marriage? I hope the individuals who are adamant enemies of same-sex marriage are also standing on street corners protesting straight people who are married with no kids. It's irritating to listen to all this hate against homosexuals destroying the idea of marriage when there is a show on television called *Married at First Sight.*

I need to stop reading the news.

I arrived at the airport before my report time. All that stress about being late was for nothing. By the time I landed, my frustrations had moved from same-sex marriage to the idea of transferring to JFK if our LAX base doesn't get more flying hours. It's been great for the past ten months, but I'm starting to see the benefits of being based on the east coast. Most importantly, better seniority. I miss my seniority. What's the point of dealing with airline passenger's bullshit if I'm not benefiting from my seniority? Sure, my commute is quicker right now, but my schedule sucks more than a Mormon elder on his mission. Maybe being based in LAX is fueling my hatred for the company, because right now, I can't stand the management at this airline. I feel like I'm in a dysfunctional relationship being locked in a cabinet under the stairs with no escape. I'm Harry Potter, and members of management are Uncle Vernon and Aunt Petunia.

I will transfer out of LAX if I go back on reserve. Even if I don't go on reserve, I have to decide if I want my seniority back, with a better schedule, or drag myself through the turmoil of being based in Los Angeles. I wish someone would tell me what to do. I need a guardian angel to hold my hand and lead me through this chaotic industry.

Thankfully, the flight loads were light today. I flew three flights, and none of them had over a hundred passengers. That hasn't happened in a while. I'm all about making money for the airline, but once in awhile, it's nice to get a break from full flights.

An older woman in 1E lost her son this morning. Heartbreaking. As she told me the story, all my problems seemed insignificant. At least I am alive, and I haven't recently lost someone I love. I don't know how her son died, but she kept repeating, "I talked to him last night, and he said, 'I love you.' Now I'll never talk to him again." I wanted to hug her, but she was in the middle seat. You really have to enjoy every moment of your life because you never know when you'll say your last goodbye. That's why I always tell my friends and family I love them. My airplane could crash at any moment, and I want people to know that they are loved.

Our last flight was delayed by an hour which extended our time between flights from two and a half hours to three and a half hours. I tried napping in the flight attendant lounge after we landed from Tucson, but my mind refused to quiet down. When I finally dozed off in the recliner, Matt called me, which was probably for the best because I need to sleep tonight. There were only forty-six passengers on the flight to Oakland, and they were all in my section. Three passengers ordered coffee which made me want to scream. Who needs coffee at eleven at night on a fifty-five-minute flight? My mood was sour all day, and I knew that if I didn't get to bed quick, I'd turn into something out of *Tales from the Crypt*. We waited thirty-five minutes for the hotel van—it should arrive within ten minutes—and typically I'd have been agitated, but my exhaustion and thinking about the women who lost her son made me numb to everything. I didn't shower tonight. I changed into my pajamas and threw myself into the middle of the king-sized bed. I could stay here for a week.

Wednesday
OAK—JFK

I opened my eyes at six A.M. but it was too early to crawl out from under the blanket. That was a mere five and a half hours of sleep, so I rolled over and fell back to sleep for a few more hours.

A friend texted me today asking if I had the authority to book him into a better seat on a flight he purchased from my airline. His text finished with: *the upgraded seats are too expensive.*

Was he joking? I respond sarcastically: *Sure. Let me email the airline right now and tell them to give you a better seat.*

He replied: *Do you need my reference number?*

That answered whether he was joking or not. I informed him that I had no authority to assist him with his request. He never responded back. Friends of airline employees think we have magical powers. As if me, a simple flight attendant, can call reservations and say, "Hi. I'm Joe Thomas, ID number 01972. Could you possibly hook a friend up with a different seat? He paid $59 for a middle seat in the back row, but I'm sure you can move him to first class.

When I write it out like that, I realize how stupid it sounds. Airline employees have no power in assisting a friend to snag a better seat or helping with discounted fares. I can't even manage a Tuesday off for a doctor's appointment.

I walked over to the coffee shop across the street from the hotel and started editing the first draft of *Fasten Your Seat Belts And Eat Your Fucking Nuts*. Finishing this book must be my top priority in the coming months. If I have a single moment of free time, I need to be working on making this book better. I love the title, I want the words inside the pages to be as large as the title on the cover. My fear is being found out that I don't know what I'm doing when it comes to writing a book. I feel like a fraud, and I suffer from imposter syndrome daily. Individuals tend to be their worst critics and I take that to the extreme. My insecurities overpower me when it comes to my writing. That's why I refer to myself as a storyteller and not a writer. I'm confident I tell funny tales, nobody can take that away from me, but writing it out and bringing it all together, that intimidates me.

I napped for three hours and kept having dreams that I missed the hotel shuttle van to the airport. One dream was with Matt, and he abandoned me on the side of the road. I kept leaving him voicemail messages on his cell phone, and then Conrad Grayson from *Revenge* showed up. The second dream involved Evan. Evan and I were driving in a New York City taxi, and I kept screaming to the driver, "I'm late. Drive faster." The taxi driver ignored me and continued telling us that he had a lunch date scheduled with Kristin Chenoweth.

I saw a fellow co-worker at the airport, and he brought in our airplane from JFK. Sadly, he and the other flight attendants left the aircraft in shambles. They didn't swap the beverage carts around for us, which is my biggest pet peeve. Working a JFK flight is often stressful before the aircraft door even closes.

A passenger fell on her left knee inside the airport and the gate agent provided her with a bag of ice for the swelling. Five minutes after boarding, the knee lady spilled the entire bag of ice at row seventeen. She rang her call bell and barely had any ice left in the bag. I took the bag and scooped ice into it, but informed her that's all we had to spare for the rest of the night. We don't have an ice machine on the airplane.

Then a non-English speaking couple was seated in 15A and 15B. Next to them was an extremely hot guy in 15C. He's not part of the story, but I wanted to remind myself that his perfect chiseled body was in 15C. As boarding continued, a passenger stopped me in the aisle to show me his boarding pass which was for 15A. This happens at least once per flight because airline passengers don't take the time to read, or in this case, don't speak English. The lady sitting in 15A was supposed to be in 12B. I tried explaining that she was in the wrong seat, but she smiled and then ignored me by looking out the window. I knew what I had to do. I remembered the bag she put in the overhead bin, so I took it out—that got her attention—and walked it up to row twelve and placed it in the overhead bin. I walked back to row fifteen, and pointed at her, "You. Asiento numero doce b."

She moved. The Latinxs were both in middle seats, and it wasn't right to ask the gentlemen assigned 15A (a window seat) to occupy a middle seat.

Before we closed the airplane door, a female passenger in 25C asked for a blanket. I informed her how much they cost and she made a face, "No freebies anymore, huh?"

I held back reminding her she was on an airplane flying from Oakland to JFK and not in a day spa in Sedona, Arizona.

During beverage service, I stood in the aisle talking to one of the other flight attendants when an Asian woman yelled at me, "Cigarettes? You sell cigarettes?"

I laughed out loud. When an older Asian lady yells at you on a full airplane in the middle of the night, requesting to buy cigarettes, you laugh your ass off.

When we landed in JFK, the parents sitting in 1B and 1C delayed us heading to the hotel because they were unable to undo the seat belt securing their child's car seat. That pissed me off. When they boarded in Oakland, I offered them a seat belt extension to aid them because most often, the airplane seat belt is not long enough to allow adequate wiggle room to undo the seat belt from the car seat. They declined a seat belt extension, and now the seat belt was so tight we needed the jaws of life to release it.

The parents became furious and yelled at me, "We have a connection to catch."

I snipped back, "Then you should have used the seat belt extension as I suggested."

Maintenance came on the airplane to detach the seat belt from the seat to release the car seat. It was the definition of a shit show. I hope that family missed their connection for being such assholes and not listening to us in the first place.

When we stepped outside to catch the hotel shuttle van, it drove off without us. After a red-eye flight, all you want to do is take a shower and go to sleep. The next shuttle arrived twenty minutes later, and after we boarded it, my co-worker started berating the driver. It wasn't the driver's fault—I blamed that family with the car seat—but she started verbally attacking him. I was embarrassed. I told her to chill out, but she acted like an angry chihuahua. I wanted to throw her off the van at top speed, but I was too tired to move.

I asked her, "How would you like it if a passenger yelled at you like that?"

She didn't answer me; she knew she was wrong. In the heat of anger, sometimes it's hard for people to forget that they should treat people as they want to be treated.

Thursday
JFK—LAX

Day sleeping is painful on my body. My body is old and likes to sleep like a normal human, not like Count Dracula.

There seemed to be no complications when I arrived at the airport, but that ended quickly when the captain found expired airplane manuals in the flight deck. Within seconds, a swarm of airline personnel swooped in and raced around searching for new manuals, or a new airplane. This caused a delay and our expected forty-five-minute early arrival into LAX was ruined. I think our airline should change their motto to: It's Always Something.

Maintenance arrived, brought new manuals, and we ended up departing an hour late. I guess it's better than being canceled and stuck in JFK for another night. Listen, I'm incredibly negative lately, so I'm trying to be positive about this shit show of an airline.

And to clarify, I said, I'm trying, I can't make any promises how long it will last.

It didn't last long. I'd say, somewhere over Indiana.

We had a large group of Christians on the flight. One of the flight attendants said, "Well, if we crash, hopefully, they know Jesus and we'll be saved."

I never laughed so hard in the galley. I said, "After the way you talked to the van driver this morning, you'll be the first to burn up."

The airplane was packed with Christian teachers and their students. One of the ladies looked like she was on the television show, *Sister Wives*. She shyly asked, "Are Bloody Marys free?"

I broke it down for her, "No."

The school principal, who was also the pastor, asked the same question about Bloody Marys. What's with the Bloody Marys? Is that the drink of choice for Christians? Do they think it's divine and was named after Mary of Nazareth? I think it was named after a Queen in England. Or was that a queen in Brooklyn? Honestly, I can't remember. And while I'm on the topic of drinks that Christians order, I wonder if Catholic priests order the Suck, Bang, and Blow when they're traveling for NAMBLA conventions?

I decided to mess with the pastor. "I was going to come and find you when a member of your flock started acting up, but you're just as bad." He chuckled. I smiled my altar boy grin, winked, and walked away.

I love flocking—yes, flocking—with Christians. With all these Christian jokes, I expect nothing less than a penthouse suite overlooking the lake of fire in Hell.

These Christian passengers ran me up and down the aisle hard. They're probably still bitter that Proposition 8 was overturned. I wanted to remind a few of them that greed was a sin, but they were too busy asking for drinks that I didn't have a chance to get a single word out. I'm not exaggerating, this one lady had two cups of coffee, two orange juices, a bottle of water, and a Diet Coke. I wonder if she's saving some of it for Jesus.

In JFK, provisioning omitted the cheese plates from the catering carts. Apparently, telling the lady in 18A that we had no cheese plates was as upsetting to her as if we had said—I don't know—both engines have failed. Her eyes filled with tears and she yelled, "This is unacceptable. I wanted cheese with my wine. What the hell am I supposed to do now?"

Her crocodile tears and dramatics were a bit much. I offered up an alternative, "Instead of wine and cheese, why not beer and beef jerky?"

She did not seem amused.

I chuckled and moved on to the next row. The moment I stopped laughing at 18A, I met 19C who asked, "What channel will I find the movies?"

I explained to her the movie channels and with a straight face, she asked, "How do I get to those channels?"

I thought, *telepathically lady. Think about what channel you'd like to watch, and it will happen.* I responded, "Use the remote control."

I stepped into the back galley and forgot I was at work, "If I don't get off this airplane soon, I may stuff a red wine down someone's throat."

The cheese issue was out of control. It wasn't an issue, it was a debacle. Every passenger wanted a cheese plate, but we didn't have any to offer. I needed cheese for these passengers. I was desperate, so I walked down the aisle counting all the male Mexicans who I knew were carrying around some extra string cheese. Listen, it might not smell great, but that didn't matter. What mattered was, how would it taste with a robust red wine?

Can you imagine the complaint letters I'd get after serving that kind of cheese?

I work one trip after being off for three weeks, and I start eyeing male passengers for their dick cheese. I'm a lunatic. Could it be time for a career change? Yes. Can it happen? No. I let too much affect me on the airplane. Why do I care if there is no cheese for these people? We have fuel, strong wings, and sober pilots—that's all we need. Cheese can't fly us safely across the country.

Enough writing about this cheese bullshit. I'm on the sofa drinking a glass of wine, and I don't have any cheese. You don't see me crying. I'm getting a stomach ache from thinking about these past four days. On second thought, that's probably the Pad Thai I had for dinner. It burned going down, and I'm sure it will burn coming out. Now that I think about it, the male flight attendant I worked with had the same Pad Thai for dinner, and he spent fifteen minutes in the lavatory.

We landed twenty minutes early, and one of the flight attendants offered to drop me off at another airport to catch my flight home. This is the first time I've commuted to Oakland. Grateful as I was for the ride, he drove so slow I wondered if I'd make my flight. I offered him gas money, but he declined. I work with him again next month, so I'll have to do something nice for him.

When I boarded the flight to Oakland, I gave the flight attendant cookies, and she looked at me like I was handing her a poison apple. I don't know what she was thinking, she's no Snow White. She's more like the hag. There were twenty passengers on the flight, and I had an entire row to stretch out.

The flight landed after midnight. I patiently waited for Matt outside the terminal for twenty minutes hoping that my shoes and pants weren't stolen by the time he arrived. You don't fuck around in Oakland. It's the kind of town where you bend over to tie your shoes and realize they've been stolen.

I'm done writing tonight, it's time for bed. I've only been gone for two days, but it felt like two months.

PAIRING 013: MEANWHILE, SOMEWHERE IN SEATTLE

Sunday
SFO—LAS—LAX—DEN—LAX—SEA

It's days like today when I wish I lived in a base city. Today was brutal; my alarm went off at six A.M., I left the apartment at seven A.M., caught a flight at 8:21 A.M., flew to Las Vegas, and landed in LAX at noon. My report time was 2:21 P.M, and then after working a Denver turn, I flew to Seattle. The flight arrived in Seattle at 9:45 P.M., and we pulled up to the hotel at 10:45 P.M.

Let me start at the beginning; I'm working with two flight attendants that I'm meeting for the first time, Beth and Jasmine. I arrived in the flight attendant lounge early, so I printed out pairings for the three of us. When Jasmine walked in, I introduced myself, "Hi, Jasmine, I'm Joe."

She corrected me, "It's Jasmine with an s, not a z. Like this...*Jassssssssmine.*" She pronounced it loud enough to make sure that everyone in the airport heard her.

The moment she spent ten seconds sounding out her name, I knew I wouldn't like her.

Being a smart ass, I responded, "Cool. I'm Joe, with an o-e."

I guess when I say the name Jasmine, I sound it out with a z. Does it really matter? I'm thinking about getting on the interphone and screaming, "Beoooooootch. The guy in 12C needs a seat belt extension."

I wonder if she'll like that.

The FAA recently fined one of our flight attendants because their manual was not compliant. Terrible, but flight attendants are notorious for being irresponsible and out of compliance. I'm sure I'll get shit for saying that, but it's the truth. Every flight attendant knows they are responsible for keeping their flight attendant manual up-to-date, but when someone gets dinged by the FAA, it's always "woe is me." I wonder if a GoFundMe account will be started for the manual violator? That happens a lot in this base.

The first flight to Denver was uneventful, and that was a bad sign for the rest of the day. We landed in Denver, and the gate agent struggled to open the airplane door, which freaked me out. After waiting fifteen minutes, another gate agent arrived and opened the aircraft door. He made eye contact with me, and I could sense his frustration boiling over.

Behind him stood a middle-aged gate agent who said, "Sorry, I'm afraid of the door."

Why does this bitch work here? How can you be afraid of the airplane door? Her job is to open the airplane door. That is literally her job. Am I fearful of a Diet Coke or pretzels?

During boarding, a mother, father, and obnoxious out-of-control child in his mother's lap sat in 1A and 1B. A solo traveler sat beside them in 1C. It was clear that the guy in 1C wanted nothing to do with this family. The lap child was already bouncing from his mother to his father, and we hadn't even closed the airplane door. Then a young couple boarded and sat in 1E and 1F and they were all over each other the moment they sat down. Her tits flopped around inside a loose tank top, and her boyfriend wore basketball shorts. I tried not gagging watching their tongues attack each other while I sat on my jumpseat.

Our flight was less than two hours long and the little shit sitting on his parent's lap in 1A and 1B was a demon sent from the depths of Hell. The mother stood in the galley and was continuously in my way while I did beverage service. I had to remind her the seat belt sign was illuminated about a hundred times. She stood in front of my beverage cart, I asked her to move, and then her spawn started banging on the airplane door. I had to tell the mother to control him. I know the demon can't open the airplane door from this altitude, but that's not the point. The point is to manage your fucking kid on an airplane. The rest of the people on the flight shouldn't suffer because you brought your asshole kid on the plane. That's the one thing that pisses me off about people with children. They think because they have a kid, they're given a pass, and when their monster acts out in public, they easily shrug their shoulders, and all is forgiven.

No. Fuck that. Parents should be held accountable when their brat doesn't know how to sit on their lap, suck a few fingers, and stop screaming at the top of their lungs.

While I was cleaning up my galley, his mother held him in her arms while he repeatedly kicked the partition that separates the airplane cabin from the galley. I wanted to kick him all the way to the back galley like a kickball.

She smiled and asked, "Are we in your way?"

I refused to lie, "Yes."

She finally sat down with her kid, but he struggled like a pro wrestler. The father barely paid any attention to his kid; all he did was hand over cubes of ice for the toddler to suck on. I decided right there that I was not doing the Heimlich if the demon started choking.

The Seattle flight did not start out well, either. Do they ever? We had to check about thirteen bags in LAX, and the gate agent kept giving me dirty looks. Listen, if there's no room for suitcases in the overhead bins; there's no room for suitcases in the overhead bins. I'm not a magician. Am I expected to stuff luggage inside my ass? The gate agent handed me paperwork for a passenger, but it had the wrong flight number.

She said, 'Are you ready to close the door?"

"This paperwork is wrong. Is this passenger on the plane?"

She huffed and puffed like she was about to blow me down. All gate agents care about is closing the door on time. That is all. This chick was no different. I said, "If you had brought the correct paperwork, we'd have been able to close the door on time." She did not like that, I expect the delay code will be placed on me. That's another thing they care about, sticking it to the flight attendants.

In row seven, we had an extremely obese man. It took him ten minutes to walk the three feet from the wheelchair on the jet bridge to the airplane door. He was traveling with his wife, and I saw another passenger seated in the row with them. There's nothing worse than spending hundreds of dollars to fly two hours and be crushed to death between a human and the fuselage. I found out we had two open middle seats in the exit row. I offered the crushed passenger another seat, but he refused. I think he was smiling. He must have liked that close human touch. Who am I to judge? Better him than me.

I gave the pilots *Flight Attendant Joe* business cards and told them to look up the blog. They're staying at a different hotel, and when we were climbing into our van, the first officer yelled, "Stay outta trouble. Don't do anything I wouldn't do." Something tells me he'd be fun to hang out with for the night.

We had a long van ride to the hotel, but when you are finally off the airplane, and away from passengers, it doesn't matter how long the journey takes. I'd take a rocket to the International Space Station to get away from airline passengers. Being away from demanding assholes gives me pleasure.

As we check in to the hotel, Jasmine assigned all the rooms. Not surprisingly, she grabbed the room on the 10th floor, she gave Beth the room on the 6th floor, and I got the fucking basement.

I'm acting bitchy. It's actually the fifth floor, but the view out my window looks like I'm in the parking garage. I'm the lead flight attendant on this trip, and I know this will sound childish, but I want the better room. That confession felt fanfuckingtastic. If I could, I'd jump around and stomp my feet, but I'm too tired. Usually, I don't care what room I get, but tonight I'm annoyed, exhausted, and still put off by Jasmine, correcting me on how to say her name.

Monday
SEA - ANC - SEA

I definitely needed sleep more than anything else. I acted like a total bitch to Jasmine last night. I stormed off the elevator without saying a word. I'd be embarrassed if I cared what she thought, but alas, I don't.

I love the word, alas, I use it whenever I can.

Matt called to tell me the new neighbors living upstairs knocked on the door, asking him to turn down the volume of the music. It was 9:30 A.M., and my husband does not listen to music loud. These new neighbors may be working my last nerve. I'm not going to get crazy yet, but I'm afraid it may be coming soon.

I felt fatigued after having such a long day yesterday, so I stayed in the hotel and tried napping. It sounded like the hotel was demolition the room above mine. I put the pillow over my head, but it didn't work. I finally fell asleep for an hour, but then woke up, showered and waited in the hotel lobby for the van to the airport. To be a better person, I apologized to Jasmine for being an asshole last night. She told me not to worry about it. It was difficult not bringing up the fact that she corrected me saying her name.

I guess I'm still an asshole.

I'm glad I had a large coffee to assist with my Anchorage red-eye turn. We stepped into the front galley of the airplane, and an FAA inspector was sitting in the front row. I casually checked my uniform pants to see if I shit myself. Thankfully, the coffee hadn't kicked in yet. Coffee works as a laxative on me. Who needs MiraLAX when there's Starbucks?

I played it cool while placing my luggage in the overhead bin, but I was nervous until I found out Mr. FAA was traveling in the flight deck. I still had to make sure we were on our toes and following procedures, but I felt relieved having the FAA inspector hanging out in the flight deck instead of up my ass with his pen, pad, and manual.

The passenger in 1D had hip surgery a few days ago, and after he sat down his wife climbed over him and fell on his hip while straddling his legs.

He screamed, "Fuck." which was fantastic as two older passengers stepped into the galley. I figured they understand the pain of hip surgery. A cute young gay couple was traveling in 1B and 1C wearing matching orange shirts. After boarding, I walked down the aisle checking that seat belts were fastened and I elbowed one of the queens in the head. I apologized but worried he'd send a tweet about it. Passengers love Twitter.

Alaskans don't know how to fly on an airplane. I'm sure some do, but most of the ones I've encountered do not. The population of Alaska is around 730,000, and I think only 30,000 have ever stepped foot on an airplane—and that's overestimating. I'm not trying to be mean, I'm stating facts. Alaskans have mastered alcoholism, but not flying on an airplane. It's like having an aircraft full of children who have untamed beards, haven't showered in months, and are allowed to drink copious amounts of alcohol. Thankfully there weren't many drinkers on the flight, except for one dude who ordered a double Jack Daniels with a beer chaser. When I attempted to collect a payment, he questioned the total. I informed him the price of the two Jack Daniels and the beer totaled twenty-one dollars. He stared at me.

I guess they don't do math in Alaska, either.

We had about an hour to kill in Anchorage before our flight back, so I grabbed some coffee and walked around taking pictures and people-watching in the middle of the night. Ted Stevens Anchorage International Airport is particularly active at one A.M. It's fascinating. The only airport close to being as busy as Anchorage is Las Vegas, but even that's a stretch.

I found a cute pair of socks in the gift shop, but the cashier moved at a glacial pace. I became worried that I'd be late for boarding until a gentleman standing in front of me in line noticed I was in uniform and waved me in front of him.

I smiled. "Thank you. Where are you heading tonight?"

He answered, "Seattle."

I told him I'd remember him. I contemplated shoving a reindeer dog down my throat before heading back to the airplane but didn't need the extra calories that late at night.

We met the new pilots, and I'd flown with both of them in the past. Boarding went slow, chaotic, and more complicated than usual. I hate to say it, but I think Alaska is the Dominican Republic of the United States. These people had no fucking clue what they were doing. We were all frustrated with how slow boarding was commencing, but then I overheard the captain say from the flight deck, "Why won't the flight attendants tell these people to hurry up?"

What's up with Captain No-Patience? I'm not getting terminated for telling passengers to hurry up and board. Jasmine made the appropriate announcements over the PA, and that's all we can do. It's not my job to place passengers in their seats physically.

When the gentleman who let me cut in front of him at the store walked onto the airplane, I upgrade him for being helpful to me in the store. That's a lesson to the world, be kind to a stranger, and it will come back to you. People don't understand that being kind to your flight attendant will benefit you.

Even with Captain No-Patience bitching about a slow boarding, we still closed the aircraft door five minutes early. Mostly everyone slept throughout the night. Well, everyone but Miss Terry in 1D and her service dog, Francis. Miss Terry spent most of the flight cooing and talking to Francis like a baby. Without warning, Miss Terry would burst out with, "ah-ha" or "ooh-ooh, that's my baby," and I sat on my jumpseat trying not to jump out of my seat and slap her and her dog. Not so much, Francis, she was innocent. I looked over to find Francis attempting to sleep, but Miss Terry continued petting her so hard I was afraid Francis would have no hair when we landed.

Sure, I baby talk to my cats, but only when they are awake. When they are sleeping, I leave them alone. As much as Tucker loves me, if I woke him up to talk to him like a newborn, he'd vomit up his dinner on me. I wanted to walk over to Miss Terry and remind her that Francis was trying to rest because she had a job to do when we landed. I thought, *what's Francis' job? Reminding Miss Terry to take her Lithium?*

While picking up trash during the flight, Miss Terry informed me that Francis had stamps in her passport. I smiled and nodded but privately disagreed. Francis doesn't have any stamps in a passport; Francis doesn't have shit. If Francis has a doggy passport, it's because she's trying to escape your crazy ass. A teenager sitting across from her caught my eye, and we'd bust out laughing throughout the flight. It made the night go by faster. Miss Terry talked and mumbled to the point that if a blind passenger were seated in the row, they'd think Miss Terry was traveling with a group of friends.

That made me sad.

Before we landed, a male passenger moved to an upgraded seat without permission. If I'm lucky, that only happens once per flight. I'm generally not that lucky. I politely reminded the gentleman that there was an additional fee to sit in an upgraded seat. He brushed me off, "I have a pinched nerve."

I smiled, "I'm sorry to hear that. I hope you have a credit card, too."

He had a pinched nerve, but no credit card.

Whenever I work a red-eye flight, my energy level is excellent until four A.M. That's when I turn into a pumpkin. My eyes get heavy, and I have to stand up and pace around the galley to keep myself awake. It's one of those moments when I wish I could stick my head out of the flight deck window for a burst of fresh air. Something tells me that a 500 mile per hour burst of air at 36,000 feet will wake anyone up.

Or kill them.

After the fifty-minute van ride to the hotel, we waited in the hotel lobby for rooms. The front desk staff acted surprised when we arrived like they had no idea we were coming. I'm pretty sure we're the only airline crew that stays at this hotel because it's miles away from the airport. It's far enough to catch a flight from Seattle to the hotel. We might as well land in Seattle and layover in Calgary. It makes sense, no other airline hates their crew as much as mine. My room was on the 22nd floor, which was better than last night.

Tuesday
Seattle

I suppose three hours of sleep is sufficient. If I hold up a bank or rape a poodle, I hope people can find it in their hearts to forgive me. I'll blame it on exhaustion. I had planned a day trip to Olympia today, but missed the first bus and then abandoned that idea as fast as I came up with it. I'm so easily persuaded to do nothing. I had bratwurst and Doritos for lunch. I can't bitch and complain about being fat when I eat 3,000 calories for lunch. After lunch, I hung out in the hotel lobby and worked on a few blog posts. I bumped into the first officer as he was on his way to Subway to get a six-inch. I don't know why he's going out for a six-inch, I've got something about that size he can snack on.

I'm a pilot predator. Double lock the flight deck door guys, and don't let me in.

I went to happy hour, got buzzed, and decided to check out a gay bar down the street from the hotel. I'd call it tragic, but that would be too kind. I walked inside, used the restroom, and walked out. What do you expect from a gay bar, on a Tuesday, in the suburbs of Seattle?

Wednesday
SEA—LAX—LAS—LAX

I woke up only once last night and didn't even look at my phone to see what time it was. The alarm went off at 4:40 A.M., and I jumped out of bed with no problem. The flight to LAX was routine, but I felt fatigued all morning. A pilot from another airline boarded the airplane and didn't say anything as he walked past me. I checked the manifest, and he paid full fare, probably paid for by his airline to position him in LAX for work. He was seated in 23E, a middle seat, and although we had an open seat in the exit row, we didn't move him.

You don't address me when you walk on my airplane, I don't upgrade your seat.

The other day, a reader asked me on the blog, "Do you go out of your way to be extra nice to mean passengers to turn their mood around?"

My answer was politely, "Fuck no." I don't reward bad behavior. You get nothing extra from me if you aren't respectful. Rewarding bad behavior is why we have so many entitled pricks running around the planet. That's why kids are growing up into the assholes of tomorrow.

That pilot could have said a simple, "Hi. I'm with Such-and-Such Airline. I'm on a full fare in 23E." I'd have moved him before he walked past row one. His young ass would have been stretched out in the exit row, and not crammed between two frustrated-looking hipsters.

By the second flight to Las Vegas, I was feeling like I could fall asleep handing out a Sprite. This trip was easy, but it messes with your sleep schedule and drains your body. By the time I was in LAX, I wanted to curl up and sleep on my commute flight home. The gate agent handed me my seat assignment early, and I moved over to the side of the gate, found an empty seat, and became enthralled watching a man and woman argue. It was verbally aggressive. The guy raised his voice like he was inside a bar, and every other word out of his mouth was "fuck this" and "fuck that." The wife, or girlfriend—or baby momma—was almost brought to tears. At first, the entire family was seated on the floor about ten feet away, but then my luck turned for the better, they took seats right next to me.

The woman said, "If you want to break up with me. go ahead."

He spit out, "You stupid bitch."

This was more dramatic than when Sam had Frank kill Lila on *How To Get Away With Murder*. I felt terrible for the kid having to listen to his parents talk to each other so hatefully. That kid will most likely grow up to be an alcoholic and abusive husband. I hope not, but statistics rarely lie.

When I boarded the flight, I handed a bag of cookies to the lead flight attendant, and she gasped, "Oh lordy, what are you doing? Oh my goodness. Thank you. Thank you. Thank you."

Honey, it's a bag of cookies, not Henry Cavill's underwear.

As I found my seat, she jumped on the interphone and publicly thanked me again. Her husband must get the best blow jobs when he brings home a loaf of bread and a gallon of milk. If it's take-out, he's getting anal.

Matt agreed to pick me up at the airport, but we both forgot that it was during rush hour (in the San Francisco Bay Area, rush hour starts at one P.M.) and it took him an hour to pick me up when it should have taken twenty minutes. When he pulled up to the curb, he was annoyed, and who could blame him. I wanted to take full responsibility for his frustration, but he reminded me that he agreed to pick me up, I had nothing to apologize for. Matt may be the most rational human being I've ever met.

After dinner, we watched *500 Questions*. I don't know what makes these people geniuses, this one dude didn't even know who Malala was.

PAIRING 014: WORKING TOWARDS A COMMON GOAL

Saturday
SFO—LAX

It's Memorial Day weekend. Sadly, my seniority in LAX is terrible, and I can't hold off the holiday. I thought being based closer to home would help me rediscover the joy I once had for this job, but it's only brought me a different set of frustrations. I had a dream last night that I had sex with a childhood friend. That's the best part, the worst part was after the sex, I was taking a shit in a gas station restroom while two flight attendants stood over me asking each other work-related questions. Then I crumbled all the toilet paper into a tight ball, but couldn't wipe my ass with the two of them standing over me. I asked them to leave, but they ignored me.

Matt started reading the first draft of *Fasten Your Seat Belts And Eat Your Fucking Nuts.* I'm in complete panic mode that he's reading the book. Partly, because he's the first person to read it besides me. Writing a book is a complex process, and it's personal, especially when it's nonfiction and about your life. While I'm editing content, he's editing the style and technical aspects of the book. He worked on the first chapter today and provided some positive feedback. I think our collaboration will work out well. Honestly, this is an enormous step in our relationship.

We've been together for over a decade, and it's hard for me to take his criticism without wanting to throw one of the cats at him. For example, if this were five years ago, and he made as simple a suggestion as, "I think you need a comma here," I'd believe I was worthless and be ready to burn my book at the nearest Baptist Church.

I struggle when Matt gives me constructive feedback. It doesn't have to be about my writing, it could be about making the bed. All he has to do is hint that I might be doing something incorrectly, and I transform into DEFENDER MAN, ready to defend my honor with rage, sarcasm, and bitchiness. Before he started reading the book, I sat him down and asked him to be extremely delicate when giving me feedback. We both know how my brain works, and that I'm always ready to overreact to something I deem insulting, and he agreed. I'm crazy, and it's important that my husband knows that. And he does.

I took the seven P.M. flight to LAX, and I'm sleeping in the lounge tonight. It happens so rarely that I can't be upset about it. I have a long layover in Orlando tomorrow so I will be able to rest. On the flight to LAX, I sat in my window seat watching the California coastline, and it calmed my nerves like a cup of Earl Grey with a shot of whiskey.

In other news, Ireland voted for marriage equality. The first country to vote it in by referendum, particularly notable for such a Catholic country. What's up with the United States? Are we living in the Dark Ages? Our citizens are so hell-bent on making this a Christian Nation that the federal government has to get involved. That's pathetic. Gays don't want special treatment, we want to be invited to the party.

I walked into the crew lounge, and it was packed with flight attendants and pilots. After an hour or so, they departed for home or red-eye flights to the east coast, and I was left alone for the night. I hung up my uniform in the closet, blew up my air pillow, and curled up with my blanket on a recliner. I started reading a book to help me doze off when another flight attendant, who had missed their commute home, came in and is spending the night in the recliner next to me. I hope they don't snore. Better yet, I hope I don't fart.

This sounds terrible, but I've seen this flight attendant before, and I have no idea if he's a she. I can't tell. Maybe he/she is they? I have no clue, and it drives me insane. His/Her name is something like Pat too. Is it Pat? I have no confirmation. I hope this mystery doesn't keep me up all night.

Update: It took me a few minutes, but I found out that he's a he. Now I can move forward and learn his name.

Sunday
LAX—MCO

I never found out that guy's name last night, and he was gone before I woke up. As I changed into my uniform and brushed my teeth in the sink, I felt like a trucker in a truck stop. I met the other two flight attendants, Diane and Mary. I've flown with Diane before, but this was my first time meeting Mary. Mary immediately rubbed me the right way with her bubbly personality. We have so many bitches in LAX that it's nice to work with someone kind. I quickly found out she has only been at the airline for two years, so that makes sense. Give her five more years, and she will be a bitch like the rest of us. It's Mary's husband's birthday today, and he's flying to Orlando with us and staying on the layover with her.

We had the guy who runs our security department on the flight in 2C. He's big, buff, and got me so overheated the WiFi stopped working. My loins were blocking the WiFi connection like his wife cock-blocked our flirting connection. It doesn't help that I haven't touched myself since Tuesday night and my balls are the color of blueberries. If I sneeze, my sac is going to blow out one of these airplane windows.

While letting the pilots out for a lavatory break, Mr. Security told me to flex while I stood in the front galley to show the passengers I meant business. I almost passed out. I felt like I needed to strap the defibrillator to my chest for the remainder of the flight. From the front galley, it looked like he had an extra carry-on in his khaki pants. It helped to focus on him instead of the passenger in the front row wearing flip-flops who looked like he had run a marathon in his bare feet. If your feet look like they went through a meat grinder, you need to wear shoes.

We landed in Orlando, and the temperature outside was ninety-five degrees with a feels like temperature of a million degrees. I can't believe I once lived in this humidity. I'm spoiled now that I live in California. Anything under sixty-five degrees and I need a sweater to wear with my shorts. Our new crew hotel is on International Drive, which is better than staying across the street from the airport. We got to the hotel, checked into our rooms, and I didn't see anyone from my crew for the rest of the layover. I'm okay with that. Exploring by yourself is healthy. After downing a glass of red wine, I walked to the Orlando Eye. It's like the London Eye but in Orlando. Does Orlando really need this? This is the vacation capital of Earth, but do they really need a Ferris wheel? Apparently, they do, or they think they do. I paid the overpriced admission fee, and after watching a 4D movie and an ad to visit Orlando, we stepped into a car that whisked us 400 feet above Orlando.

My Ferris wheel car was packed with me, two cute lesbians, and three rednecks from Brevard County. It reminded me of the boat from the book *Life of Pi*. I immediately started wondering who I was going to have to throw out when we stopped at the top.

That's a no-brainer, the Brevard County hillbillies.

The views from the top were uninspiring unless you enjoy looking at the horizontal landscape. Central Florida is remarkably flat, and at one point, I saw the ocean but realized it was only a sinkhole. I told the employee, "You should serve alcohol on here like they do in Las Vegas."

He got snippy, "This is a family ride." I wanted to stab him in front of the hillbillies. Please stop trying to make this a family ride. It's a Ferris wheel in Orlando, not Dollywood.

After spending five minutes on the wheel, I couldn't wait to get off and contemplated jumping. I decided against it because the hillbillies would think it was a reality show called, *Gay Sacrifice*, and toss out the cute lesbians right behind me. I'll sacrifice myself, but I'm not taking young lesbian love with me.

At first, I relished in the idea of walking around alone, but after the Ferris wheel ride, I was lonely and wanted company. I'm never happy. I filled my loneliness void by text messaging multiple people while having dinner at Hooters. I ordered a beer, devoured my chicken wings, and had to fight the waitress off with the chicken bones. It was clear that she wanted me, or she was flirting for a big fat tip. I went back to my room and rested for the remainder of the evening. The bed was an A+. I decided I'd only leave to piss in the middle of the night, and even that might be pushing it.

Monday
MCO—AUS—HOU—AUS—LAX—OAK

I spent twelve hours in bed. The alarm went off at 10:30 A.M., but I changed it to noon and didn't climb out of bed one minute sooner. I had no coffee. I had no breakfast. At the airport, I ran into a few co-workers I hadn't seen for a long time, and then Dee came up to visit me on the airplane.

She asked, "Did you get any food from the Memorial Day cookout?"

I had no time to stop for food. What does Dee do for me? She leaves the airplane and comes back a few minutes later with two full plates of food: hamburgers, sausages, potato salad, everything was on those plates. I can't love this woman enough.

We took off for Austin, and there was a feeling of calm inside the airplane. All the passengers were watching news stories about horrendous thunderstorms in the Austin area resulting in severe flooding. One passenger walked up and informed me there was a tornado a few miles from his house. I thought quietly, *this is God pissed off at how homophobic Texas has become. Or still is.* Recently, Ireland passed same-sex marriage, and they were rewarded with double rainbows across the sky. Texas has floods, devastation, and Ted Cruz. What? That's how most irrational Christians would think. Listen, you can't say God only gets pissed when He's destroying New Orleans after a gay pride parade.

We circled around Austin for almost an hour, but with the storms beating up the skies, the pilots diverted to Houston. After we taxied off the runway, there were no gates available, and we had to sit on the tarmac for hours. Not an hour—that would be easy—but hours. I started panicking thinking the passengers would protest and we'd end up like most characters from *Game of Thrones*, but they were oddly calm and understanding.

When a gate opened up for our aircraft, we parked and offered any passenger the opportunity to deplane in Houston, but their luggage would continue on to Austin. Who the hell thinks that's a good idea? Apparently, nobody, because no passengers chose that option.

I wanted to leave. I raised my hand to volunteer to get off the airplane and never return, but the captain laughed at me. I wasn't joking. Hell, they could keep my luggage. Sell my clothes and donate the money to the passenger whose house had probably been destroyed by a tornado. We offered passengers water at the gate, and most of them remained in their seats, except for the occasional lavatory break, and stayed composed during the diversion. It was creepy as fuck. After all these years as a stewardess, I do not expect passengers to remain this peaceful during a diversion. In fact, I don't expect much from airline passengers.

I've had a lady blame me for ruining her honeymoon on a thirty-five-minute flight to Key West because her television was inoperative.

But these Austin passengers were different, where were the outbursts? Where were the tears? Where were the angry tweets and combative behavior? There was nothing but apologies and empathy for the flight attendants and pilots. I learned a valuable lesson that under the right circumstances, passengers and crew can band together to work towards a common goal. All of us wanted the same outcome, to land in Austin as quickly as possible. We were in this together, and I've never felt that camaraderie with my passengers. One gentleman came to the back galley and said, "I'm sorry you guys have to deal with this today." He caught me off guard, I turned my head and gave myself whiplash. I took three ibuprofen in case my neck hurt later.

After a total of four hours in Houston, we were airborne and flying to Austin. To clarify, we departed Orlando five hours earlier and still had not landed at our first airport destination. The only thing that kept my patience in check was how wonderfully our passengers managed their expectations. That's the trick with air travel, manage your expectations. Personally, I try not having expectations when I report for work. Who am I kidding? I barely have any expectations on humanity at this point. Having no expectations rarely works out as I planned, but that's how I start each work trip. I expect delays, I expect exhaustion, and I expect asshole passengers. That way, if none—or all—of those things occur, I am prepared. I checked the flight status of our Austin to Los Angeles flight, and we were delayed only an hour before the last scheduled departure of the evening.

I passed the information along to Mary. Initially, our flight to LAX had about twenty available seats, but I didn't think that would last with these storms and delays. Our trip was delayed, and I was afraid they'd move people over to our flight, and it would be full.

She didn't seem concerned. She shrugged her shoulders and didn't say anything. When we landed in Austin, the gate agent opened the airplane door, thrust the manifest at me and yelled, "We're full."

I was the lead flight attendant, and Mary was the mid-cabin flight attendant. When she heard the flight was full, and that her husband would be left behind in Austin, I figured she'd blow a gasket. Lose her shit. Act the way I did once when my husband got stuck in Austin on his way to Las Vegas. I go to ten when I'm stressed, she was at a four. Whatever medication she takes, I need some. But then Mary blocked the front door chatting with the gate agent while all the passengers lined up behind her waiting to step off the airplane.

After a few seconds, I interrupted, "Mary, step out of the way so the passengers can deplane."

Flight attendants can be harder to manage than passengers.

After deplaning, news came in from the flight deck that our pilots only had seven minutes before timing out. I can't begin to explain the ins and outs of pilot duty times. It's incredibly complicated. It's complicated enough that some pilots don't understand it, which makes me nervous because they fly the airplane. Here's the simple explanation (and don't hold me responsible if my definition is wrong): from the moment the captain releases the airplane brake, they have a limited time when they must be off the ground.

If the airplane doesn't take off within that period (in this case seven minutes), the pilots time out. When the pilots time out, they can not fly for the rest of the day. The airplane has to be brought back to the gate, the pilots go to the hotel, and the airline has to find new pilots to operate the flight. In a city like Austin, there are no extra pilots to stand in for pilots who time out. It would result in a cluster fuck, and because of the storms, there were no additional hotel rooms available in Austin. We'd be sleeping on the airplane, which sadly, is not that big of a concern for most of the airline management.

At boarding time, the captain informed me that we'd have to board fast, taxi out to the runway, and depart quickly. We barely had a minute to spare. I felt like a character in a James Bond movie trying to diffuse a bomb. I didn't mention that to the captain because "diffuse" and "bomb" are not the best words to use on an airplane. Every second counted, and that's not an exaggeration. It was intense, but I felt alive, a feeling I haven't known at this job in years. Most often, I feel like my soul is being crushed in a vice, but this excitement was electric. Communication was flawless between the Austin station manager, the pilots, and myself. The airline should run each flight this stressful because we'd be perpetually on time. On second thought, I should never repeat that sentence again.

I felt terrible for our captain; he looked beat down. His eyes were bloodshot, and he looked exhausted. He had that recently-divorced look etched across his face. You know the look, where he signed off the papers on his second divorce and lost custody of his colorful socks.

We boarded the airplane, and all the passengers knew we were on a time crunch. The station manager continued making announcements at the gate instructing passengers that if they weren't on the airplane, in their seats, and ready to go, they'd be spending the night at the airport. In all my years, I've never experienced such a flawless boarding.

Honestly, we should scare passengers more often.

Passengers marched onto the airplane in a single file. Their bags went up in the overhead bin with no issues. They sat down, fastened their seat belts, and were ready to go. Nobody tried using the lavatory or asking for water to take an imaginary pill.

Mary informed me, "My husband is getting on the flight in an hour." The station manager was beyond helpful, making sure he got on the next flight. The teamwork between everyone involved to get this airplane off the gate and in the air was incredible.

When the airplane door closed, I read the safety demonstration faster than I've ever read it. I wish I could speed read like that while I'm reading a book. We taxied to the runway, and the moment we lifted off, the entire airplane erupted into loud applause. I thought, *I hope we don't crash while the passengers are clapping. That would suck.*

All that and we still had a three-hour flight to California.

Over Arizona, I wanted to lie down on the galley floor and take a nap. When we landed in LAX, I learned that the pilots working our flight to Los Angeles were deadheading to Oakland and then catching a van to the hotel by the San Francisco International Airport.

I asked, "Do you mind if I tag along in your van ride to the hotel in San Francisco?"

They did not mind, which turned out to be an enormous win for me because I didn't want Matt driving all the way to San Francisco International Airport that late at night. I flew on the flight to Oakland, took the van ride to the hotel by SFO, and then I took a shared ride home.

I walked into the house after three A.M.; I was supposed to be home at eight P.M.

Pairing 015: Layovers Are Fun

Friday
LAX—OAK—LAX—SEA

I took a quick nap in the crew lounge for a few hours and had an exciting dream; I was driving a Jeep with the top down. I drove through a massive forest, but then I came to a clearing where I viewed a large lake with pristine water. The water was transparent enough to see the white sand at the bottom. It hypnotized me. The water beckoned me to dive into its cold stillness. I drove towards the beach, but when I slowed the Jeep down, I noticed large logs floating in the water. As I drove closer, I realized the logs were crocodiles. Hundreds of them feeding off cow carcasses floating next to the beach. The frightening part was people were hanging around and swimming in the shallow parts of the lake. The lake was a Venus flytrap.

I have an irrational fear of alligators and crocodiles. I don't know where it comes from, but it may have started in 1988 when my grandparents took me to Gatorland Zoo in Kissimmee, Florida and I saw an alligator for the first time. Seeing an alligator in your high school science book, and looking at one directly, are completely different experiences. I remember walking away from that zoo—glad to be alive—believing I had stared death in the eye. To clarify, when I say that I have an irrational fear, I expect an alligator to ring my doorbell and eat me.

And I live in Northern California.

After that dream, I had to get my mind off of being dragged into the water by an alligator, drowned, stuffed under a rock to tenderize, and then eaten throughout a fortnight. I had a few hours before report time, so I pulled out my laptop at an empty table to work on my book. After five minutes of editing, another flight attendant sat at the table with me and struck up a conversation. I did my best to get some editing done, but this guy was a constant distraction. I call people like that, assholes. You see me doing something, and instead of respecting me and moving the conversation to someone else, you insist on doing everything in your power to distract me. I can only nod my head so many times before I give myself a migraine. The same shit happens on the airplane. There I am, reading and minding my own business somewhere over Boise, and the other flight attendant wants to tell me about how, after her fourth can of cranberry juice, that dang UTI is still burning.

Nobody cares about your burning UTI, Lorretta.

I met my crew, and they were okay. The captain commutes from San Jose, and she rubbed in that she took a later commute flight and landed in LAX with time to spare. Damn, I took the earliest flight because I was afraid to be late, and I've been waiting for seven hours in the crew lounge. Why am I based in LAX and waiting seven hours to start my trip? I could fly across the country in less time and have an incredible schedule in JFK. What am I doing in this base? Dying slowly? Hating my life? Should I jump into the airplane engine? Yes, to all that.

On our flight to Sacramento, the guitarist from No Doubt was in the first row with his family. He was down-to-earth, and his kids were well-behaved. There's nothing better than a celebrity with well-behaved children. I told him and his wife I'd be singing No Doubt songs for the rest of the night, and they both laughed.

I don't know what happened on the return flight to LAX, but the passengers were off their rockers; ordering two, and even three drinks, on a one-hour flight. If you're that dehydrated, you might want to make an appointment with your doctor, not empty out my soda cart. The lady in 2D had her garbage on the tray table, and when I came by collecting trash, she rudely tapped her fake press-on nails rapidly on the table. I hope she wasn't demanding me to pick up her garbage off the tray table, because the last time I checked, my crew ID didn't read "Assistant to 2D". A few rows down from 2D, as I walked down the aisle with a trash bag, a woman handed me the air sickness bag. It felt extremely light. My curiosity got the best of me, I stopped, opened up the air sickness bag (I know, I'm a brave guy), and all that was inside was a used napkin.

A fucking napkin.

It may have been caused by fatigue—that's my excuse if she writes in a complaint letter—but I emptied the napkin into the trash bag, handed the sickness bag back to her, and said. "This isn't a garbage bag."

During boarding for our last flight to Seattle, I got my second wind and joked with passengers walking on the airplane. A pilot stepped into the galley and we instantly connected. He's definitely the attractive dad bod type. We were attempting to get all the passengers in their seats and close the overhead bins when the gate agent stormed on the airplane, "Can I close the door?"

I'm really tired of gate agents pushing us to close the aircraft door before all the passengers are seated. There was no rush; we had ten minutes before the door had to be closed. It's every airport and an everyday occurrence, but what good would complaining do?

The Seattle flight went smoothly. While doing beverage service, I stopped at row five and addressed the gentleman seated in 5B, "Good evening. What would you like to drink?"

His eyes glazed over. I handed him a napkin, and he stared at it. Now it felt like a game. I asked him again, "Would you like something to drink?"

The gentleman sitting in the window pulled the menu from the seatback card and opened it up to the list of drinks. They perused the menu while mumbling to each other under their breath. I was extremely annoyed. Thankfully, it was a three-hour flight, and I had time to waste while waiting for him to sound out the menu.

The passenger in 5B looked at me, "I'll take a water."

That caught me off guard. I furrowed my eyebrows while pouring him some water. He spoke English, I did not see that coming. Not only did he speak English, but he also spoke English better than me after I finish off a bottle of Pinot Noir.

After we landed, a female passenger stopped in the front galley during deplaning. She smiled, "I want to say, you are wonderful. I've been flying this airline for three years, and I've never met anyone as good as you. Everyone should be like you, you've got it. Can I write into the airline for you?"

I was completely honored. The funniest part was I was fatigued and hardly grinned. I barely put in 50% on that flight because I was tired. Can you imagine how that passenger would feel if I was operating at 100%?

I thanked her, "You made my night." It doesn't even matter if she writes a compliment letter to the airline, which passengers rarely do. I appreciated her taking the time to stop in the galley and spread some kindness. That's all flight attendants ask for, a little love from our passengers. We aren't in this job to be bitches to the flying public. We're flight attendants because most of us are extroverts who want people to be happy and have a great time. Unfortunately, that's not what the general public believes. I'm disrespected so often that when someone compliments me on a job well done, it means a lot.

The front desk clerk demanded that all the flight attendants provide a credit card number to use the refrigerator in the room. I could have let it go, but I'm an asshole when I'm tired. I began debating with the front desk clerk while my co-workers gawked at me. I informed her that I had recently spoken with the airline (that's a lie) and our contract states we are not required to hand over a credit card on layovers (not a lie). She stood firm with her request and refused to hand us a key to the refrigerator until we each gave a credit card number. I backed down. I was getting nowhere, and there were six of us waiting for hotel room keys.

Now that I think about it, I remember hearing a rumor that the crew was taking items from the refrigerator and not paying for them. At this hotel, the fridge is also the minibar. The hotel staff usually gives us a key to store our food, but if the crew is stealing, then I understand the hotel's dilemma. I'll apologize to the front desk clerk when I see her tomorrow.

This is the second time I've been a dick at this hotel in the past month.

Saturday
SEA-FAI-SEA

The *Flight Attendant Joe* blog hit over 6,000 visits last month. That's so incredible. Who reads this shit? Whoever they are, I want to thank them personally.

I tried writing today, but nothing good came out. At this rate, I'll never finish the book. Waking up early and commuting to LAX and waiting around for seven hours to begin my day is taking its toll on my mind and body. I can't decide what's the better scenario: be based in LAX, only an hour flight from home, or transfer back to JFK. This is when I wish I were back in therapy so Melinda could tell me what to do. Who am I kidding? Therapists don't tell you what to do. They let you decide what to do so you can mess up your life and continue needing them. It's an endless cycle.

While sitting in the hotel lobby this afternoon, one of the flight attendants I'm working with walked up to me and stated, "I barely recognized you out of uniform."

Was her comment friendly or rude? Honestly, I couldn't tell. I decided to forgo leaving the hotel and went back to my room, closed the curtains, and decided to nap for the rest of the day.

I slept a solid three hours and woke up in a great mood. I've decided to rent a car tomorrow when I'm back here so I can explore. After booking my rental, I walked to the nearest coffee shop and told the barista, "I have to stay up all night, and I need something strong." I ordered an iced Americano with three espresso shots and then stopped at the cupcake shop and ate two mini cupcakes.

Danny Bonaduce walked past me in the hotel lobby while I waited for my crew. He looked fantastic. I told one of the flight attendants, and she said, "Who's that?"

I hate young people.

Our flight to Fairbanks was slightly delayed because the airplane coming from Dallas was late. That's nothing new; I expect all my trips to be delayed. Now, when my flights are on time, that's cause for a celebration. A female passenger had a service animal that kept barking at other passengers while we all stood at the gate. Service animals shouldn't do that. They should serve their master, not cause a commotion. I walked over to introduce myself, I didn't say anything rude, but I let her know that I had my eye on her…and her little dog, too.

We had a full flight to Fairbanks and the second passenger who walked on the airplane admitted, "I can't read. What's my seat number?"

At least he's honest. I'd rather have you admit you're illiterate than have you standing in the aisle blocking the other passengers trying to find their seats. On the flight back from Fairbanks, we only had ninety passengers, and surprisingly enough, I think they all knew how to read.

Sunday
Seattle

Sleeping all day sounded divine, but that would screw up my sleep schedule. I walked the few blocks to the car rental office to pick up my car. When I stepped inside, three other customers were standing in front of me, and each needed special attention. I have the worst luck at car rental offices. We're only renting the cars, not buying them. The first customer in line had a credit card that kept getting declined. He pulled more cards out of his wallet, but each failed. I snickered at the fact this dude was attempting to rent a car with no money—or credit. He finally got the hint and stepped outside to make a phone call.

Next up was the second guy in line. He sauntered up to the counter, and cooly asked, "Can I have the car you were going to give that guy?"

That's shady. This guy should be a real housewife. That poor dude was barely outside, and this asshat was trying to scoop up his compact car. Human beings are selfish creatures. I wonder if dinosaurs were that shady when they roamed the planet? Dinosaurs had more important things to worry about, like the end times.

Next was an older woman who spent fifteen minutes yelling at the employee about her sick kid. She ended her rant with, "…and you don't even care about him."

Guess what, bitch? They weren't the only ones. Shut the hell up and rent the car. If we were in the *Big Brother* house, I'd win on the first day. I'd get all three of these fools to fight each other, and all I'd have to do is bring up car rentals.

When the lady finished complaining, she grabbed her keys and walked out. I had almost reached the counter when I heard the bell ring on the front door. I turned around, and the first customer made his way back into line. He stood behind me, but I stepped aside and motioned for him to go first. Don't ever say I'm an asshole. Okay, I'm an asshole, but most of the time it's all talk.

He thanked me, and I smiled. In all honesty, he was there before me, and even though I joked about his credit card dilemma, I felt terrible for him. That's an embarrassing situation that once happened to me at a bookstore.

When it was my turn, I asked the employee, "I need to drop this car off tonight. Do you have night drop?"

He frowned, "Nope. We open at six in the morning."

I did not laugh. I answered, "Looks like all your customers have a problem today." Unfortunately, I have a five o'clock van to the airport in the morning, dropping the car off late than that was not an option. After all that bullshit, and waiting almost an hour, I walked out with no rental car. It's frustrating, but I had to find the humor in the entire situation. Out of all four of us in line, I had no initial complaints or problems, and I ended up being the only one to walk out with no car.

Even the dude with no credit card rented a car.

I walked out, devastated. Okay, that might be over-dramatic. Let's say I was slightly annoyed because it sounds butch. The sun shined bright in the sky, so I decided to hop on the bus and explore a park a few miles away. The bus ride was entertaining, to say the least. One passenger yelled at himself for the entire twenty-five-minute ride while I attempted to read *The Catcher in the Rye*. I wanted to shout back at him, but he was obviously mentally unstable, and I didn't want to bring any attention to myself. I already felt like all eyes were on me because I was reading a book on the bus and not following in my fellow passenger's lead. You know, screaming at the dirty windows and eating cookies off the floor.

Layovers are fun.

I walked to a restaurant outside the park for lunch, and the food sucked. I've already forgotten what I ate, that's how bad it was. My layover did not turn out how I had planned. Next time I'm here, I'll keep my ass in bed. I strolled around the park and spoke with Matt on the phone. I miss him. Being based in LAX reminds me of my seniority when I first started. I've had shitty seniority and survived it, WHY AM I DOING THIS TO MYSELF AGAIN?

The bus ride back to the hotel was uneventful. I suppose the crazies take the 10:20 A.M. bus to the park and never leave. I went for happy hour and ordered chicken wings. I've been eating a large number of chicken wings lately, that can't be good for my health. I chatted with Adam on the phone and ordered a beer, but decided not to drink it. Who says I have no control? I left a full beer at my table and walked back to the hotel. I wish I could have given the beer to the dude on the bus.

It's time for bed, 4:40 A.M. comes quickly.

Monday
SEA-LAX-LAS-LAX

My body felt like it was breaking down, that's how goddamn early I had to climb out of bed. While I stumbled around, getting dressed, each one of my organs screamed at the other one to fail so I could die. That's how tired I was, I'd rather be dead than heading to the airport. It was quiet on the van ride. There's nothing worse than an early morning chatterbox. That's why flight attendants and pilots aren't allowed to carry knives, we'd stab each other for discussing stupid shit at five o'clock in the morning.

I'm one of those people who refuses to function without coffee. Without that early morning bitter juice, I can barely form a complete sentence. I'm not ashamed to admit that I'm addicted to caffeine, and at this point in my life, I don't care. Let caffeine kill me, I'd rather die from the joys of a coffee buzz than from an infected pressure ulcer that I received at Saint Madonna of The Vogue Nursing Home and Rehabilitation Center. Seriously, if there were such a thing as a coffee drip, I'd walk around with a bag of Veranda Blend hanging from an IV pole. Why is that not a reality? (I'm talking to you, Starbucks.) The second I swallow that first sip of the potion, my brain wakes up, and I function as a human being.

Our first flight was delayed for forty-five minutes. I'm telling you, do not choose my airline if you want something delivered on time. I hope to God nobody is ever waiting on a heart transplant, and their new blood pumper is packed in dry ice on one of our airplanes, the dry ice will dissolve before the aircraft departs.

I sat with the first officer and shared with him a meme I made about how big titties bounce in the hotel van. I shared my blog with him and told him I was writing a book, he wasn't impressed. Our airplane arrived, and we boarded the flight. At some point before 10,000 feet, I mentioned to my co-worker seated next to me that I needed a ride to another airport to commute home.

The passenger in 1D overheard me and offered, "I can bring you to another airport."

I smiled, "Thank you, but I'll be fine."

During the flight, the captain told me that we were keeping the same airplane for our Las Vegas turn. That's helpful on a long day with multiple flights. Each time we step onto a new aircraft, we have to do security checks. It's less work keeping the same airplane all day. Sadly, the captain lied. The moment the airplane door opened, the gate agent corrected him. We did have to swap aircraft for our Las Vegas turn. We grabbed our luggage and followed each other to the new gate, which was right next to the one we parked at. We passed a group of flight attendants leaving the airplane we were about to board. It would have been easier for all of us to keep the same aircraft we were already on, but that would be too easy. Airlines like to make things difficult. I'll never understand the logic around here.

The captain working with us to Las Vegas gave us a thorough flight deck briefing. One of the other flight attendants told me that the captain was weird and delayed flights for stupid reasons. During the briefing, he reminded us about three recent airline incidents that have been in the news. Thankfully, I'm a blogger, and I keep up with airline news.

He ended the briefing with, "...if any passengers give you a hard time, please diffuse the situation and resolve it."

The instant we closed the airplane door, an elderly woman in 1D stood up and shuffled to the lavatory. I made no attempt to stop her; I'm not going down as the flight attendant who forced some old lady to shit herself in row one. That's not happening while I'm the lead flight attendant. By the time the slides were armed at the aircraft door, the geriatric ladies daughter had come forward from her seat to assist her mother. I smiled and stuck my head in the flight deck to politely inform the captain that an elderly lady was in the lavatory.

He asked, "How long will she be?"

How the hell am I supposed to know how long it takes an old lady to use the lavatory? What am I, a shit psychic? If I had to estimate, I'd say she was pushing a thousand years old, so I'm guessing it might take a long time. I can't be sure, but if someone cut her in half, she'd have more rings than a giant sequoia.

"I don't know how long it's going to take, I didn't ask her."

He frowned, picked up the interphone, and announced, "We need everyone in their seats right now."

I doubt that made her shit any faster. I was afraid she'd push hard and have a heart attack. I think that's happened, no need to pull out the AED while parked at the gate. I believe the term is referred to as vasovagal syncope. I'm glad that nursing education still comes in handy.

When she finally emerged, I smiled at her and closed the flight deck door before the captain had a chance to utter anything inappropriate. You know it's severe when I worry about other people being inappropriate.

Grandma destroyed the lavatory with her stink bomb. I choked reading the safety demonstration, and I had to fight off the mid-flight attendant from manually releasing the oxygen masks. I sprayed enough Febreze to refresh an entire 5,000-square foot house, and all that Febreze did was laugh at me. The last time I smelled something that offensive, I was a nurse, and my patient died and shit the bed. Grandma spread pre-departure death in the lavatory, and I decided to use the back lavatory for the rest of the flight.

After landing in Las Vegas, we started reboarding for our return flight to Los Angeles with new pilots. We went through pilots today like prostitutes go through tricks.

These Las Vegas flights are ridiculous; they remind me of the Hogwarts Express, but instead of magical students on a train, we transport call girls on a plane. They were seated throughout the aircraft—little bedazzled pieces of pimp candy strewn around like sprinkles.

I had two of them seated in row two, and the mid-cabin flight attendant leaned over and whispered, "She's an ABG. An Asian baby girl. They dress slutty and wear a lot of makeup. Have you heard of that?"

"No. Why would I need to know that?" I was already annoyed with this Asian baby girl and her tramp stamp. When she boarded the airplane, ABG dropped her luggage in the aisle and stated, "I need all my bags in the overhead bin."

She had three bags, which was one over the limit. The flight wasn't completely full, so instead of checking her third bag, I politely said, "Well, the small one can go under the seat in front of you, and we'll put these two in the overhead bin. But so you know, this one," and I pointed at the third bag, "should have been checked."

ABG scratched her scalp with her long lime green press-on nails and shrugged while sliding into the row and sitting down. I helped her with her bags, but her high-pitched voice pierced my brain like death metal music.

On my commute flight home, I sat in a middle seat and was grateful to be on my way home. You know I'm tired when I don't bitch about a middle seat. I was homeward bound and focused on enjoying a few days off. This job has drained all the happiness from me. One reason is I miss being home on the weekends. My seniority is atrocious on the west coast. I sound like a broken record, but these feelings have saturated me. The LAX base may be a closer commute, but it's still crushing my soul. I'm never happy. What's more important, a shorter commute or seniority? At this airline, I can't have both.

I missed the train, and instead of waiting an hour for the next one, I ordered a shared car ride and was picked up by an awkward guy who refused to open his trunk. Instead, he put my luggage in the back seat. My first thought was that he had his last three riders mutilated in the trunk. I grasped my suitcase in the back seat with one hand, and with the other, I held onto the door handle in case I had to escape.

I'm happy to be home, in my pajamas, and not in the trunk of that BMW.

PAIRING 016: PMS: PISSY MALE SYNDROME

Sunday
LAX—BOI—LAX—PDX

I'm taking Lamisil for a few toenails riddled with fungus. Each morning that I'm not jaundiced or have liver pain, I think I might survive this treatment. In eleven weeks, I expect to have beautiful nails. Right now, my big toenail looks like it should be attached to a velociraptor.

I woke up two minutes before my alarm this morning and still hadn't listed for my commuter flight. I called the airline last night and spent thirty minutes on hold and then finally hung up without speaking to customer service. Matt made coffee this morning, and I barely had time to finish one cup. Chaotic morning leaving for the airport, and I was flying on another airline, which increases my anxiety level. I brought the crew candy, and the gate agents name was Alyx (Alex), which I think is a unique way to spell it.

The airplane pulled away from the gate and sat on the runway for fifteen minutes. I wanted to panic, but I held myself together because I'm flying on a different airline. I read Orwell's *Animal Farm* while listening to a little girl screaming at the top of her lungs in the row across from me.

My mood lifted when I stepped into the flight attendant lounge. Laura was there, and her presence makes me feel better. Even when she's eating a Chipotle rice bowl, she's terrific. She's Zoloft without the dizziness. Laura informed me about a second audition that she's landed for a series that would film in New York. I have my fingers crossed for her. In the time that we caught up in the lounge, Laura told me about a new guy she's dating who's not in show business. Hollywood must be a difficult place to date. I imagine everyone dating in Hollywood is douchey and trying to get in your pants.

Hollywood sounds like the airline industry.

Laura drove her own car on the first date so she'd have a ride home without depending on this guy. That's the best advice to give your teenage daughter—or any woman—who's going on a date. Drive your own car, and don't be dependent on some random dude. I had to make out with an ugly guy once for a ride home, it wasn't fun.

I boarded my flight and met Captain Lex, who I follow on Instagram. He follows me on social media as well, and once he knew my identity, he stated his surprise that we worked for the same airline. I love being incognito; I'm practically Batman. While standing in the flight deck chatting with him, I stuck my foot in my mouth. I started talking about his life and his pet iguana as if we were old high school buddies. Now I look like a stalker.

We did a quick Boise turn, and on the way back to LAX, a passenger moved to the exit row. When the mid-flight attendant informed her it was an upgraded seat, the lady yelled, "No," and didn't move. Luckily, she finally paid. That's too short of a flight for nonsense.

The flight to Portland was filled with people who should have been riding on a bus. After we closed up the aircraft, the gate agent knocked on the airplane door to reopen it. I immediately stepped back and did not address her. We have to acknowledge the gate agent before the aircraft door is opened, and I didn't want her to open the door before I disarmed the emergency slide. I went to the flight deck and told Captain Lex we were disarming the slides. He agreed, so I made the announcement to the other flight attendants to, "disarm your doors," and the moment my door was disarmed, the gate agent opened it. I don't know what came over me, but I yelled at her. I can't even remember what I said, but it had to do with me not giving her the authority to open the door. The gate agent apologized, but I don't think some of these agents understand how safety-orientated we are. The best part is, she opened the airplane door to let on an underage minor who's traveling standby.

This kid's mom is a gate agent in Portland. It took me a few seconds to realize that we opened the airplane door—after it had been closed already—for a standby passenger. I've seen the aircraft door reopened for a revenue passenger, but never for a standby. I wonder if one of these gate agents will get in trouble? Probably not. It seems that the only people held accountable at this airline are the flight attendants and pilots.

When I checked into the hotel, I opened my luggage and realized I only packed gym shorts. At least I looked comfortable while at late happy hour with the crew. I wanted to go straight to bed, but I felt a little nightcap would do wonders.

I can't shake this feeling of anger and frustration. Granted, I'm usually angry and frustrated, but this is entirely different. It feels like I'm walking around in a cloud of aggression where I'm ready to snap at every human I encounter. Maybe I have my man period, it wouldn't be the first time.

I've decided not to set my alarm for tomorrow morning; I deserve the sleep.

Monday
PDX—ANC—BOI

Yesterday I felt angry, this morning I was depressed. Maybe I'm bipolar. I have this feeling of hopelessness that I can't shake. I'm not myself; it's like my brain is fighting against me. I crawled out of bed, showered, and ordered a shared car ride to Target. The lady who picked me up gave off the impression that she was new to America and new to driving a car. Even though Google Maps directed her, she had no clue where to go. When the Google Maps voice alerted, "Turn left at Rose Road," this bitch turned right.

I kindly asked her to shut off the directions and listen to me, and within five minutes, we were pulling into the Target parking lot.

She asked me, "Do you want me to wait and give you a ride back?"

I answered, "No. I'd rather walk."

My stomach has been hurting; I may have an ulcer. It wouldn't surprise me because I've been internalizing everything lately and it's bound to mess me up. I bought some Pepto, a pair of old man shorts, and then walked the two and a half miles back to the hotel.

I spoke with my friend Mike on the telephone. He's in Florida visiting his new boyfriend for the week. He delivered some tough love and reiterated that my life was remarkable, and I needed to focus on the positive stuff. That seems so easy, I don't know why I make my life difficult. When I arrived back at the hotel, I decided to rest.

I'm one of those people who must convince myself it's perfectly fine to do nothing. I think I'm missing out on a layover if I'm not continually moving. I definitely felt manic today, so I shut the curtains, turned the air conditioner down to sixty-four degrees, and passed out.

I woke up at four P.M. and did a Google search for "man period" and Irritable Male Syndrome (IMS) appeared. There's an actual explanation for a man period. I'm pleased that I can now refer to this emotional rollercoaster by its exact name.

The next time someone asks, "What's wrong, Joe?"

I can politely reply, "I'm suffering from Irritable Male Syndrome. It's a real thing; I Googled it."

After crawling out of bed, I looked up my flight, and it's two hours delayed. On my way to get dinner, I called Crew Scheduling and informed the scheduler that our flight was delayed, but that our report time had not changed.

His response was typical, "We're not changing your report time because there may be an airplane swap."

Not in Portland, dickface. I know for a fact that we have no additional airplanes in Portland. I know my tone sounds grating, but it's frustrating dealing with these schedulers who have no knowledge how the airline works. My non-airline friends know more about the airline industry than the employees managing our schedules.

The scheduler put me on hold and quickly came back, "We've pushed your report time back two hours."

I asked, "No extra airplane available?"

"What?"

"Never mind. Thank you. What about our new van time?"

177

"It should be updated on your pairing in a few minutes."

I didn't believe him. I never do. When schedulers utter their propaganda quotes back about how everything will be taken care of, I have little faith. Actually, I have NO confidence in this entire airline. When I got back to my room, I texted Sam (the other bear flight attendant) about the update, and he responded: *our new van time is 8:05 P.M.*

At least he knew what was going on. That was three hours away, so I settled back down to take another nap, but the moment I started dozing off, the hotel room phone rang. It was the front desk.

The front desk clerk stated, "Hi. This is Claudia from the front desk, your van time has been changed to nine o'clock tonight."

I asked, "Are you sure that's the correct time?"

She had more confidence than Madonna in a cone bra, "Yes. Nine o'clock tonight."

That totally confused me. Was it 8:05 P.M. or nine? I honestly didn't know. I called Crew Scheduling back and was connected with some lady who sounded like she hadn't reached puberty. I understand the department has a fast turnover rate, but have they started hiring employees right out of junior high school? I asked about our new van time, and she put me on hold. I figured she had to chat with Satan about it because he obviously runs that department. She came back a few minutes later and confirmed that our van time was 8:05 P.M.

At that point, I couldn't sleep because my brain was stimulated, and my mind raced. Shouldn't schedulers be held accountable for disturbing a flight attendant on a layover? Technically, I called them—so I know my point doesn't make sense—but they should still be held accountable. We are already blamed for enough bullshit.

I met Sam and the other flight attendant in the lobby at 8:05 P.M., and there was no van outside to drive us to the airport. Was I shocked? Was I surprised? None of the above. I was disappointed. I called scheduling while Sam called the van service company. The employee at the van service company answered first and confirmed there was no van time set for flight attendants at 8:05 P.M.

Crew Scheduling finally answered my call, and within the first five seconds of the conversation, I struggled to understand the guy on the other end of the phone. He didn't appear to speak in English. In fact, it sounded more like I was receiving attack coordinates from ISIS. I relayed my dilemma, and every time he spoke, I responded, "What? I'm sorry, I don't understand you." That happened five times until I asked, "Can you put a supervisor on?"

I'm not trying to be a dick, but he spoke like there was an entire bag of Werther's Originals stuffed in his mouth. He put me on hold, and then came back on the phone to talk to me, but it was gibberish. I hoped the message he was trying to convey wasn't all that important. Again, I asked to speak with a supervisor, and he abruptly placed me back on hold. I fought the annoyance bubbling up inside me. I remember once while conducting flight attendant interviews, we declined hiring an applicant because a few of the managers questioned her accent and how her voice would sound over the interphone. That's some bullshit to think about when I've got Bobcat Goldthwait on the phone gargling marbles.

A supervisor eventually picked up the call. It would be easier to get members of the Westboro Baptist Church to host a same-sex wedding in Topeka, Kansas than getting a flight attendant supervisor on the phone. At least I understood this guy, but I retold the circumstances for what felt like the tenth time. I should be compensated for each time I repeat myself to another airline employee.

Here's the thing about any representatives of the scheduling department: whenever explaining something to one of them on the phone, they stutter and pause as if they're shocked that we are calling and asking questions. Each time a scheduler answers, "This is Jerry. How may I help you?" I expect it's their first day on the job and that they know zilch about flight attendants or the airline industry. And I'm usually right. I have no proof about this, so don't quote me, call it intuition. The real indicator is the fact that they put you on hold for any question. You could ask, "What time is it?" and they'd say, "Please hold." That's not an exaggeration, ask any flight attendant or pilot. It happens every single time I call scheduling. It never fails, but I think that's how micromanaged the airline industry is.

With the supervisor, I began losing my patience because I had already explained the mess we were in with scheduler, Mr. Werthers, but I had to stay calm. Our calls are all recorded, and I can't begin to remember what was said, but as we went back and forth in the hotel lobby, Sam waved at me to catch my attention, "The van service is sending a taxi, but it won't be here for another thirty minutes."

That was unacceptable, especially when two schedulers told us our airport van time was at 8:05 P.M. I explained to the supervisor, "We aren't waiting for thirty minutes. We're jumping in a different taxi and heading to the airport. I'll expense it."

I heard a loud sound, and I'm pretty sure his head exploded all over the wall. He tried talking me out of hailing a taxi and instead, persuaded us to wait for the airport van. I shut him down. First, that would make us late for our report time, which would delay the flight. Why did I care more about a flight departing on time than a supervisor? Second, if you don't want flight attendants expensing their taxi rides to the airport, have the fucking ride ready when you say it's going to be available. How difficult is that?

After I ended the call, I asked the bellhop to summon a taxi; it pulled up to the hotel in about three seconds.

The ride to the airport was uneventful, and I sat in the front seat, shooting the breeze with the driver. When we pulled up to the terminal, Sam and the other flight attendant stepped out of the taxi and grabbed our luggage from the trunk while I settled the bill.

It should have been a smooth transaction, but then the driver said, "Oh no."

I turned my head as the receipt printed out from the machine. Instead of it reading: $61.00, it read: 671.00.

My first instinct was to choke her, but then I remembered it was an accident. I fantasized about strangling her the way Homer Simpson strangles Bart, but killing a taxi driver outside the Portland International Airport sounds like a Quentin Tarantino movie. And who am I to judge, I make mistakes all the time. I calmly asked her to refund the wrong price and recharge the card with the correct amount.

She sighed, "I can't do that."

All this drama and I hadn't even stepped inside the airport. I answered, "Now we have an issue. Can you call someone?"

She started ringing up the correct charge and while she apologized up and down—I did feel bad for her—she tried contacting their dispatch department. When someone on the other end of the phone answered, they confirmed her original statement. Nobody at this taxi company could solve the issue until tomorrow morning. My neck became red, and I began to sweat. I had to get away from her before my temper blew up her yellow taxi. I smiled and said I'd contact my credit card company if I didn't see the problem resolved on my credit card statement within the next few days. I'm surprised I maintained my composure, but I still can't stop thinking about how this was all caused by bad management and scheduling.

After we walked through security, I called Matt because I needed him to tell him everything was okay. I work myself up over situations and then act like Henny Penny. Even though I tell myself over and over in my mind that nothing terrible has happened, it's hard to understand that the sky is not falling. Matt does a great job at jolting me back into reality. Sure, not having a ride to the airport to do your job can be annoying, but it's not the end of the world. It's failed communication, not an airplane broken up into a million pieces. Priorities. I told myself that over and over as I made my way to the gate. It calmed me down until I walked up to the gate agent and found out there was no airplane, and nobody knew the whereabouts of our pilots.

While standing at the gate, a passenger walked up and asked the gate agent where he was seated. Was he unable to read or simply think she was psychic? I couldn't tell you. She took the boarding pass from him and said, "You're seated in 25A."

He snipped back, "Oh, Y'all got me in the slave section."

I turned around and walked away. After the yellow taxi ride, I had no energy to deal with an angry passenger. Our pilots arrived after we were at the gate for fifteen minutes. They sauntered up like they were in a slow-mo rap video.

"Where were you guys?" Sam asked the captain.

"We took the nine o'clock van."

My neck almost snapped off. The nine o'clock van? I could feel my pulse racing at the tip of my earlobes. Then he continued, "I called the front desk and told them to call you and let you know the van was changed to nine, and that if you had any questions, to call my room."

Claudia, the front desk clerk, never relayed that part of the message. I was mentally exhausted and ready to call in fatigue and go back to bed. At that moment, as if things couldn't get worse, the passenger in 25A walked back up to the gate, slapped his ticket on the counter, and demanded a full refund and upgrade because of the delay.

If it were my last day, I would have told him to sit down and have a seat, on another airline.

After the airplane landed, we waited for the passengers to deplane. I took that as the perfect opportunity to recant my experience about my overcharged taxi ride to anyone who'd listen. Sam was drained by my complaining and rolled his eyes, but to hell with Sam. Was his credit card overcharged? No. It was not. I started with the pilots, "Guess what happened to me…" and ranted only stopping to catch my breath. I wish the story ended with, "…I got a blowjob at the hotel."

Well, I did get screwed in the ass by my airline, so that almost counts.

The airplane we flew to Anchorage should be sold for parts. Nothing worked. We even had to get an air start because the APU was broken and that made the airplane hotter than Chris Hemsworth with his shirt off. If you are wondering what the APU is, don't overthink it. All you need to know is that airplanes use magic to stay in the air. And Jesus helps out if you're flying in and out of the Dominican Republic. The coffee makers didn't work, the carpet was disgusting, and half the televisions were inoperative.

The guy seated in 1C stood in the galley while provisioning restocked the front galley. I kindly asked him to step out of the way to allow provisioning to finish their job, and he glared at me. Not a stare; but a glare. An evil glare, which anyone would agree is much worse than a stare. After he moved, I couldn't let it go. I had to have the last word. Or in this case, the first word even though his glare said a mouthful.

I moved close to his face, "Didn't mean to upset you, I didn't want you to get hurt."

He ignored me.

We landed in Anchorage, and the cleaners came on the airplane. They were slightly aggressive if you ask me. I stepped off the aircraft to stretch my legs and wash my hands in the airport restaurant. I love scrubbing my hands in a real sink after being on an airplane for hours. There are clean airplane hands, and then there are clean airport restroom hands.

We began boarding, and some heavy-set guy walked on with a car seat. I politely reminded him to put the car seat in the window, and sarcastically, he responded, "Oh. Alright."

I thought to myself, *I'm trying to save your life in case of an emergency asshole.*

Boarding took a long time because most of the passengers were slow as tar. We only had ninety-eight passengers, but the way they moved, you'd think it was 10,000. I had ten passengers in my section, but because of my mood, that was nine too many. I had only one drink order, and then everyone fell asleep. I wish I could have curled up in the exit row and taken a nap, but that's not allowed.

Stupid airline rules.

I should be sleeping already, but if I don't jot this shit down in my journal, I'll never remember it. At the airport, the hotel van driver annoyed me. At least I didn't have to pay for a taxi again.

See Joe, think positive.

As the van driver lifted my suitcase into the back of the van, I politely said, "Be careful."

He spent the next ten minutes bemoaning that because he's seventy-nine years old, he can lift anything and do anything. Why in the hell is a seventy-nine-year-old lifting crew bags into a van? What is this, North Korea? Second, if you can lift anything, then lift the van, bitch.

Tuesday
Boise

I had a dream last night about Caitlyn Jenner tucking her penis between her legs; I never want to think about it again.

I slept for four hours, maybe three. Honestly, I don't care. Anything under seven hours of sleep is inhumane. I crawled out of bed at noon and walked to Starbucks and then strolled around Barnes and Noble. I'm still cranky today. Knowing that it's IMS makes it a little easier to understand, but nothing stops the transition from Flight Attendant Joe into Cranky Ass Hoe. The change happens within seconds. One minute I'm giving someone a compliment and the next I'm stabbing them with my mind. I walked all the back to the hotel. Honestly, it was less than two miles, I shouldn't make it sound like I walked to a different country in a blizzard. I sent in my expense report to be approved for the taxi ride and emailed my base manager and supervisor with details regarding the horrible job scheduling did handling the airport van. I don't expect anything will be done, but I still need this situation documented and my money reimbursed. On a positive note, the taxi charge went through for the correct amount.

I met up with my Sam at the hotel bar. I enjoyed the company, but I really wanted to be alone.

Wednesday
BOI—LAX—LAS—LAX

Go-home day is my favorite day of a trip. I attempted making coffee and realize I left my coffee thermos on the airplane yesterday morning. I had a meltdown in the hotel room. I cursed, and after saying a list of profanities that would shock a sex worker, I was still upset.

Our airport van pickup time was at 5:30 A.M. and I was still ironing my shirt at 5:17 A.M. That's cutting it close, even for me. I made it down in time for the van and also had a moment to get a cup of free coffee from the hotel, which I quickly tossed into the trash because it tasted like dirt.

I approached the gate with a look of disgust ready to attack anyone who looked at me. Sam shook his head, he probably couldn't wait for the trip to be over. I've been a complete asshole this entire trip. I'm positive working with me when I'm having my man period is no fun for anyone. I thought about defending my actions and educating them about IMS, but as I placed my luggage behind the counter, the gate agent recognized me and said, "Hey, we found your coffee cup on the plane yesterday."

She handed me the stainless steel thermos, and I felt harmony. I'm addicted to coffee. I can't function without it. I wouldn't even get that upset about starving to death on a deserted island as long as they had coffee.

I was in a better mood when we landed in LAX. When I met the pilots taking us to Las Vegas, they seemed bearable. Captain Ginger had a thick German accent, and First Officer Chatterbox I'd seen before, but couldn't place from where. After boarding completed, Chatterbox immediately got on the interphone, and it all came back to me. She's a stand-up comedian or thinks she's a stand-up comedian. I'm all for entertainment on the airplane, but Chatterbox was out of control. While she held the interphone hostage, the gate agent closed the aircraft door. I waited nearly three minutes to alert the flight attendants in the back to arm their emergency slides. Three minutes seems like forever when you're trying to do your job. I complained to Sam about it, and I think First Officer Chatterbox overheard me, but I didn't care. Listen, go fly the fucking airplane. That's what you are paid to do, not hinder my ability to finish my duties by telling bad jokes for cheap laughs from our passengers. How would she like it if I went into the flight and started telling jokes to ATC?

After she entertained the passengers, she slammed the interphone into place and began walking into the flight deck. I stopped her, "You know I need that right?" She disregarded me, which confirmed she heard me lamenting about her antics.

We landed in Las Vegas, and it was hot as balls after a five-mile run. The jet bridge was roasting, and I wondered what any of our Jewish passengers were thinking regarding our German captain pulling an airplane up to a scorching hot jet bridge. We met our new pilots, and they were both so sexy, I could barely talk to them. The captain I had flown with long ago. Let's say that if the captain is an eight, the first officer is a twenty-four. Why can't we all be on a twenty-four-hour layover somewhere instead of a forty-five-minute flight?

Maybe my man period is caused by my job? While waiting in the flight attendant lounge, I chatted with another flight attendant about becoming a first-class purser. I think I'm going to apply. It's time to transfer to JFK and change things up, do something different and exciting. I saw my base manager and reminded him to approve my expense report from the taxi ride. I know he's a busy man and that's why I didn't make a scene about it. Please approve the expense report so I can get my money, that's all I want.

I saw a co-worker who I'm writing about in my book, but I didn't tell her she's in the book. When I took my seat on the airplane, I put on my headphones, turned on some Madonna music, and quickly passed out. The flight attendant woke me up for landing because my bag wasn't under the seat in front of me. I was embarrassed.

On the train home, while I was in a seat, a Middle Eastern guy who had forgotten to put on deodorant stood over me. I had to cover my nose the entire ride. Biological warfare on the train right out in the open.

PAIRING 017: PICKLEBACK SHOTS

Wednesday
SFO—LAX

The alarm went off at four A.M., and I felt like a zombie walking through the house. I dropped Matt off at the chaotic domestic terminal of San Francisco International airport. I kissed him goodbye and drove away, missing him the moment I pulled onto 101 South. Matt is flying standby to North Carolina, on an airline that I don't work for. Even though he will be at the bottom of the priority list, he's confident he'll get on the flight. I expect to see him later today. Because it's the 4th of July holiday weekend, flying standby will be challenging. Flying standby during a holiday weekend is like gambling in Las Vegas, there's a high probability you will walk out a loser.

At home, I tried napping, but Matt continued texting me on his status. Around 5:30 A.M. I received: *I'm 25 on the standby list.*

We chatted back and forth for a few minutes, and once the sun came up, I didn't fall right back to sleep. He never got on the six A.M. flight and didn't make it on the 7:50 A.M., either. None of this surprised me. As he sent me updates, I grabbed my phone, read the text, and nodded to whichever cat was in the room thinking, Daddy Matt's not leaving San Francisco today.

He texted: *The gate agent said the eleven A.M. flight looks good. I'm going to wait for that one.*

Judging by our text exchange, he seemed to be staying remarkably calm. If he was stressed about being bumped from flights like a drunk Bostonian on his way to Florida, he hid it well. Lucky for me, I fell asleep and woke up at eleven A.M. to a text message: *The gate agent doesn't know what she's talking about. What should I do?*

I responded: *Come home and figure out a new plan.*

While his standby plans unraveled, I packed for work. I'm done with this job. I'm at the point where I must convince myself to go to work. The notion of jamming my finger down my throat to vomit crossed my mind 1,000 times, but that was my approach to skipping high school. I can't be the guy who hasn't matured since high school. But honestly, I hate the entire concept of going to work. Oddly enough, I only feel this way when I'm on my way to the airport. I wonder if other flight attendants or pilots experience that? The instant I unzip my suitcase and place it on the bed, a wave of anxiety and panic washes over me. It's hard staying focused and calm. I stay silent while Matt drives me to the airport. I take deep breaths attempting to remind myself that everything is fine. Once I'm at the airport I'm a different person. I cruise through security, pulling my luggage behind me as if I own the airport. I step on the aircraft, greet the crew, take my seat, and the rest is smooth sailing until it's time to venture back to work again. That makes me wonder: do I hate being a flight attendant, or do I hate the process of leaving home to go to the airport?

I think I know the answer.

Matt took Uber home, and we worked out a new plan. He'd fly to JFK and then down to Charlotte. It seems too stressful, and I think it's ridiculous for ordinary citizens (not flight attendants or pilots) to fly standby over a busy holiday, but he's gonna do what he wants to do.

Honestly, I have other issues to work out, like this overwhelming anxiety I get about leaving for work. I've suffered this affliction since my teenage years. I despised junior and high school, but it never stopped once I was out of high school. It continued until my adulthood. When I was a nurse, I'd throw myself out of the house to go to the hospital. I can count on one hand the number of jobs I've had where I wasn't a basket case on my way to work. The moment I arrive on duty, I'm fine. It's as if a switch in my head yells at me, "Okay Joseph, pull yourself together, we're here." In high school, I'd hide in the bushes at the end of the road, wait for my parents to leave, and then creep back in the house and watch soap operas all day. Listen, there's nothing you can learn in high school that Erica Kane can't teach you on *All My Children*. That's a fact. I may have failed algebra, but I got an A+ in manipulation 101.

When it was time to catch the train to go to the airport, I asked Matt to drop me off at the station near our home. The temperature was approaching ninety degrees, and pulling my luggage five blocks in full uniform was not how I wanted to start my night. I'm miserable. I am off today, but I'm flying to LAX a day early. I feel guilty complaining about this nonsense. I should be ashamed of myself, but here I am, whining like I'm being sent to work in a mine that might collapse. If I expressed this to another soul, they'd slap me with a seatbelt extension.

Two ladies sat with me in the exit row. Thankfully, I was in the window seat. The one in the middle seat opened the seatback menu card, turned to the full-color destination map, and asked her friend, "What country is that?"

Her friend replied, "Cuba."

Then the curious middle seat occupant asked, "Oh. That's why it's gray. Where's Mexico?

Her friend pointed to the map, "It's right there, under the states."

We were still at the gate, so I fought the urge to open the overwing exit and fling her dumb ass onto the tarmac. I controlled myself, which says a lot for my patience. I'm sorry, but if you don't know where Mexico is on a map, your education failed you. It's Mexico, not Brunei. In her defense, the airline requires that you be fifteen years old and speak English to sit in the exit row, they never said anything about being dumb as fuck.

I checked into the hotel that gives airline crew a discount. The front desk clerk assigned me a room on the first floor, which was unsettling. As part of our contracts with hotels, the hotels are required to put flight attendants and pilots on rooms above the first floor. They are also not supposed to put us by ice machines and elevators, but that rarely happens. After all these years, when I'm traveling for personal reasons, and I'm given a room on the first floor, I make an odd face and wrinkle my nose, "Do you have anything on a higher floor?"

What do I think will happen? A rogue migrant worker will break into my first-floor room and steal my passport? If someone named Julio Angel Miguel Juan Carlos Jorge Castillo can pass himself off as Joseph Thomas—he can have the passport.

As I'm writing this, I plainly heard two loud popping noises outside that may or may not have been gunshots.

Welcome to LA.

Hopefully, somebody dropped something heavy…twice.

Thursday
LAX—SLC—BOI—SEA

The hotel had a free breakfast buffet. That's a win. Nobody broke into my first-floor room, and I didn't hear any more gunshots. That's two more wins. I wonder if someone shot the guy who I imagined wanted to steal my passport. That sounds plausible and ignorant all in the same sentence.

There was a flight attendant in the complimentary breakfast room heating up something in the microwave. I was seconds away from ordering a shared car ride to the airport when she approached me and said, "I requested the hotel to pay for a taxi. Would you like to join me?"

I accepted her invitation. I was impressed with her ability to get the hotel to pay for a free ride to the airport; I couldn't even get a room on the second floor.

I met up with my crew in the flight attendant lounge, and I'm thrilled to be working with them. Once again, at work and in uniform, I'm ready to fly. I got a text from Matt while I was in the lounge and he's in Charlotte and on his way to Asheville. I'm glad it worked out for him.

If it were me, I'd have said, "Screw this. I'm going home."

Flew to Salt Lake City and the flight was remarkably full. I think when the airline figures out how to charge passengers to sit in the lavatory and the galley floor, you'll see a new low in air travel. There were 143 paid passengers with thirty-three standby passengers. I think the standby list read: a husband, his wife, his other wife, a third wife, and their twenty-nine children.

The flight was jam-packed with LDS members. Having all these Mormons around reminded me of their efforts to block same-sex marriage in California. Would I be able to tell one of these passengers, "I don't mean to be rude, but I don't believe the angel Moroni visited Joseph Smith and told him where to find golden plates buried in the ground. And because of that, I can't serve you a ginger ale."

I wonder if the airline would support me? Or, better yet, would these religious zealots see the irony in my sarcasm? The bottom line is, religious beliefs belong in your private life, not at your job where you collect a paycheck. That ran through my mind while standing in the aisle with my beverage cart looking out over the sea of magic-underwear-wearing and same-sex-attraction-disorder-claiming passengers.

On the flight to Boise, our first passenger was a woman in a wheelchair seated in 1D. After she boarded, a family of ten walked onto the airplane. I'm serious this time, a husband, a wife, and their eight children. I felt terrible for the wife's carry-on; and by carry-on, I mean her uterus. I thought of the gate agent saying, *Excuse me, miss, you're only allowed a carry on and a personal item. That uterus dragging behind you will have to be checked.*

The family was scattered throughout the airplane. The only two seated next to each other were the husband and wife. I wish I were lying, but I am not. I assume the kids ranged in age from eighteen to three hours old. I rescind that comment; three hours old may be pushing it. My guess is, that newborn was delivered at the Qdoba in the airport food court with a side of guacamole.

I shook my head in disbelief as the wife handed me a handful of boarding passes and asked, "Is there any way we can all sit together?"

I answered, "We'll do our best, ma'am."

We got four of them seated together. The flight was full of other LDS Church members unwilling to trade seats because they were also flying with their own caravan of offspring. As an airline passenger, it's essential to select your seat when you purchase your ticket. That's not always an option when you buy your airline tickets through a third party service. The advice I give my friends is, purchase your ticket through the airline's website directly. You may pay a little extra, but you'll be happy when you aren't stuck in a middle seat on a transatlantic flight to Paris. And that's my advice for friends who haven't birthed the population of Monaco. If you are a Mormon, it's important enough that there should be an addendum to *The Book of Mormon*:

> *"And I said unto him: purchase tickets directly from the airline. I know it may be cheaper to purchase through a third party; nevertheless, your asses won't be seated together on your flight to Sal Tlay Ka Siti."*

A young man and his little sister were seated next to the older lady in 1D. He was twelve years old, and she was six years old. Maybe it was his cousin, or perhaps it's his wife. All I know is, they like 'em young.

Midway through the flight, an older woman in 1D needed help opening her bag of nuts. I had started trash service and was wearing rubber gloves, so I informed her I'd follow up in a few minutes to deal with her nuts. Before I go any further, I'm well aware that I should have removed the gloves, opened her nuts, and then put on new gloves and continued with trash. I know my job, thank you very much. However, she was old, and I didn't think to wait another five minutes would kill her. Nevertheless, when I returned a few minutes later, she was eating her nuts. No harm was done.

I bent down, "Oh, you got the package open?"

She smiled and pointed towards the boy next to her, "No. But this nice young man opened it for me."

I found his parents a few rows away, and the second I approached them and brought up their children, the mother asked, "What did he do?" She began standing up.

"They're fine. I have to tell you, your son is polite. I rarely see polite children on flights anymore. Good job."

They beamed bright enough to illuminate the entire airplane. I wouldn't be surprised if that mom ends up pregnant by the end of the flight.

After the plane touched down, the pilots slammed on the breaks. We heard bags banging around inside the overhead bins, and all the passengers lurched forward violently. The young man in 1E stretched one arm out in front of his sister and the other one in front of the older lady to protect them. I wanted to yell over to 1D, "You'll make a fine second wife to him and his sister."

It really made me proud of this kid, and he's not even mine. Sometimes I need to see things like that to have my confidence restored in humanity.

The flight to Seattle was average if you consider passengers carrying tents and sleeping bags onto an airplane average. I'm working with Kelly and Carrie. Kelly admitted she hated people as much as I do, which I find hard to believe. I quizzed her a lot, "Do you give money to charity? Do you let people cut you in line? Do you despise humans and wish dinosaurs would come back?" We spent the flight comparing notes trying to prove the other one hated people more. Also, I find Kelly attractive. She's a tomboy, which makes perfect sense. If I had to do her, I would, although she'd probably wear a strap-on and give me the ride of my life. Carrie is sweet, and we worked together a few months ago on a trip to Las Vegas. She's the one who likes boys and girls. When I stood in the galley and announced, "I hate people," she disagreed and said, "I don't think you do."

She's definitely mistaken.

After a quick shower, I met the ladies in the hotel lobby, and we ventured out for drinks and food. It was eight P.M., and the sun was still high in the sky. We hit up a restaurant for a few drinks, I had a glass of wine, and while I noshed on a flatbread, Kelly and Carrie tongued oysters on the half shell. I've never had oysters, and I never plan on ingesting those slimy creatures. Even though Kelly tried her hardest to get me to swallow one, I declined. I couldn't do it. I didn't want to do it. My throat closed up, thinking about letting one of them mucousy monsters slide down my esophagus.

By 10:30 P.M., we were assembled at an unnamed bar watching the bartender pour Jameson into three shot glasses. Kelly, who's also a bartender, convinced me to do a pickleback shot. A pickleback is where you shoot some whiskey and then chase it with pickle brine. I was skeptical as the bartender poured the pickle juice into three separate glasses. Then my mouth began watering awaiting the brine that would soon slosh around my tongue. I believe drinking too much pickle juice can cause dehydration, cramping, and diarrhea. Drinking pickle juice is like licking a salt lick, which doesn't sound great for you, either. We did two of these shots and after that, plus two beers, I was enthralled with Kelly's spaghetti strap top. I didn't ask her to remove her tank top, but at one point we took some pictures with our tongues touching, and I thought, *how do flight attendants get away with this shit?*

I told Kelly and Carrie I put in to transfer to JFK and I'll find out next week if I get the transfer. I put a transfer in a few months ago and quickly removed it. I'm a chicken shit. I had a solid plan about transferring, but the moment I put the bid in and hit enter, I regretted it and canceled the request. Not this time. Why can't I make a fucking decision? It would be easier if people told me what to do. I never think of myself as being a cult follower, but when I say I wish people told me what to do, I sure do sound like one. The girls hounded me about how much I'll hate being base in JFK.

I said, "Have you been based in JFK?"

They both said no. I can't take advice from someone who hasn't walked in my footsteps. Sometimes I listen, but most often I shrug off their warnings. I'm currently hating my life right now and questioning if I should quit this job, but then I have layovers like this where I have so much fun I can't fathom not being a sky waiter. Why wouldn't I give myself a chance at a different base? It wouldn't be so bad, and Evan lives in New York.

How bad could it really be?

Friday
SEA—FAI—PDX

Hungover this morning. I forgot to charge my phone last night, and it was dead when I woke up, which is precisely how I felt. I went out for breakfast at a small diner and ended up spilling water all over the floor. The owner told me, "Leave it."

I never planned on cleaning it up. I dragged myself back to the hotel and slept for the entire day; pickleback shots will end your life if you aren't careful.

After I woke up, I went to grab food, and a homeless couple asked me for money. I informed these two panhandlers I had no cash. I lied. I had two twenties, but I doubt they could make change. On my way back to the hotel, I passed by the same homeless couple. They asked me the same question, and I lied again. I felt terrible, but that didn't stop me from reminding them they had already asked me for money when I walked by the first time.

I went to Jimmy Johns, not the bank.

During boarding, the gate agent alerted Captain Brian and me that a family of three checked in, but one of them wasn't on the airplane. To make matters more confusing, the passenger who wasn't in their seat had checked a piece of luggage. How does that happen? Where was the person? I felt uneasy.

Captain Brian said, "It's the 4th of July holiday weekend, and we need to be on a higher alert about this type of stuff."

The gate agent stared at Captain Brian. I was ready to cancel the flight and go back to the hotel. We discussed removing the missing passenger's luggage, but it wasn't an international flight, so bags didn't have to match with passengers. Safety isn't as important as everyone thinks. I guess they don't believe airplanes can blow up over the state of Washington.

We closed the airplane door, without the missing passenger, and departed for Fairbanks. Turbulence rocked the airplane as we ascended to 10,000 feet. Carrie whispered, "Something seems wrong."

My heart started pounding. The airplane rocked from side to side, and I patiently waited to lose one of the wings. I kept calm and didn't let Carrie know I was expecting to die, "Maybe we're too sensitive."

"You're probably right," she said.

We leveled off, and that was the end of that.

A passenger in 15D stopped me while walking down the aisle and said, "Hey, the flight attendant on my last flight told me to tell you that I'm active military."

I looked at him and wondered what his point was. I answered, "Ok. Thanks."

What did he want me to do? Sing the national anthem while I completed beverage service. I observed him for a moment, and then my eyes shifted over to his portly wife sitting next to their two kids. She rolled her eyes at him, and then I realized they wanted free shit. Fine. I decided to play along and see what they ordered.

He ordered two snack boxes, and after retrieving them from the back galley, I whispered in his ear, "It's not our normal policy to give complimentary stuff to military personnel when they're not in uniform."

I have no problem offering free stuff for the military. Hey, I love America. But for a passenger to come on with his wife, two kids, and assume that they deserve complimentary food when he's in civilian clothes, that's tacky.

Sadly, it didn't end there.

When I came back down the aisle later in the flight, he ordered a few more snack boxes and dared to show me his military ID card. Unless that card had a credit limit, he could put it away. He and his wife were greedy, and I had no tolerance for them. I asked Carrie to deal with him for the remainder of the flight. That reminded me of last year while working a trip to Anchorage. I had a different military guy demanding a first class seat. Nobody should assume they're getting anything for free. Well, unless you're me flying standby, I expect everything for free.

There were twenty-seven kids on the flight. I was unaware there was a Disney World in Fairbanks. We had an unaccompanied minor on the plane. Her name was Miracle and the way she ate, it was a miracle she didn't throw up all over herself.

We had a quick turn in Fairbanks and had enough time to get off the airplane, stretch, and buy some coffee. Captain Brian, who is one of the hottest captains at our airline, bought coffee for Carrie and me.

I told Carrie, "You're gonna have to give one up for the team now that he bought us a coffee."

Captain Brian laughed and said, "Wait until you see what I make Joe do."

Schwing! I blushed and ran back to the airplane to change my underwear.

A family of eight started down the jet bridge, two parents and their six kids. Their toddlers were carrying their own car seats onto the airplane. Were they priming these rugrats to work in a sweatshop? I had to help this family; I grabbed car seats, backpacks, and children like I was a father shopping at Walmart, trying to help these parents get on the airplane faster. These people have never heard of birth control. I've seen this situation before; they must be on their way to Salt Lake City.

When we arrived at the hotel at five A.M., a butch lesbian was cemented in place behind the front desk. I say cemented because her legs were thick enough to need a wheelbarrow to move her. How butch was she? She made Captain Brian look like a drag queen.

The lesbian highlighted our names with a pink marker on the sign-in sheet, and I yelled, "You guys, we're all up in the pink."

Carrie laughed out loud. I've never been anywhere near the pink, so I didn't even chuckle.

Saturday
PDX—LAX

I slept for three hours and then went for a walk. I was drained; it felt like all the air had been replaced with water. I decided to spend the day perusing Powell Books, shopping at Target, and enjoying some Indian food from a food truck in the park. I placed my uneaten food in the trash can and a homeless woman claimed it before I was three feet away. It made me emotional, I wish she would have asked for the food. The homeless in Portland and Seattle are different than in San Francisco. In San Francisco, they'll shit on you and walk away. In Portland and Seattle, they want your money and food. I'll take that any day. After my Indian food downtown, I walked back to the hotel and vegetated until it was time to catch the shuttle van to the airport. We had fifty-six passengers on the flight to LAX. It's Independence Day, but with a flight load that low it felt like Christmas.

After taking off, I resumed complaining about passengers, and Kelly set me straight, "We have like ten people on the airplane, and you're still bitching."

We landed twenty-five minutes early and deplaning went smoothly until a partially blind passenger decided to use the lavatory. I worried I'd miss my commute flight home while she searched for the toilet seat. My instinct was to assist her, but after practically sweating to death a few years ago during "Operation: Tomato Ass," I decided to stay far away from the lavatory.

She finished in the lavatory quickly, which tells me that she couldn't find the roll of toilet paper. I sprinted off to catch my flight home. I wish Matt were home, but he's still in North Carolina.

PAIRING 018: IT'S LIKE FLYING WITH ROMAN POLANSKI

Tuesday
Home

Matt asked me, "Now that you are becoming a public figure, do you want to be known as the flight attendant's flight attendant?"

I made him elaborate.

"You know, stand up for flight attendants or build relations between passengers and flight attendants."

"I want to make people laugh and tell stories. I'll let Heather [Poole] be the flight attendant's flight attendant."

I spent a few minutes pondering his question. I never started writing to be anything more than a funny storyteller. My desire to write and express myself stems from performing in community theater.

Who am I kidding? Joe, stop lying to yourself. You know perfectly well that the day you were dragged out of your mother, you were born to entertain. It's true. I bet a few seconds after my eyes adjusted to the light in the delivery room, I grabbed the forceps out of the nurse's hand, used them as a microphone, and told my first joke, "Testing. Testing. Is this thing working? Did you hear about the doctor who came too late to the delivery? (Pause for dramatic effect) The lady was already pregnant."

Listen, I didn't say my first joke was great; I was five minutes old.

When I acted in community theater, I commanded everyone's attention. I was a star. Sure, I wasn't Lin-Manuel Miranda taking bows after performing in *Hamilton*, but I was the star of the Emma Parrish Theatre in Titusville, Florida.

Google it, I promise, it's a real theater.

When I become a flight attendant, I had to give up the theater. It was a difficult choice to make, but I made a promise to myself that my new career wouldn't extinguish my creative light. I have a lot to share and, dammit, whether people want to hear me or not, I'm going to share it. That's why I focused on documenting my life with a blog. Writing has filled the void left by the theater and satisfied my desire for attention. This declaration may not be shocking to most people, but I'm an attention whore. I LOVE attention, especially when I'm entertaining people with a story. It's more than attention; I need acceptance. My insecurities push me to crave feedback from people in the form of laughter. When I make somebody laugh, it's instant gratification that people accept me; or think I'm a lunatic. To be honest, even if they laugh at me and believe I'm a lunatic, I'm content with that too. All humans need acceptance; I think insecure people go to greater lengths to obtain it. Trust me, I've been known to make a total ass out of myself to receive approval from complete strangers.

I've found sharing my stories through writing to be the easiest way to accomplish my hunger for recognition. Writing is my drug of choice, but hand me a microphone, and I'll not shy away from embarrassing myself for a few laughs. Hardly anything is off-limits when I'm at my computer writing a juicy personal tale. To share that tale—on paper or in person—is akin to the best orgasm you can imagine.

I'm not exaggerating. Here's an example: when meeting friends out for dinner, I start preparing what jokes I'm going to tell while I'm IN THE SHOWER. As the introverts and modest citizens of the world stand on the sidelines, absorbing everything, I'm standing in the center of the room dishing it all out. On more than one occasion at a random bar, my friend Mike has asked, "Are you done, Joe?"

Writing and storytelling have become the best outlet for my super-sized ego.

Here's some big news, I'm transferring to JFK. It's happening. I'm excited but extremely nervous, kind of like my high school prom night when Wanda tried slipping her hand down the front of my pants even after I complained about a migraine. It's time to abandon the LAX base and say *adios* to these shitty schedules. It is an injustice that my LAX seniority doesn't allow me to take a Friday off. I think there are flight attendants in JFK, who have been with the airline for twenty minutes, holding better schedules than me.

At least in JFK, I'll have a schedule with weekends and holidays off. I'll hold decent trips and not stress about requesting the time off for the simpler things in life, like masturbating.

I have to get to LAX earlier than usual tomorrow morning to meet with my supervisor. If you ask me, it will be a waste of time.

She will ask, "What are your goals here at the airline?"
I will respond, "I have none."

That's an honest-to-Madonna answer. I have not one single goal at this airline.

I stand corrected, I do have a few goals. At this point, I want to fly as little as possible, avoid complaint letters from passengers, and write books. Probably not the best thing to say at a one-on-one with my supervisor, so I'll merely deny having goals. I've gone above and beyond at this airline, and I have nothing else to give. I've been on the Standards Advisory Team. I've been a flight attendant supervisor. I've given all I can to management, and now all they will get out of me is handing out Diet Cokes and bags of nuts while I collect stories for future books.

I started reading *Mindfulness For Beginners* by Jon Kabat-Zinn. It's way over my head, but I'm pushing through it. If it's this intense for beginners, I can't even imagine how mind-blowing it is for people who've studied this for years. I can barely be mindful enough to read it.

Wednesday
SJC—LAX—HOU

On my commute flight, I sat in the exit row next to a small lesbian lady. Even with my questionable gaydar, I knew she was a lesbian. Honestly, it had nothing to do with my gaydar, and all to do with her buzz cut and the possibility that she had a U-Haul frequent customer card. Without my knowledge, Ms. Birkenstock checked out my *Flight Attendant Joe* bag tag and looked up my blog.

When we landed in Los Angeles, she informed me that she read a few posts. She smirked and said, "You're very funny."

I love lesbians.

By the time I got to the crew lounge, my new favorite lesbian had liked the *Flight Attendant Joe* Facebook page.

I'm getting famous one lesbian at a time.

My supervisor pulled me into her office and tried having a conversation with me. I stared at her like she had frosting on her chin. Whenever she asked a question, I stated, "I plead the fifth."

That's not true; I simply acted dead inside and responded with one-word responses. My goals were never addressed; my supervisor finally gave up, and she went to lunch. She probably cried in her car while eating Taco Bell because nobody respects her. I hate being an asshole, but I think a rock would be better at supervising people.

Thursday
HOU—DEN

I had a long day, and I'm not in the mood to deal with people. I barely have the mindset to write my feelings out in this journal. I'm that fucking annoyed. I'm currently working with a flight attendant who seems nice but is extremely frustrating. Let's call him Bruce. Honestly, I believe Bruce has a social interaction disorder and shouldn't work with the general public. I don't know where he should work, and I don't care, as long as it's far away from me. I wanted to trip him on the jet bridge as he sauntered up to the gate area. Wishing pain on a co-worker is not how I conduct business, I'm not based in Miami. Seriously, that's not how I'd typically handle someone who has a disorder, but he pushed me to my limit. If the idea of tripping him makes me feel better, then so be it.

He says the most inappropriate shit at the worst time, and that's saying something coming from me; I've been daydreaming about knocking him to the ground for the past six hours.

I don't even know where to begin with all his shenanigans. It started during boarding, I was helping a passenger put her carry on in the overhead bin at row five, and he stood in the front galley yelling out to anyone who'd listen, "Joe's famous. Hey everyone, that guy is famous. Look him up. He has a blog, it's called *Flight Attendant Joe.*"

It stressed me out. I shook my head and rolled my eyes while helping passengers with their bags. I'm far from famous, but I do try my hardest to keep my airline private. All I need is a passenger to search for my name online during boarding and tweet: *I'm on [Airline] flight 567 & I've got some dude by the name of Flight Attendant Joe as my flight attendant. Who is this guy?*

Each time Bruce announced anything over the PA, he lied. I figured he was a Republican, "I've been at this airline for twenty years."

I leaned over, "No, you haven't. And nobody gives a fuck how long you've been here."

"Yes, they do, Flight Attendant Joe."

He pushed me to my limits today, "Please stop calling me Flight Attendant Joe in front of the passengers."

"Okay…Flight Attendant Joe."

We had a thirteen-year-old unaccompanied minor on the airplane and Bruce continued saying that she looked "old enough" and that her parents should lock her up and not let her out until she turns eighteen years old.

I was working with Woody Allen. Something tells me that Bruce considers Roman Polanski a role model.

He was relentless on the jumpseat as we landed in Denver, "If I were gay, I'd do you."

I didn't have the heart to tell him that chocolate breaks me out, but I played along anyway, "You would?"

"Oh yeah, Joe. Totally."

"Bruce, I think you'd do your tote bag if you had the chance."

He laughed, "Damn you, Flight Attendant Joe. You're funny."

As we walked through the airport to find the hotel shuttle van, we stepped past the TSA exit, and Bruce pointed at me and announced to anyone listening, "You should probably check that flight attendant's bags."

I was appalled. No, that's not the word—I was livid. Who the hell says that to a TSA agent? Truthfully, TSA could rummage through my luggage all day long, and I'd have nothing to worry about, I'm not a drug mule. I don't even travel with a dildo. Why bother? I barely have enough time to sleep during a layover, the idea of cleaning a dildo during an eleven-hour layover sounds impractical.

I reprimanded him for drawing attention to me as we left the airport. He shrugged his shoulders and smiled. Again, he's got a disorder, but that's not my problem. I decided to play his game. I said, "You better rest up tonight because I'm coming for you tomorrow."

Then I thought, why wait until tomorrow? As the van driver loaded our luggage into the back of the van, Bruce asked, "Can I sit up front?"

I turned my head towards him, "Sit up front? Have you lost your mind? I thought you were supposed to sit in the back of the van."

Uncomfortable laughter is the best sound after a long day.

Friday
DEN—LAX—SJC

Bruce gave me a ride to Long Beach Airport to catch an earlier flight home. After sitting on the jump seat next to him for three days—I could barely stand being around him— but a ride is a fucking ride. I think if you keep Bruce away from thirteen-year-olds and off the interphone, he's endurable. Anyway, I jotted down his employee number to put him on my avoid list. He may have offered me a ride, but that doesn't mean I can handle him on the airplane ever again. I tend to manage disruptive people rather well, but Bruce was a menace to my mental health.

PAIRING 019: I'm Not My Mother

Friday
JFK—OAK

This is my first day back in JFK. It reminds me of the first day of a new school year, but not high school—where students are treated like adults—but preschool, where we're put in time out if we forget to put our toys back in the correct place.

I psyched myself up last night and had a pep talk in the shower before heading to the airport, "Okay, Joe. You wanted a better schedule, and you received one. You deserve this seniority. Don't be a little bitch and complain the moment you get to the airport. Be a man and don't cry. Okay, don't cry in front of a passenger or co-worker. You can do this."

I estimate that pep talk will last until a passenger complains about having to pay for an upgraded seat.

The gate agent issued me the last open seat on the airplane, which was an aisle seat with no leg room and the mid-cabin flight attendant jumpseat positioned awkwardly in front of me. Commuting across the country is not as painful as I remember, especially when the lead flight attendant sneaks you food from first class.

I walked into the JFK supervisor's office sporting a huge grin, introduced myself to the woman sitting at a desk next to the glass door, and with disdain she asked, "What do you need?"

Welcome to John F. Kennedy International Airport, Joe Thomas.

To say the least, the administrative secretary was off-putting. I instantly remembered why I hated JFK back in 2008. It's simple, the supervisors at JFK were bad flight attendants who didn't want to sit on reserve, and somehow, they become leaders in management. I don't know how that works, but it's a running theme in the airline industry: bad flight attendants turn into horrible supervisors.

My first flight out of JFK went smoothly. Mary, one of the flight attendants on my trip, is friends with Evan. That doesn't surprise me, Evan is the mayor of JFK. He is acquainted with everyone at our airline. You think that by saying everyone, I'm speaking in hyperbole, but I promise you that I am not. He probably knows future co-workers who are still in training bound for JFK after graduation. It's uncanny how in-the-know Evan keeps himself. When I meet another human being, I instantly forget them if I don't take notes about their behavior in my journal. Evan can remember a flight attendant he bumped into for two seconds on a layover in Honolulu.

I have Alzheimer's. Evan does not.

What can I say about Mary? She's charismatic. That's the perfect way to describe Mary. My first impression of her was that in a past life she was a gay man.

Nevermind, I think she's a gay man in this life, too.

Every other word out of Mary's mouth is, "Yaaaaaaaaaaasssssssss." And that's being kind, I could have added a few more a's and s's to make it more realistic.

Our first conversation went like this, "Do you know, Evan?"

Mary, "Yaaaaaaaaaaasssssssss."

"He says hi."

Mary, "Oh my God. Yaaaaaaaaaasssssssss. Evan is fabulous."

I added, "He is. He said the same thing about you."

"Yaaaaaaaaaaaaaaaaaaaaaaaaaassssssssssssssssss."

If she were a fembot in *Austin Powers: The Spy Who Shagged Me*, that would have been the moment her head exploded. I popped four Advil and smiled. She's cute though and fits my personality well. During our briefing, Mary started talking to me in gay lingo (a language that I haven't spoken since turning forty years old), and I asked her to speak to me in mainstream American English, not Fire Island English.

On our way to Oakland, I opened a mayonnaise packet to add to my expensive airport sandwich. I squeezed the packet hard and the mayonnaise squirt out onto my apron. I laughed and zinged, "Wow. This looks like my chest before bedtime."

The other flight attendant, Diane, stared at me. I thought, *Great! My first trip back in New York, and I'm destined for a human resource intervention.*

On a happy note, a passenger traveling with an emotional support animal bought the lady next to him a drink because she didn't complain about his oversized dog. It pays to be friendly to strangers. I wish more passengers were friendlier to their flight attendants, but wishful thinking like that only ends in disappointment.

Saturday
Oakland

Matt drove over to Oakland to hang out with me during my long layover. We went to the CatTown Cafe and hung out with strange cats for an hour. I hope Tucker and Harvey don't find out; it's like I'm cheating on them when I love on other cats. They probably know, I think that's why Harvey doesn't cover his shit in the litter box. We had a lovely day, but Matt's driving stresses me out. It's a touchy subject. It's like he's waiting for me to say something about his driving so he can respond with a snippy comment.

I'm afraid to cough because he'll say, "Does my driving make you cough?"

No. It makes me pray to a God I don't believe in.

Sunday
OAK—LAX—LAS

It's Mother's Day. I'm not a fan of Mother's Day. Honestly, I'm not a fan of any holidays that aren't my birthday. I'm an only child and I celebrate my birthday as a national holiday.

All joking aside, Mother's Day is a painful reminder that my mother, Irene, and I had a turbulent relationship. I'm talking damage-to-the-aircraft-type turbulence; where even when you have your seat belt fastened, you're in danger of being tossed around. I enjoy scrolling through social media witnessing all the love that people have for their mothers, but after a few minutes, it becomes overwhelming. I'm envious of anyone who had a stable and healthy relationship with their mother. I want to remember Irene in a positive light, but it's complicated. The scars from my childhood run deep. I've forgiven Irene for all the bad life choices she made that affected me, but I simply can't forget them.

A few weeks ago, I was chatting with Adam about the aftermath of being raised by my mother, Irene. He said, "You should focus on what your mother did teach you. She taught you how not to be. She showed you how not to live your life, and you are doing an awesome job at it."

And because of that conversation, I posted a picture of my mother and me on social media today. After looking at it for a few minutes, it made me sad. It's a great picture, but when I view it, I imagine a child who was verbally, mentally, physically, and emotionally abused. A child with no say in the chaotic world he was thrust into. A child who, against all the odds, turned into an adult who has never abused the people he claims to love. When I see Irene I see a woman so weak and broken that she never had the courage, strength, or self-esteem to stop her abusive husband from hurting her only son.

That's my history and the reason I focus all my energy on comedy; I mask my pain with comedy.

Masking My Pain With Comedy should be the title of my forthcoming memoir.

After we departed for Las Vegas, I reminded Diane and Mary to call their mothers. I may dislike Mother's Day, but I still think children should do their duty and call their mothers.

Diane asked me, "Did you already call your mom?"

I responded, "My mom is dead; I can't call her. That would be impossible." Even if we could call Heaven, I imagine being put on hold and then having to talk to Jesus when he answered, *Hi Jesus, It's me again. Is my moth— Oh, at the Divinity Dive Bar again? Just let her know I called.*

Diane stood up from sitting on the jumpseat, "I'm sorry."

"Don't be." I reassured her, "You didn't kill her. Budweiser and Winston 100s did."

Mary put her hand up to her mouth and chuckled. I continued, "I use comedy to hide my immense pain. Don't worry, you won't find me hanging in the lavatory."

Diane and Mary both gasped.

So far, the three of us had been lucky on this trip, but on our flight from Los Angeles to Las Vegas, we flew with two dick pilots. I've had years of experience with pilots, so I'm unfazed by their dickery. The captain looked like he shit his pants a week ago and hadn't been home to change.

As we started boarding, I asked the first officer if he cared for a beverage. He answered, "Yes. I need hot tea with two Splendas and a cup of ice."

I glared at him. Yes, I know I asked him what he wanted to drink, but I didn't expect him to order like he was seated in first class. I expected him to ask for what most pilots request—water. Pilots take home enough money to make a televangelist blush. Their wallets overflow with dollar bills that any coffee shop would love to collect, but they save those George Washingtons for the strip clubs in Jacksonville.

As I grabbed a hot cup, I looked over at him and asked, "Would you like me to slap you, too?" He didn't flinch, which led me to believe he's into that sort of thing.

After checking into the hotel, I invited Diane and Mary to join me on my day of debauchery. They declined, which meant I'd be hitting Las Vegas on my own. I paused for a moment while changing out of my uniform and thought, *Is it smart to drink by myself?* I knew the answer. I put my hat on backward, grabbed my hotel key, and let the door slam behind me thinking, *What's the worst that could happen?*

I rode the monorail a few stops to MGM Grand to walk the Las Vegas Strip. I never tire of this urban playground. In a perfect world, I'd have one Sin City layover a month to quench my appetite for vice. And that appetite consists of day drinking, tossing my money into slot machines, and people watching. Nothing says Las Vegas like watching a group of rednecks throw back a few Colt 45s while hollering racial and homophobic slurs out to a chaotic crowd and then ending up in handcuffs outside of Planet Hollywood.

As I meandered down the street, dodging white guys in wife beaters and Latinos flashing sex worker cards in my face, I downed a few beers because no one was around to suggest I drink water and stay hydrated.

Where's a friend when you need one?

With the sense of an underaged drinker holding a fake ID, I found myself standing at the booth to purchase tickets for the High Roller. The High Roller is proof that there is no God. If God existed, He wouldn't make alcohol this accessible to weak human beings. And that's what happens when you step into the open bar car and take a ride on this impressive Ferris wheel, you become a weak human being.

I stand corrected, I become my mother.

Let me break down what it's like experiencing liver destruction in real-time. When you pay for the open bar car on the High Roller, you get thirty minutes of unlimited drinks, which is the time it takes the entire wheel to rotate once. There are two separate lines for the Ferris wheel, the non-drinking observation car line, and then the open bar car line, which is basically the alcoholic line. I stood in the alcoholic line. Not to be judgy, but nobody is sober in the alcoholic line, even at 11:30 A.M.

Now that I think about it, nobody is sober in Las Vegas at 11:30 A.M.

I felt like I had drunk enough alcohol to keep up with spring breakers at the Jersey Shore. At this point, if I bumped into any co-workers, I'd have told them I was auditioning for the television show *Drunk History*. In my mind, it was the truth; I was making history, and I was drunk.

Once I stepped into the open bar car, time moved quickly. I imagine it's like being on Neptune if Neptune had a Ferris wheel filled with liquor and I had a spaceship to get there. Thirty minutes cleaning the apartment goes by much slower than thirty minutes of an all-you-can-drink Ferris wheel ride. The open bar car holds about fifteen ~~drunk~~ patrons. I squeezed myself inside, the door closed, we lifted into the sky, and all mayhem began.

The bar is situated in the middle of the car and managed by a single bartender. I gulped down two Jack and gingers, and then I had no idea what else to order. We hit the fifteen-minute mark, and I scrambled to ingest more alcohol.

You may be shocked, but that makes perfect sense to me; I'm my mother's son.

I asked the bartender, "Can you make me something sweet?" She acknowledged me and proceeded to dance around the bar at top speed. I scanned the horizon and watched an airplane depart from McCarran International Airport. When I looked back at the bartender, she had three plastic cups on the counter and was pouring different color concoctions into each one. With both hands, she picked up all three drinks and placed them in front of me.

I asked, "Which one is mine?"

She began making another drink and answered, "All three, honey. I didn't know what to make you, so I made you those."

We looked at each other and she laughed, "This is Vegas baby."

Hello Jesus, it's Joe again. Cancel that message to my mother, just let her know that I'm probably going to be up there before the day is over.

I sighed, took all three drinks, and tried to remember how much money Matt gets from my life insurance policy if my body spontaneously combusts.

I made my way to Harrah's and bought another drink. As I said, one of those times when traveling with a friend would have been convenient. You know, someone to pull your hand away from the drink, hand you a bottle of water, and call you a taxi back to the hotel. Instead, I was alone and found myself sauntering up to a group of black guys partying at the entrance to the casino. I'm not gonna beat around the bush, I tried becoming their best friend. My memory is fuzzy, but I believe I brought up the group Bell Biv DeVoe and then asked, "What happened between Whitney and Bobby?"

To make it worse, I yelled out, "Bobby!" a few times, too. You know, ignorant drunk white people shit. They tolerated me for a few seconds and then one of them brushed me off. I think his exact words were, "I think it's time for you to go."

I started bawling. I don't think my new friends saw me crying, but I heard them howling with laughter as I stumbled away, so my guess is they saw the tears. My ass barely made it through the casino before I bumped into a housekeeper and started wailing like I had lost my house at the roulette wheel.

I cried, "I'm sorry for how awful white people are. I'm not like that, but they still didn't want to be my friend."

If this were a Netflix movie, she'd have called for security to detain me. Instead, this lovely human being took me by the hand, and we began to pray. I couldn't tell you what we prayed about, all I can say is we stood among the gamblers and high-end prostitutes while tears flowed down my face.

What am I saying? It was Harrah's. There are no high-end prostitutes, simply tramp stamp hoes.

She took her lemon-scented wet hand and wiped away my tears. For a split second, she was the mother that I wanted; the mother that I needed. A kind-hearted woman who probably assisted intoxicated white guys all day long, but at that moment, she paused from her daily grind to make me feel important and loved.

Now that I think about it, it might have been a urine-soaked hand, but I didn't care at that point. I leaned against her housekeeping cart to stabilize myself, placed my hand in hers, and with bowed heads, we prayed to Jehovah.

I thought, *if she's not one of Jehovah's chosen ones, this prayer ain't gonna do shit.*

Whatever we prayed about together is lost in a hazy shade of intoxication, but if I had to guess, I'd bet money that we prayed I didn't vomit on her freshly mopped floor. While my angel went back to replacing urine cakes in the men's restroom, I walked outside the hotel and fell flat on my ass.

I made it all the way to a bench outside Westgate Las Vegas. I managed to dial Dee's number; when she answered, I started crying. Dee may have thought it was a crank call, but after realizing who she was talking to, she encouraged me to calm down and go to bed.

I cried, "I need my bed."

Did I need an intervention?

I didn't need an intervention: I needed water, ibuprofen, and sleep.

When I drink, I think of my mother, Irene. She was an alcoholic. I believe the correct term is a functioning alcoholic. The alcoholism trait was planted in her genes the moment she was conceived, she had no input in the decision, like having blue eyes or being a fabulous homosexual. Her father was an alcoholic. Her uncles were alcoholics. Her brother was an alcoholic. Because children of alcoholics tend to gravitate towards chaos and drama, she had two failed marriages to alcoholics. Irene was the poster child for Alcoholic Anonymous but never spent one hour in a meeting. While most people drink a few cups of coffee in the morning, Irene drank beer. Don't get me wrong, she had coffee too, but she chased it down with a six-pack. I can distinctly recall being in high school and hearing the sound of a beer cracking open at six A.M.

The fear that I carry my mother's DNA sleeps in the back of my brain like a restless child. My challenge in life has been to not become my mother, and the word challenge is an understatement. It's been a full-time career protecting myself from the bad behaviors she instilled in me. But I've learned over the years that I am not my parents, and I don't have to be. There's nothing written in stone that says we must turn out like our parents. Just because they fucked up on an hourly basis, doesn't mean we will. It's about breaking the cycle of bad behavior, something I've been telling myself for decades. It's pushed me to be a healthier person mentally, but even though I understand that, it's hard not waking up from a night of drinking and think, *Great, Joe. One more night like this and you might as well change your name to Irene.*

The fear of becoming an alcoholic has weighed me down for years. I go weeks without drinking alcohol and don't even think about having a drink, but back there deep inside my emotions, where that restless child sleeps, the fear haunts me. Will that little child always be there? Will he forever remind me that I'm not my mother?

I hope so. Listen, I have many issues to deal with as an adult, thinking I'm on the road to becoming the next Norman Bates is not one of them.

When I was old enough to live on my own, I refused to keep alcohol in the house. It sounds shocking, but it's the truth. There's no need to fabricate at this point. I didn't keep alcohol in my house until I began dating. It only takes a few eye rolls from a potential boyfriend to change your behavior after you cheerfully state at dinner, "I don't keep alcohol in the house. That's a sign of being an alcoholic."

That's what I believed. And why wouldn't I believe that? I grew up in a house that had more alcohol in the refrigerator than food. My father stashed bottles of vodka around the house like Easter eggs. I've learned to stop fearing the idea that I'm addicted to alcohol, but it hasn't been an easy thing to convince myself. My saving grace is the fact that I am in my forties now, and committing myself to a life of alcoholism sounds like a lot of heartburn in the middle of the night. I'm not perfect, and I don't claim to be. I struggle with all the emotional baggage that my mother left on the front door of my first apartment. Some of it I tossed out, some I sold in a yard sale, and some of that baggage, I continue to work on to this day.

After that confession, I'm drained and exhausted. Also, this sounds completely alcoholic-like and embarrassing, but I don't remember how I found my way back to the hotel, or better yet, how I located my room last night. If I had my own reality television show, that would solve the mystery.

On second thought, some things are best left unknown.

Monday
LAS—JFK

Las Vegas beat me up. Sucker punched me in the gut, took my wallet, and kicked me when I was lying face down outside the hotel. I deserve it, I instigated a fight that I was destined to lose. When you go head to head with Vegas, you will lose. Vegas has been knocking cocky tourists off their pedestals for decades, and yesterday I learned a valuable lesson, I can not consuming alcohol like a twenty-two-year-old.

Hell, I can't drink like I'm forty years old anymore.

I woke up at five A.M. and my alarm was set for 8:30 A.M. I tried sleeping a few more hours, but I needed water; I needed it bad. I'd have consumed Lake Mead if I had a car to get me there. After dragging myself around the room shaking every last droplet from the few plastic water bottles strewn about, I stuffed my head under the sink, turned on the faucet, and let the water flow down my throat. My mouth felt like the Grand Canyon in July.

After taking a cold shower, a hot shower, and another cold shower, I put my uniform on and headed down to the lobby to catch the van to the airport. Chatting in the van to the airport, we discussed that Mary had slept the entire layover, Diane had banked about $500 from gambling, and I had lost my dignity somewhere between Harrah's and my hotel room.

Three older New Yorkers sat in 1A, 1B, and 1C on the flight back to JFK. They conversed with me for the entire flight. They were friendly, but I was hungover and smiling hurt my entire body.

My favorite passenger was an eighteen-year-old cat named, Movie Star.

When we landed in JFK, I felt better and decided to walk to another terminal to take a different airline home. Halfway to the terminal, I changed my mind and decided to commute home on my own airline. As I walked back to my airline's terminal, I changed my mind another two times. All this back and forth made my brain hurt. In the end, I commuted home on my own airline which was for the best because I was rewarded with an entire row all to myself for the six-hour flight.

The flight attendant who I had worked with years ago pulled up the beverage cart, "Would like something to drink?"

"May I have seltzer water?"

"Sure. Would you like a wine or something else?"

I reached for the barf bag and put it on my lap, "Please, don't trigger me."

PAIRING 020: PHOENIX IS HOT AF!

Tuesday
SFO—JFK—MCO

I prayed that Tropical Storm Colin might cancel my commute today, but no such luck.

The gate agent assigned me a seat by the mid-cabin door. She cheerfully stated, "It's a window seat without a window."

I responded, "So, it's not a window seat?"

She shrugged her shoulders and handed me my ticket.

The second passenger on the airplane complained the moment he stepped into the aisle. He didn't like his seat assignment and figured anyone within earshot cared about his fucking problem. If anyone had a problem, it was me. I was the guy assigned the window seat without a window, that only makes sense if you are blind.

Do I really have grounds to complain if my biggest problem is that my free airline seat is missing a window? Are there more important things I could lament over?

You be the judge of that.

Not only was his seat an issue, but he also began complaining that there wasn't enough overhead bin space for his bag. That seemed curious; he was the second passenger to board the airplane, and he only had a small duffel bag. The overhead bins had ample space. Maybe not enough space for Mariah Carey's luggage, but enough for a businessman heading to JFK.

Then a guy and his wife stopped at the row behind me. I'll call them Mr. and Mrs. Asshat. Thom, the flight attendant, stood at his jumpseat—in the same row that I was seated—greeting people as they found their rows.

Mr. Asshat loudly slammed his bag in the overhead bin and said, "I need water. My wife has to take a pill."

I'll never understand passengers who walk on the airplane and begin barking out orders. I understand that airline passengers have expectations that come with the price of their airline ticket but to start yelling out demands like a real housewife on vacation in the Bahamas; that's absurd.

Let me clarify: handing out water to a passenger who needs to take medication is not the issue; the issue I have is the tone passengers use when interacting with customer service personnel. That's my problem. That's what makes me want to shove a bottle of water up their ass and watch them wiggle around trying to drink it. What happened to people being polite? Why do passengers lose their manners when they walk on the airplane?

I think they never had them in the first place.

I sound ridiculous calling out passengers' behavior as I confess my desire to slam a water bottle up someone's ass, but if they showed us some respect, I wouldn't entertain violent fantasies. I'm creating excuses for my extreme opinions, but ask politely, and I'd withhold water bottle anal until later in the flight—like when a passenger orders a cup of decaffeinated coffee twenty minutes before landing.

Not only did Mr. Asshat want a bottle of water, but he also wanted the entire row. You read that right, he paid for two seats but demanded the whole row on a full flight. With his type of entitlement, they'd need to operate this flight on an Airbus 380.

Mr. Asshat began harassing Thom and demanding his own row, Mr. Asshat yelled, "My wife has an ailment. Are you going to care for us or not?"

I thought, *I don't believe the cost of an airplane ticket entitles a passenger to free medical care.*

The only ailment I noticed was the malignant tumor of a husband seated next to her. Honestly, I have no clue what Mrs. Asshat's illness was because I didn't turn around to investigate. Unless she suffered from all her bones broken, I didn't think she needed an entire row. If all her bones were broken, I'd have suggested throwing her in a box and shipping her via FedEx to New York.

Mr. Asshat informed Thom, "She needs to be able to prop her leg up."

Thom responded, "We'll see what we can do for you, sir, but every seat is occupied on today's flight."

"Is someone sitting in the row with us?" He questioned.

"Yes."

When did propping up passenger's legs become the airline's responsibility? If a person requires that much care on a flight, they should hire a private jet that comes with a nurse.

I did notice that when Mrs. Asshat walked down the aisle, she had no limp. She never uttered a single word during the entire flight, which now makes me think she was a victim of sex trafficking.

Every few minutes, Mr. Asshat jumped up from his seat, moved into the aisle, and asked, "Is someone sitting in the window seat?"

Thom smiled, "The flight is completely full. All the seats are occupied."

Mr. Asshat asked often enough that Thom simply ignored him. At one point, Thom walked away and began closing overhead bins, and I continued hearing Mr. Asshat ask, "Is anyone sitting here?"

I wanted to recommend that he place Mrs. Asshat in the overhead bin, but the last thing my airline needs is to be on CNN for stuffing an Asian woman in the overhead bin.

The woman sitting next to me grinned at me a few times. I smiled back until she opened a container of foul-smelling yogurt and hogged the armrest. I leaned against the wall, trying to ignore her, not so much her, but her stinky yogurt. After the flight departed, she reached into her backpack and pulled out a container of stuffed grape leaves, or dolmades. Usually, I love dolmades, but not at eight A.M. As she slurped out the rice from the leaf, I contemplated throwing her out of the airplane without a parachute over Colorado. How can anyone eat something like that for breakfast? I can barely eat a slice of bread before nine A.M., and she's eating oily rice packets.

Adele blasting in my ears didn't help; it made me want to turn to my seatmate and sing, *"Hello, it's me. I was wondering if you could put those nasty fucking grape leaves away."*

A five-hour flight, all this drama, and I hadn't begun my workday. Once the dolmades went away (no worries, they made a comeback) I informed my neighbor there was a charging outlet under her seat.

She thanked me and asked, "Do you work here?"

"Yes. I do."

"I thought so. I've never seen another passenger so confident in their seat."

While I helped clean the airplane, I heard a black guy randomly state to someone on the other end of his phone call, "Can I get a break from this white supremacy?"

Wednesday
MCO—CLE—PHX

Slept soundly, but I feel jetlagged. The entire Orlando flight last night was easier to manage than my commute sitting in front of the Asshats.

I'm working with Gloria and Jane. Gloria reminds me of Laura Branigan, and after telling her that, I sang "Gloria" to her the entire flight. She might not like it, but I don't care.

A woman boarded the flight to Cleveland with her three kids, and they were seated in different rows. All four of them were assigned middle seats a few rows apart from each other. She stepped into the galley and pushed all the boarding passes towards me, "The gate agent told me you could seat us all together."

Do I look like I'm part of a coven? Can I make magic happen on a full flight? The only thing my wand does is take up space in my underwear. I hated showing no empathy, but I disliked how she approached me, "It's a full flight. We'll see what we can do. Please take your assigned seats."

When she stopped in the middle of the airplane, she spoke to Gloria. I'll never know what Gloria told her, but a few seconds later the mother erupted into uncontrollable hysterics in the aisle. Her cries were audible from thirteen rows away. I looked down the aisle, and Gloria rolled her eyes and threw her hands up in the air. Boarding had ceased, and while I watched their conversation go back and forth, I kept apologizing to the people held up in the galley and on the jet bridge.

A few minutes went by, and there was no resolution. The ladies' kids stood in the aisle with their little suitcases staring around, lost in the chaos.

I heard, "That's not gonna work for me," through her tears and gasps.

A gate agent finally walked on the airplane, and I asked him to handle the situation. Instead of marching down the aisle and taking control, he leaned against the galley counter, waiting for it all to work itself out.

I said, "You can't get anything accomplished standing in the galley. You gotta get all up in there and handle this mess."

He exhaled with frustration, upset he had to do his job. As he walked down the aisle towards Gloria and the disruptive passenger, I followed. I didn't want to be involved, but I'm nosey. By this time, the passenger had on her sunglasses and continued crying as if instead of her kids sitting in middle seats, they were dead. I know she was in distress, and I don't want to sound uncaring, but she was being a dramatic asshole. She was seated so close to her children that she could have comfortably leaned forward from her seat and tapped them on the shoulder to make sure nobody was molesting them.

Honestly, she could have only touched one of them. The other two were further away, but being next to one out of three is better than none.

The gate agent surveyed the area asking other passengers to switch seats, but you should never expect people to move. Airline passengers are not required to compromise their experience to accommodate you. Be a better airline passenger by not imposing your lack of planning on your fellow passengers. A responsible traveler chooses their seats as soon as possible, not when they've arrived at the airport with three screaming kids in tow.

I'm gruff, but it was a long day.

Thankfully, her fellow passengers swapped seats to allow her to sit closer to her kids. It's important to note that when the situation favored her, the waterworks stopped like a Florida rainstorm. I immediately felt hoodwinked by this lady. Not many people will stand by and let a woman sob uncontrollably on an airplane, but the truth is undeniable, she manipulated everyone to obtain an outcome she didn't deserve. Oh, she deserved something, she deserved an Emmy for her performance, but she didn't deserve being rewarded for her disruptive behavior.

I struggle with people rewarding bad behavior. This is something I think about not only on the airplane but in my daily life. My sensitivity to it comes from having a mother who used manipulation like I use water to wash dishes. If she wasn't manipulating, she was sleeping. I spent years falling prey to her games, giving in so I'd get a break from the negative reinforcement, intimidation, and guilt trips. But giving in to manipulation and inappropriate behavior is like being held captive by someone who knows that if they torture you long enough, you'll give them the code to their safe deposit box. Protecting myself from manipulation is on my mind constantly; I probably obsess about it. The moment I sense I'm being manipulated, the walls of my fortress go up, and I'm ready to attack.

But on the airplane, unless I want to be terminated, I can only ask, "Would you like cream and sugar with your coffee?"

Unable to pull this lady aside and call out her bullshit, I simply turned around, walked back to the galley, and thought, *I feel bad for her kids.*

It wasn't lost on me that throughout the entire flight, she'd let her three kids walk to the lavatory alone. I wanted to step up to her, tap her on the shoulder and say, "You realize that when you let your kids go to the lavatory at the back of the airplane alone, they are further away from you than where you were all originally seated."

I kept that to myself.

When we landed in Cleveland, Jane walked up to the front galley looking pale and clammy. At first, I thought it was because she's British, but then I found out she was ill. While we waited for our incoming airplane to land, she confessed, "I was in the lav throwing up the entire time we were landing."

In my fatherly tone, I said, "You need to call in sick."

She hesitated, "I need the hours."

I put my foot down, "Are you gonna be throwing up the entire flight?"

"I don't know."

"Then you need to call in sick. You can't be getting the rest of us sick."

While Jane dialed crew scheduling, Gloria and I grabbed a cup of coffee to get us through the rest of the night. We met the captain, and he informed us that he had a check ride scheduled. He was stricken with fear. In all my years, I've never witnessed a pilot fearful over a check ride.

Annoyed and irritated? Yes. Acting like a vampire was hiding in the flight deck to drain his blood? No.

It made me ponder, *should I be worried about this guy?*

I understand that having an employee from the FAA watching your every move can be daunting, but not fearful to the point that the flight attendant questions your ability to fly the airplane. I thought as we walked down the jet bridge, *Pull yourself together. You're shaking so bad your coffee is spilling all over your arm.*

Passengers notice fear quickly, and if they sense a lapse in a pilot's confidence, they're liable to stampede off the airplane like an angry mob trying to get inside Walmart on Black Friday.

I asked him as we stepped onto the airplane, "Why are you so freaked out?"

"You know, man. You push one wrong switch, and it goes on your permanent record forever."

I responded, "I understand. I get written up for forgetting to give a passenger a napkin."

As long as it's not the nose-dive-into-the-ground switch, I think we'll be fine.

Charlotte, the replacement flight attendant for Jane, was operating her second flight ever. That's what I call a newbie. Her shoes were barely scuffed, and her breath didn't smell like pilot balls. Charlotte's excitement about being a flight attendant was a refreshing twist from working with co-workers who continuously complain about everything from ice for beverages to delays.

Once Charlotte completed her security checks, we began boarding, and a fellow airline employee walked on while I helped a passenger in row two with their crutches.

Her name was Linda. Linda interrupted me, "Will we have to help you clean in Phoenix?"

I answer, "Yes."

Linda demanded, "I need gloves."

I froze in place while holding the crutches above my head, positioning them into the overhead bin. Linda needs to learn some manners, it's probably not the best idea to be a dickhead towards the flight attendant while he's holding a weapon.

I rolled my eyes, "I'll bring them to you when I have a chance."

Then to make me dislike her even more, Linda placed her large carry on bag over row one but was seated in row ten. When I walked to the front galley, I checked the manifest to make sure she worked for the airline.

She did.

When a passenger places their bag over row one but is seated in the back of the airplane, I walk the suitcase to their seat, grab their attention, and show them that I'm placing their bag by their row. If you're seated in row ten, your carry on luggage does not belong over row one.

Linda was no exception.

I put a pair of gloves in my pocket and walked towards the exit row closing overhead bins. I placed Linda's suitcase over her row and addressed her, "Your bag is right here," then I pulled the gloves out of my pocket, "And here are some gloves."

I started back towards the front and she waved at me with both hands, "Can you put this bag in the overhead bin?"

I gritted my teeth, "Your backpack goes under the seat in front of you."

Before we closed the airplane door, I began conducting a compliance check and Linda's husband handed me his empty coffee cup and a few soiled napkins. The only time you should hand trash to the flight attendant is when they have a trash bag in their hand, or they are conducting a trash pick up with the trash bin. Let that be a lesson to airline employees, I understand that passengers who aren't associated with the airline industry might not know that, but airline employees and their travel companions should know better.

That's what happens when airline employees from other departments travel on the airplane, they have no clue how to act.

Thursday
PHX—JFK

It's hot as balls in Arizona. I'm sure if you live in Phoenix ninety-two degrees at nine A.M. is perfectly normal, but for us Northern California residents, it's brutal. When it gets over eighty degrees in Silicon Valley, we act like Mt. Shasta erupted.

After a full breakfast—which only cost $6.99—I realized why people put up with living in the sister city to the planet Mercury. Things are cheap in Phoenix. I bet the homeless in San Francisco could afford a two-bedroom apartment in Arizona. I was in full tourist mode and began walking to the Capitol building, but I started melting and summoned a shared ride service. My water bottle was empty, and I'd been outside for only ten seconds. I'm shocked that there aren't bodies lined up on the side of the road of people who have dropped dead. Arizona feels like you could drop dead at any moment. Say goodbye to your loved ones when you go to the store or check the mail.

It got hotter every second, and not simply hotter, but I think the temperature rose five degrees every minute. I don't know if this is accurate, but it may have reached 200 degrees before the end of the day.

Humans shouldn't live in the desert.

At the airport, every restaurant and coffee shop after TSA was closed and there were hundreds of passengers waiting to board flights. I know I exaggerated about the temperature, but there were hundreds of passengers awaiting flights without the ability to get coffee.

When we get to the gate, the agent said, "The quicker you board, the sooner you can leave."

No shit. This might be Charlotte's second flight, but I've been at this rodeo so long I've been branded. The back galley was a mess, and the beverage carts were not swapped out for our flight, which upset me because we passed the last crew as they walked out of the airport and they were all smiles. Had I known they didn't do their job, I'd have tripped them into a cactus.

We began boarding, and a husband and wife carried their infant onto the airplane in a car seat. I said, "Don't forget the car seat goes in the window seat."

The dad stopped, "We don't have a window seat." I pulled him aside to wait in the galley with the baby while the captain ran to get a gate agent.

The family was assigned middle and aisle seats. The gate agent supervisor came down and addressed the father, "You'll have to hold the baby in your lap; there aren't three seats together."

The father became frustrated, and I didn't blame him. He calmly reminded the gate agent that they had purchased three seats. Without saying a word, the supervisor stepped over to row one and asked the lady in 1A if she'd switch seats and take 2E. I'd never have the balls to ask a passenger to change from a window to a middle seat on a red-eye.

But the woman said yes. I'm pessimistic and believe people put their own needs before others. I'm bitter. I know it's not my best quality, but after flying around in a metal tube for years, it doesn't take too long before you become jaded from the airline industry. For me, I believe it was the time I watched a passenger step over another passenger, who had passed out on the galley floor, to ask me for another Sprite. After that, I deemed all passengers to be selfish monsters. But I have to remind myself, that isn't true. There are good people in the world, and some of them fly on airplanes. When I witness empathy and compassion from people, especially when it's targeted towards strangers, it catches me off guard. I know I spend countless hours complaining about airline passengers, but once in a while they surprise me, and it reminds me that not all people are selfish assholes.

Later during the flight, I bought the woman who moved to 2E a few glasses of wine.

Once the family was settled, I walked up to the supervisor and comforted her, "Take a deep breath and relax."

She answered, "I get frazzled."

My neck snapped back. Frazzled? Honey, you work two flights a day out of this airport. And they are red-eye flights. She doesn't have to show up until eight P.M. and goes home at one A.M. I thought, *If she can't handle two flights a day, how does she manage the Arizona heat?*

After boarding was complete, she went into the flight deck to speak to the pilots while I completed one of my announcements. Without another word, she walked out of the cockpit, stepped off the airplane, and closed the airplane door without getting the final confirmation from me that our compliance was completed and we were ready to go.

I didn't finish my announcement; I stopped mid-sentence. I struggle to control my temper when I'm at work. It's not like when I go off on a rude person at the grocery store. I have to maintain my composure on the airplane, but she irritated me. I hung up the interphone, grabbed a piece of paper to jot down a note, and walked over to the airplane door. She was on the jet bridge, chatting with another gate agent.

I waved until I caught her attention through the airplane window and held up the note for her to read:

YOU DIDN'T CHECK WITH ME
BEFORE YOU CLOSED THE DOOR.

She mouthed, "I'm sorry,"

During the safety demonstration, the lady in 2D was on a video call with her boyfriend. She reminded me of a Playboy bunny who flies in coach. I spent an ample amount of time trying to get this little bunny to follow the rules. I asked her twice to fasten her seatbelt when the seatbelt sign was illuminated. During our taxi to the runway, she refused to cancel her video call even though I had asked her multiple times. I should have been more aggressive about her non-compliance, but after an exhausting boarding, I refused to argue. As we started to take off, she was still on her call. We made eye contact, and I swiped my hand across my neck, telling her to end the call. I hope she didn't think I was suggesting she was about to get cut.

To be honest, I don't care what she thinks.

Pairing 021: Red Uggs

Friday
Queens, New York City

The Universe was looking out for me today.

I landed in JFK early this morning, and I start another trip tomorrow. I rented a hotel room by the airport for the night and planned on sleeping in the crew lounge for a few hours until check-in time at the hotel. While we were walking off the airplane, one of the other flight attendants suggested I call and ask the front desk clerk if there were any rooms available right away.

She said, "The most they can say is say no."

Well, the hotel said yes. In a chipper voice not typical for Queens, the front desk clerk had a room for me and sent the hotel shuttle van to the airport to pick me up. I was showered and in bed by seven A.M.

The room is decorated nicely, but my view is obstructed by the hotel's air conditioning ducts. Not a small obstruction, but large enough for me to read the label of the air conditioning company on the gray steel against the window.

I napped until eleven A.M. and then walked to the grocery store about a mile away. Hands down, it was the nastiest grocery store I've ever stepped inside. If LaGuardia reminded Joe Biden of a third world country, I can't imagine what he'd say about this store. The building looked condemned and I almost bitched at Google maps for directing me to a closed grocery store. The sign above the entrance hung sideways, and the awning flapped in the wind. There were two carts in the cart bin, and they were from two different stores. The store looked like it was pillaged by humans after the zombie apocalypse. The inside was cramped, filthy, and smelled of rats. I figured the cockroaches carry groceries out for the elderly shoppers. I picked up some items to make a cheese board and bought a $6.99 bottle of sparkling chardonnay. I had no idea $6.99 chardonnay was a thing, but I like it.

I spent the rest of the day inside my hotel room watching Netflix. The only thing waiting for you outside a hotel next to JFK is a homicide. I chatted with Matt on the phone while he's in North Carolina visiting his cousin. Matt talks highly of his cousin's son, John. John is learning Russian—for fun—and I can tell that Matt wishes he had a nine-year-old who wanted to learn a foreign language. If either one of us had a uterus, we'd probably have a fourteen-year-old right now. I know Matt imagines a life where we have a kid, but it's impossible for us living in Silicon Valley. Sure, people have kids around here, but these people squeeze ten human beings in a one-bedroom apartment and have bunk beds set up on their balconies. And if I had a child, I wouldn't want them growing up in an apartment. I'm not saying there's anything wrong with that—I lived in an apartment my entire childhood—but I'd want to give my child what I didn't have. A house with a yard and walls not connected to noisy neighbors.

Saturday
JFK—LAS

I had a great night's sleep and left for the airport early to get coffee and breakfast. I found a quiet place to sit, but before I knew it, the entire area was filled with people.

A New Yorker with a hairdo straight out of 1986 sat behind me alone and exhibited her verbal diarrhea, "Fuck this airline. Fuck all of them. A three-hour delay. That's fucking bullshit."

I figured she saw me sitting there, in my uniform, and wanted me to know that she was dissatisfied. I didn't give a damn, I was disappointed that I had to hear her whining while I tried sipping my coffee in silence.

There is never peace at the airport, no matter where you find yourself.

During boarding, a woman with a fear of flying walked up to the galley from her seat and asked to meet the pilots. I don't know what they said to her, but she came out of the cockpit smiling. They probably showed her their penises, I assume pilots will take any chance to show their dicks off in the flight deck. Right before we were closing the airplane door, there was a maintenance issue regarding the waste and water levels. While maintenance tended to the problem, the lady in 13E rang her call bell.

I walked over, "May I help you?"

"We have a short circuit. I hear it in my headphones."

"Excuse me?" I asked, shutting off the call bell light.

"It's a short circuit. Oh, Jesus. Can you hear it?"

This was going to be a long flight. I responded, "What's a short circuit sound like?"

"A pop. It's a popping sound. Oh. Oh. I can hear it." She removed the earbuds from her ears and winced.

I tried not laughing, "Let me tell the pilots and see what we can do."

I stepped into the cockpit and passed the maintenance man who had fixed the waste and water problem. I informed the two pilots about the short circuit, and the captain looked at me like my brain was short-circuiting.

"Tell that lady to shut up," he said. "We're ready to go."

After we departed, I checked on 13E, "Do you still hear that noise?"

"It's fine. Thank you. Can you bring me a Coke?"

A flight attendant I worked with recently is on this flight, and she brought us cupcakes. I don't need cupcakes, but I ate them. There were a lot of demanding passengers on the plane, but they were manageable. Two that stick out in my mind were the lady in 1C, who looked like Bernadette Peters, and a guy in 2C who had ants in his pants and spent four out of the five-hour flight standing up. The best passenger was Larry, a cat seated with his human mom in 4E. Larry is moving to Las Vegas. I checked on him throughout the flight, but he didn't need my assistance. I was hoping he'd escape so I could spend the entire flight searching for him and not dealing with trying to get 2C to sit the fuck down.

Checked into the hotel and then walked to Holstein's at The Cosmopolitan for dinner. The hostess wrote my name down, I told her I'd sit at the bar, but she made a sad face and said, "There are no seats at the bar."

When they finally called me for a table, I saw a bar stool tucked away at the end of the bar. Why don't people do their job correctly? I should have complained to the manager, but I don't have a bob haircut, and I'm not a soccer mom named Vicky.

As per Matt's recommendation, I ordered ahi tuna sliders and an adult milkshake. My waiter, Erik, was thick, cute, and kept talking about how he shoves the ahi sliders down his throat and then plays hockey. Hockey in Las Vegas? Isn't that like cross country running in Siberia? I wanted to talk more about Erik sliding things down his throat, but then my food was delivered, and the fleeting thought disappeared.

When my adult milkshake arrived, I immediately regretted it. Erik placed the tall glass of carbs in front of me, and also brought out the tin canister of milkshake that didn't fit in the glass. I wanted to send it back. I wanted to send it all back, but it looked so tasty, and I'm not a quitter, so I drank it. Not only did I drink it, but I also scraped off the buttercream frosting the kitchen had spackled around the top of the glass. To add calories to injury, I ate all the M&M's plastered to the icing.

As I said, I'm no quitter, I'm a pig.

My blood sugar was higher than some of the patrons on the street as I shuffled to Harrah's in search of a five-dollar roulette table. I figured Harrah's would have lower limit games, but I was mistaken, you will not find a five-dollar roulette table on the Las Vegas strip on a Saturday. As the money burned a hole in my pocket, I stopped at a ten dollar roulette table and the dealer running the table was surly.

I fumbled with my money trying to tidy it up for him, and he yelled, "Just give me the money will ya."

That was the indication to walk away, but I'm stubborn. I lost forty dollars in about three seconds. I left beaten, but not ready to give up. I rode the monorail to the Stratosphere (no five-dollar table there, either) and then jumped in a taxi and headed down to Fremont Street. At 4 Queens, I found a table for five dollars and planted my ass, preparing to win big.

I lost bigly.

My sixty-five dollars lasted forty minutes, and I received two free beers out of the experience. I lost sixty-five dollars and had two beers—you do the math. The guy sitting next to me kept bragging that he had started with twenty dollars and now had a stack of chips around him that had me a nasty shade of green. It looked like he was building his own wall to keep out anyone who might try and steal his winnings. He won each time the ball landed on a number. He'd hoot, I'd smile and take a sip of my beer, but secretly hope he'd get a kidney stone and fall over. After losing the rest of my money, I tipped the dealer, Pam, and walked out.

Good old Pam, if only she were as good at landing the white ball on a few of my numbers as she was at snatching the tip out of my hand.

Outside on Fremont Street, there were crowds of families and drunk straight people. Besides me, there wasn't a gay for miles. I have the worst gaydar, but even I'd have spotted a homosexual in that crowd. A cover band sang every rock song from the '80s. The long-haired lead singer looked haggard, but he moved around the stage like he was ageless. He wore torn red jeans, a button-down shirt with the arm sleeves ripped off, and I'm sure he still gets loads of panties thrown at him on stage. I mocked the lead singer, but then found myself jamming along to Def Leppard realizing that this guy sounded like every lead singer from every rock band in the eighties. Is this possible? Were they the same person? Those ideas run through your head when you're alone in Las Vegas. When the music died, so did my mood and my time there. I taxied to the Stratosphere and enjoyed the sunset, and a few appetizers, at the Level 107 lounge. It's the perfect way to end a great day in Las Vegas.

It's layovers like this that make this job tolerable.

Sunday
LAS—SAN—PDX

A great night's sleep means the world to me now. When I first became a flight attendant, I'd sleep five hours on a layover and run around town like a maniac until my eyeballs were ready to pop out of my head and scurry to the nearest bed. I'd treat every layover as if it were my last because in the airline industry you never know when your time is up. I could be fired. I could become disabled and not be able to do the job. The airline might cease operation while I'm in the shower getting ready for my next flight. I'm not exaggerating, airlines have ceased operation during the night, leaving the employees dumbfounded in the morning.

When I turned forty, I realized my body required eight hours of sleep. If I don't get the rest I need, I'm a real bear. And that's when I'm home in my own bed. When out flying and staying in random hotels with questionable beds, it's even worse. Lucky for my mood, and my passengers, I slept nine hours last night and woke up happy. I also had time to eat free breakfast in the hotel lobby before it was time to take the van to the airport.

I walked on the airplane, and the captain asked, "Are you, Flight Attendant Joe?"

Being recognized by a pilot is the best way to start your day.

I haven't addressed the other two people I'm working with on this trip. Norman, who's in the mid-cabin, is a decent flight attendant. He's dorky, talks about gambling a lot, and doesn't drink alcohol or coffee. I understand not drinking alcohol, but coffee? What happened to you as a child that would cause you to deprive yourself of the finer things in life? Yes, I consider coffee to be up there with owning a villa in France and having a personal driver to take you to Target. I have nothing in common with Norman except that he loses money gambling in Las Vegas and that he likes dick.

Violet, the other flight attendant we're working with, she's another story. How could I describe Violet?

I've got it: a fucking disaster.

It seems that my airline has given up on trying to hire quality people. If you have a heartbeat, you're hired. It's like they sift through applicants at Goodwill and take whatever fits, even if it's tattered and torn.

It started first thing yesterday morning when Violet marched on the airplane, late, with a pair of red UGGs slung over her shoulder. Before Norman and I greeted her, she began bitching, "There's some standby flight attendant at the gate starting shit with me."

Norman and I made eye contact and then focused back on her.

Violet continued, "She's up there telling the gate agent to say something to me because I'm wearing a noncompliant jacket. Why not mind your damn business when you ain't involved in a situation. How 'bout that?"

I shrugged and watched her drag her luggage down the aisle while her red UGGs bounced up and down on her chest. In all honesty, she was most likely embarrassed for being called out for her bad behavior. Yes, that co-worker at the gate should mind her business, but that doesn't excuse the fact that Violet was in the wrong. Her jacket was noncompliant.

Airlines have strict uniform guidelines that employees must comply with. The requirements are not that big of a deal, but some flight attendants act like toddlers when expected to follow uniform guidelines. I imagine some of them throw tantrums in their hotel rooms screaming, "But I want to wear neon green nail polish today. Why does the airline hate me?'

They don't hate you, honey, they hate neon green nail polish.

I didn't care enough to discuss uniform compliance with Violet. I hope that she's smart enough not to slip on those red UGGs anywhere near the airplane. If that happens, we'll have to go to war.

After beverage service, Violet dawdled and never once went through the airplane collecting trash. Norman asked her, "Are you gonna do trash?"

She answered, "In a minute."

But that minute never came.

I'm the lead flight attendant and didn't interact with her as much as Norman. When I walked to the back galley after doing a compliance check, she was glued to her iPad binging a television show on Netflix. She had on closed captioning, so I didn't say anything to her about watching television. If she had earbuds in, that's a safety issue, and I'd have challenged her. I learned quickly that when managing Violet, you have to pick your battles. You can't question everything she says or does, or you'll spend the entire flight calling her ass out. At 38,000 feet sometimes it's not the passengers who need an ass whooping, it's your fellow co-workers. I decided to let a few things slide because I'm not being paid enough extra as the lead flight attendant to interact with Violet on that level.

Norman, on the other hand, was at his wit's end. She had pushed every last one of his buttons.

Halfway through the flight to Portland, I noticed that Violet had only left her jumpseat to do a lazy beverage service and use the lavatory. I called to the back galley, and Norman answered. I said, "Can you send Violet up here? The pilots want a break."

He said, "Here. You can talk to Violet."

Lordy, it's like getting elementary school students to play nice after a fight on the playground.

She answered, "Yes?"

That's not challenging at all. I responded, "The pilots would like a break. Can you come up?"

She said nothing and hung up the interphone.

I took a deep breath. I kept thinking, *Don't let her get to you. Don't let her get to you.*

When Norman walked up to the front galley, I asked. "Where's Violet?"

He smirked, "She didn't want to come up. She's watching her tv show."

When you don't listen to me, that's a strike against you.

On the flight from San Diego to Portland, I didn't have an ice bucket for my beverage cart. Violet offered me hers. I questioned, "What are you going to use?"

She mumbled out, "I'm doing hand service on this flight."

I thought she intended to give out handjobs, but that's not the case. What I realized was she had no plans on using a beverage cart. Here's the skinny on Violet, she's one of those flight attendants who make up their own fucking rules. It happens continuously in this industry, and it drives me bonkers. When you work with these personality types, you're living in their world. Rules and guidelines don't matter. I stand corrected, only the rules and guidelines these individuals want to follow matters. The policies they disregard or dislike are replaced with their own version. A version they think works better, but in reality, makes everyone else on the flight miserable. In Violet's mind, we were flying on an airplane with the words—Violet Airlines—painted on the outside of it.

When Violet informed us she wasn't using a beverage cart, I looked at Norman, and he rolled his eyes. I needed to conduct beverage service the correct way, so I didn't argue. If her passengers write in a complaint letter about her, that's not my problem. I may be the lead flight attendant, but I'm not here to babysit full-grown adults. On that note, I believe she's pushing me to the point where a confrontation is inevitable. Is she challenging me on purpose? Is she waiting for me to snap on her?

I fear she won't be waiting for long.

In Portland, the captain darted off the airplane first. It's entertaining to watch pilots knock over passengers attempting to be the first one off the aircraft. Where do they have to be that's so fucking important? A child support hearing?

I'm using sarcasm, it's not entertaining, it's embarrassing.

The first officer stepped out of the flight deck, "The captain lives around here and went home. Are we taking the same van together to the hotel?"

I answered, "Yes."

He responded, "Oh. I guess I'll wait for you then."

I wanted to throw myself at his feet and thank him for his kindness, but instead, I said, "That would be nice of you."

Inside the van, I observed Norman and Violet, chatting like old high school friends. At one point, it seemed like they were laughing. On the airplane, Norman wanted to grab her by her weave and toss her into the engine; now they were cracking jokes. I understand working with someone you butt heads with on the airplane but then can be cordial with off the plane. That happens in every industry. You can't stand your neighbor in the next cubicle, but take them out of the office environment, and you think, *this asshole's not that bad outside of work,* I should buy him a drink. Happens to me all the time on the airplane. Off the aircraft, Violet was tolerable, but on the plane, she brought out the worst in your personality. I made no plans with either of them at the hotel. I perused around Powell's Books for a while and then had some food at the Portland City Grill. I finished the night by stuffing two doughnuts from Voodoo Doughnut into my mouth. Now I'm in bed, and my stomach is regretting all the food I ingested in the past few hours.

I'm killing myself with sugar on this trip.

Monday
PDX—LAX—SFO—LGB-~~LAS~~-SJC

My gaydar is broken. I believed Norman was gay, but apparently, he's straight. My facial expression must have said it all when he mentioned a girlfriend, and I asked, "You're straight?"

It was an awkward exchange of words.

It was only a matter of time before Violet pushed me over the edge. I was seated in the back of the airport shuttle van this morning, so I was unaware she was wearing those red Uggs until we arrived at the airport.

The moment my eyes scanned down to those colorful boots glistening in the morning sun, I had to walk away. Words had escaped me, the only thing on my mind was pulling those boots off her feet. Instead of going to jail in Portland, I grabbed my luggage and headed straight into the airport.

I had to calm down; I took a few deep breaths, assessed the situation, and planned on approaching her carefully and professionally. Today was the last day of the trip, but we still had four flights to operate together. How stupid of me to think she wouldn't wear those UGGs at some point during our journey. I never reminded her not to wear them; I didn't believe she was that much of a jerk. That shows you how gullible I am. Flight attendants have a hard time hiding their true identities at work. You know their personality type within five minutes of meeting them at the gate, and Violet let us know she was difficult the moment she walked on the airplane. Violet liked doing shit her own way, but I couldn't let this slide. I felt disrespected and furious she had put me in this predicament. A good co-worker doesn't put you in an awkward situation where you have to call them out for their behavior. We all know our job, why can't people do it? We're all adults when we come to work on the airplane, I shouldn't have to tell a full-grown adult not to wear inappropriate shoes with their uniform.

I hate to admit this, but I was enraged. I stomped through the airport while Norman and Violet followed a few steps behind. It wasn't only the boots that triggered me, it was the entire experience working alongside Violet. She's quite a selfish, lazy human being. It's akin to dealing with a child who wants to see how far they can get with you before their sent to their room without video games for the night. What made me bubble up with anger was her boldness and fuck-you attitude targeted towards Norman and me.

Once we were all inside the terminal, and I was able to catch my breath and compose my temper, I slowed down and let her catch up, "You need to change your shoes."

Without looking at me, she answered, "I will."

"Why are you wearing them?"

She responded, "They're comfortable."

I left it alone. As long as Violet removed them from her feet, and I didn't have to wrestle her to the ground, that was a win. I'll never understand certain people. She knows she's not allowed to wear those with her uniform. And red? Not even black ones, but red? Why not wear a clown mask while doing service?

I didn't mention that because I didn't want to give this bitch any ideas.

When we stepped onto the airplane, she said, "I'm not feeling well today."

I thought, *Is that why you wore those red UGGs?* I've had a hard time letting those UGGs go.

Her voice was hoarse, and I politely told her to stay clear of me.

The captain was worried if she'd be able to conduct her job duties while she was ill. I told Norman on the jumpseat, "She hasn't been conducting her job duties for three days, why would being sick matter?"

He laughed. Our captain was correct though, it's important that the flight attendant speaks clearly in case they find themselves having to yell out emergency commands. If you can barely squeak out your boarding announcement over the PA, screaming at passengers to get the hell out of the airplane might be a challenge.

Before we began boarding, I asked, "Do you want to call in sick?"

She rolled her eyes, "I can't. I have too many sick call points."

All airlines have issues with flight attendants calling in sick. To help mitigate sick occurrences, airlines set up strict point systems to handle sick calls. Each sick call is a point, and those points add up to disciplinary action. I know all about points, I collect them like baseball cards. I'm the king of points, but it's essential to manage these points and not use them when you aren't sick, because the day will come when you need them and you'll be like Violet, unable to call in and infect everyone on the airplane. No flight attendant should work sick, but I can't force her to call in sick. I can suggest, and she can shut me down.

The captain might have been able to remove her from the airplane, but I don't know the logistics on that process.

It might depend on the severity of the situation. She had a cough, it wasn't Ebola.

Viola informed us she was fine and could do her job, so I believed her.

The flight to Los Angeles went quick, but she wore the red UGGs during service and my brain almost melted. I promise that if Violet ever makes it into one of my books, her chapter will be titled, Red UGGs.

Norman came up at some point today and said, "I can't deal with this anymore. Can you please go talk to her?"

I don't have children, and frankly, why bother having children when I work with flight attendants all day?

When I stepped into the back galley, she was sitting in her jump seat, wrapped in a blanket, with Netflix on her iPad, and wearing those fucking red UGGs. Whoever thought a pair of boots could cause so much drama?

I leaned against the back galley counter, folded my arms, "Hey. Whatcha watching?"

She looked up from the screen, "*Scandal.*"

"*Scandal,* huh? That's cool." I twirled my finger around her, "That's funny because we've got our own scandal up on this airplane today?"

Violet put her iPad down on her lap, "What are you talking about?"

"I thought I asked you to change out of those."

"My feet are cold." She wasn't backing down.

I responded, "I have a headache today, but you don't see me laying down taking a nap."

She put her iPad on the counter and flung her blanket off her shoulders, "Fine. I don't see what the problem is."

"I understand you don't see the problem, but I promise you, it's a problem."

Again, why is the airline hiring these people? Honestly, I've said it before, I don't get paid enough to be everyone's father on the airplane. I have passengers to care for, I shouldn't have to tell my co-workers how to dress. If the airline wants to make sure flight attendants are following procedures, then put ghost riders on the fucking airplane. One trip with a ghost rider and Violet would burn them red UGGs.

She blatantly refused to do service the correct way, which made Norman homicidal. I spent most of my time in the front galley, far from Violet. Norman occasionally made his way to the front to complain about something she had done, and I'd encourage him to focus on his own section and let her do her thing.

In Los Angeles, we found out we had a two-hour delay. Then a few minutes later, it was updated to a three and a half-hour delay. The trip initially ended in Las Vegas, not in JFK, and we all had plans scheduled to commute home from Las Vegas. We panicked while crew scheduling modified our trip because when they start changing your pairing, you have no clue which way they might screw you over.

Luckily, crew scheduling removed us from our flight to Las Vegas, which left us only having to fly a San Francisco turn back to Los Angeles. In San Francisco, we were in such a rush to get back to Los Angeles that we told the gate agent to start boarding the moment the last passenger was off the airplane. We declined ice and emptying of the trash cans. Norman snatched the handheld vacuum out of the gate agent's hand and began vacuuming crumbs up off the carpet.

That's above and beyond even for me.

I should write him a compliment letter. I had one flight attendant who refused to serve drinks the correct way, and another one vacuuming the floor. It's like they're from different airlines.

I'd given up the idea of catching the earlier flight home, but when we landed, the captain opened the flight deck door and informed me that we were on the airplane that was headed to San Jose. The best part, I didn't have to step off the aircraft. While we cleaned up, the gate agent called the gate and found out I was assigned 4C. I changed my shirt, sat down, and was thankful everything worked out.

I was also thankful that I didn't have to deal with Violet any longer.

Before the flight started boarding, I walked to the back galley to introduce myself to the other two flight attendants. One of them, Yolanda, screamed, "Oh my God. It's Flight Attendant Joe. I follow you on social media. I love your blog."

I blushed and thanked her.

She continued, "When is your book coming out?"

"In the summer."

"I'll be the first one in line to buy it," she added while handing me a bottle of water.

That interaction made my night, and for a few seconds, I forgot all about Violet and those red fucking UGGs. Sometimes, when you're feeling beaten down and exhausted, all you need to brighten your day is positive energy and kind words from a complete stranger.

Pairing 022: Ciudad de México

Wednesday
JFK—TPA—MEX

I landed in JFK at 8:45 A.M. and made my way to the flight attendant quiet room to take a nap. There was a sign on the door:

> QUIET ROOM WILL BE CLEANED
> EVERY WEDNESDAY AT NOON.

Assuming they were referring to every Wednesday but today, I ignored the sign and found an empty recliner in which to plant myself. A few minutes later, the fluorescent lights from the hallway illuminated the darkroom as someone opened the door and slowly stepped inside. Even though the room was dark, I instantly recognized who the person was by the glow of her cell phone, Lara. I watched from the corner of my eye as she placed her tote bag beside the recliner, placed her hands together tightly, and prayed over the chair. Once she was done mumbling, she lowered herself into the chair and began snoring almost immediately. Something tells me she was praying that housekeeping doesn't wake us all up to clean at noon.

Pray on, Lara.

When my alarm woke me up at 1:30 P.M., I realized Lara prayed the housekeepers away. Any right-wing Christian would believe that's a sign that He exists; that He sacrificed Himself on the cross so we could nap in peace. I'll go with my belief that this airline is so disorganized they haven't cleaned the room since 2010.

I changed into my uniform and went upstairs to grab a coffee. I spotted Frank (who I'm working with on this Mexico City trip), and he asked, "Why is your pairing modified? You have a different pairing number than I do."

I confessed, "I'm pulled off the Philadelphia turn on the last day. There's a new hire doing their check ride."

He snubbed me, "Bitch."

We both laughed, but I laughed harder because I'm the one working less.

We met up with our lead flight attendant, Ronald, at the gate. Ronald is funny, charming, handsome, and makes that clicking sound with his tongue that many gay men do. Evan does it, too. I can't do it; I must not be gay enough.

I'm okay with that.

Ronald leaned in and hugged me tight, "Girl! I'm so excited to be working with you." Then, without skipping a beat, he looked over at Frank and clicked his tongue tossing his hair to the side. I laughed loud enough to get the attention of the passengers within earshot. Ronald makes any flight better, his personality should be a required flight attendant item. He's the type of person who is funny without having to try. I work my ass off to be funny, it's like breathing for him.

While boarding our first flight, a pilot from a different airline took one step on the airplane and asked Ronald, "When can I get some wine?

I wasn't standing there, but I imagine Ronald clicked his tongue, handed him a bottle of water, and ushered the pilot to his seat. He was seated in Frank's section, and

Frank confirmed that during beverage service this brazen pilot ordered a glass of wine and three beers all at once. Frank set him straight by leaning down and whispering to him the rules of etiquette to flying non-rev on an airplane, which ended with, "…and put your employee ID away."

On the Mexico City flight, I was filled with anticipation watching the Mexicans walk down the aisle and find their seats. I've wanted a Mexico City layover for years, but my schedule never permitted it. There was one layover in our schedule packet for the month, I bid for it, and I was awarded it. More reasons why I'm better off in JFK than LAX: seniority and more layover options. If at anytime the airplane crashes into the Gulf of Mexico, I was meant to perish.

We had an unaccompanied minor named Tito sitting in the last row. Tito was a cool kid, but he demanded an orange juice during boarding, which put him on my shit list. Orange juice is a simple request, and I'd typically have handed him one, but not after demanding it like he was El Chapo. I have zero patience for a demanding eight-year-old.

Beverage service was overwhelming. It started off easy, many passengers waved me off as I pushed the card down the aisle. They had no idea that beverages were complimentary. Once people caught on that drinks were free, they treated the cart like an all-you-can-drink buffet.

As I headed to the back galley, two girls stopped me at row eighteen and giggled, "We don't want these drinks anymore. We want new drinks."

They thought it was fun when I gave them a dirty look as I annoyingly handed them their new order. I understand my job description includes bringing passengers drinks over and over again, but order what you want the first time.

We landed in Mexico City earlier than our original arrival time while the Miami flight came in five hours delayed. I'm telling you, I'm meant to be in Mexico City at this exact moment. We were processed through customs quickly, but I believe the agent took my twenty pesos from inside my passport. I didn't cause a scene because spending my layover in a dirty Mexican jail doesn't sound as thrilling as drinking margaritas and sightseeing. Our hotel is downtown, which was a short ride from the airport. After checking into the hotel, Ronald, Frank, and I hightailed it to our rooms for a quick refresh before tackling Mexico City at night. My room was clean, comfortable, and equipped with a king-size bed. The three items I look for in a hotel room. I noticed free bottles of water provided on the counter next to the microwave, which I appreciated. The last time I was in Mexico, I accidentally drank water in Puerto Vallarta and was deathly ill for two full days.

I'm not about to let that happen again. Before meeting the guys downstairs for drinks, I took a hot shower and put on a fresh pair of underwear. I don't recommend wearing the same underwear for twenty-four hours. I had to peel my sac off my thigh. To prevent another gastro incident, I kept my mouth tightly closed in the shower to prevent water from sneaking down my esophagus.

The last time I stayed quiet that long, I was in utero.

The three of us met in the hotel lobby. We had a beer at the hotel bar and then hit the streets to check out the gay district. Frank is straighter than a ruler, but when there is fun to be had, he's first in line. Ronald brought us to a dance club that was too loud. I guess if you're deaf, it might be manageable, but for people without a hearing impairment, a few hours inside and you'd need a hearing aid. I'm too old for loud nightclubs. This is the first time I've confessed this to myself, and the honesty feels excellent. In my twenties, I lived for the chaotic vibe of a loud nightclub. In my thirties, I'd frequent them, but leave feeling verbally abused by a loudspeaker. In my forties, I'd sooner visit the dentist. The idea of standing next to someone in a bar, but unable to have a conversation with them because it sounds like fighter jets are flying around us is not my idea of fun.

I'm really old.

"Can we go to a bar where I won't need to know sign language when I wake up in the morning?"

Ronald laughed, "Alright. Let's find you a bar."

"Thank you. Preferably one where we can hear the crickets outside." I responded.

We found a small dive bar that reminded me of a Quinton Tarantino film set. The front of the bar was completely open to the outside, but the inside had enough statues of the Virgin Mary and crucifixes to make a Catholic church jealous. I've visited churches in Rome that didn't have that many Christian artifacts.

Nothing says fun like drinking Mexican beers while reading the words to the Lord's Prayer painted over the bar.

After the bar closed, we walked to a taqueria that was not only a hole in the wall but actually had holes in the wall. I stopped counting them when I realized they were bullet holes. I know I'm stereotyping, but you weren't there. It was the kind of establishment where you catch the Dengue virus from simply walking inside. Nobody spoke English, but I mustered up enough words to order two cheese tacos and a Coke. I almost asked for a Mexican Coke but realized where I was standing. Honestly, if I asked for

Mexican Coke, I'd probably have been handed a bag filled with Mexican cocaine.

The cashier opened the bottle of Coke, and if I knew enough Spanish, I'd have asked, "I noticed the toilets don't flush, does the water run? Your hands look like you've been playing in the mud since 1987."

I raised the bottle to my lips, took a sip, and Frank said, "Whoa, dude. Use a straw. Don't put your lips on that."

I made a curious face; nobody has ever told me not to put my lips on something.

Then I realized he was protecting me from myself. I'm destined to get Montezuma's Revenge and die. I freaked out slightly but didn't want to make a scene. Enough white people are making a scene about Mexico.

The walk back to the hotel was nerve-wracking. Frank and I followed Ronald down side streets that lacked the illumination of street lights. You don't know how vital street lights are until you're in a dark alley in a foreign country. Shady transient people past by us while police officers carrying automatic weapons stood on almost every street corner.

This wasn't Ronald's first trip to Mexico City, and he warned us, "I'm serious, don't make eye contact with anyone, including the police. The cops are crooked and will harass tourists at night for money, and if you don't give it to them, they'll fuck you up."

I don't know if Ronald was being truthful, or trying to scare the white boys, but it worked. As we raced through the maze of streets, I kept my eyes pointed towards the ground until we stepped into the hotel lobby. I was safely in bed at three A.M. Although I'd been down some murder-looking scary streets, I'm in love with Mexico City.

Thursday
Ciudad de México

Today started out difficult.

Last night, while the three of us were out drinking, we tried deciding when we'd meet for breakfast. It's not easy getting three people, who barely know each other outside of work, to agree on a time to meet. That's why I enjoy solo tourism when I'm on layovers, and not hanging out with other flight attendants. It's a personal policy that I've incorporated into my work life since having too many layovers ruined by co-workers. It all boils down to being selfish and not wanting someone to dictate my agenda. But I enjoy Ronald and Frank's company, and I couldn't imagine running around Mexico City without the two of them. Frank informed us he'd sleep in until at least ten A.M. I told them that I'd be getting up early, especially in a city where I only had thirty hours to explore. And that's all I remember about our discussion. After drinking $1.35 beers, eating $1.00 tacos, and avoiding eye contact with the police, my brain was refried beans last night.

I crawled out of bed at nine A.M. and texted Ronald. When I stepped out of the shower, he had not responded. I went down to the hotel restaurant for breakfast at 9:30 A.M. and he texted me back at 9:45 A.M.: *Where are you?*

I texted him while I ate breakfast, and then Frank text me stating that he'd catch up with us later. I sent Ronald a few more messages, but he never responded. These two were stressing me the fuck out. I became frustrated and wanted to slap myself for making plans with flight attendants. The reason I have my personal policy in place is to prevent shit like this from happening. I had wasted valuable tourist time waiting around and texting back and forth. I paid the bill and left the hotel. I walked across the roundabout to snap pictures of the Angel of Independence monument and realized it had been almost thirty minutes since I'd heard from Roland; I was losing my patience. I decided to forgo the plans and hopefully meet up with them later in the day.

Roland finally called. Looking back, that was the smartest move. Text messaging is usually the root cause of all my pain and suffering. I'd have called, but I wanted to avoid paying $0.25 a minute. In the future, I'll remember that a quarter is not worth anxiety over trying to communicate in Mexico.

"Where are you?" he asked.

"I'm at the monument. Why didn't you respond to any of my text messages?"

"You never responded to me."

We learned that he wasn't receiving any of my text messages. Again, an early call costing a mere quarter would have solved my problem.

Roland met me outside the hotel, and we ventured towards Chapultepec Castle. We took pictures, laughed, mocked all the tourists, and finally met up with Frank outside a bank across from the hotel. The three of us walked a few miles to historic Mexico City. Mexico City is breathtaking and rivals some of the best European cities I've visited. If you were blindfolded, kidnapped (probably not a funny joke when talking about CDMX), and dropped off in Constitution Plaza, you'd quickly think you were in Spain. We took breaks by stopping along the way at bars and enjoying a few beers while seated at outside tables soaking up the fantastic weather.

Random musicians stopped at our table, started playing music, and then asked for donations. I immediately thought of when my phone was stolen off the table in Barcelona. You aren't supposed to let one bad experience alter your life, but that's my go-to memory when anyone approaches me at an outside table while I'm abroad. Frank handed over spare change, but I ignored them. Besides the musicians, there are children beggars. I've never experienced children begging. I don't have a problem ignoring musicians panhandling, but four and five-year-old dirty children starving while pleading for money, that's heartbreaking.

We entered the Mexico City Metropolitan Church during mass, and my skin didn't bubble up and burn off, which I took as a positive sign. I took a few steps inside and forgot to remove my baseball cap. The usher reprimanded me; I immediately removed it and mouthed, "I'm sorry."

I may not be a religious man, but I am respectful.

We planned on walking back to the hotel but ordered a taxi because we were too exhausted. Outside the hotel, Ronald recommended another taqueria a few blocks away. It was daylight, so I didn't protest. Honestly, I had to shit so bad I feared I'd never make it to my room in time.

After being seated at our table, I excused myself and found the restroom. Why is there only one restroom in a restaurant when your ass is about to open up? The toilet was preoccupied, which seems to be the story of my life. I danced around from foot to foot, worried that I did catch Montezuma's Revenge from that Coke bottle. An employee finally emerged, and I pushed past her and slammed the door shut behind me. While sitting on the toilet, I looked to my right and noticed a cell phone on the sink. The moment my brain acknowledged the phone, the employee was banging on the restroom door.

I yelled, "Your phone is in here. Please give me a minute."

The banging intensified.

I remembered where I was, "Uno momento por favor," which calmed her down. I took an extra few minutes to teach her a lesson about banging on the restroom door when someone is shitting. I don't care where you hail from, that's rude and distracting.

After more tacos and beer, we walked back to the hotel. I showered and crawled into bed; I have an early morning alarm tomorrow.

Price list of things in Mexico City using the American dollar:

Beer $1.35

Taxi ride (Three miles in traffic) $7.81

Taco $1.36

Museum fee (Two people) $7.81

Breakfast at the hotel with tip $16.75

Friday
MEX—MCO

Alarm: 3:45 A.M.

Van Pickup: 4:20 A.M.

Report time at MEX: Five A.M.

Scheduled boarding time: 5:15 A.M.

Departure scheduled: 5:50 A.M.

The security guard felt me up this morning. There were seventy-six passengers on the flight, and the gate agent wanted to board early. We politely told her—in English and Spanish—to calm the fuck down. There was plenty of time to board, and no rush boarding because customs in Orlando wasn't scheduled to open until ten A.M.

We boarded the passengers in ten minutes.

In Orlando, I used Global Entry for the second time, and I believe it's something that should come with every passport. But if everyone had Global Entry, it wouldn't be unique, and the line would be as long as the regular immigration line.

Nevermind.

At the hotel, I contacted my ex-boyfriend, Kurt, to see if he wanted to get dinner. His boyfriend recently died, and I'm concerned about him. Not Doug, the boyfriend he left me for who wanted a job reference, but a new boyfriend who died from a disease that I'm unable to recall at the moment. I can't help but think of Matt dying and the emotional devastation that would leave behind. This is how selfish I am, I want to die before my husband to avoid the pain of losing him. I'm selfish because I'm not taking into account the pain he'd experience losing me because when you die first, you don't have to worry anymore. Well, I'll be concerned about the heat in Hell, but something tells me spending all those summers in Florida will come in handy.

I can't imagine how painful it is for Kurt. When Kurt and I chatted on the phone, he repeated how much he missed his boyfriend. My heart aches for him and his loss. I believe if you loved someone once in your life, even if they caused you heartache, you can still hold a place for them in your heart. I don't think love dies, I think it turns into something different.

Kurt said, "My shift doesn't end until eight tonight, I can swing by and pick you up, and we can hang out at my house for a while?"

I snarked, "Kurt. Stop trying to sleep with me. We've been over for years."

He laughed. I instantly knew it was the first time he'd laughed in a while.

Instead of hanging out with anyone tonight, I saw a movie and had dinner alone. I enjoy hanging out with Frank and Ronald, but I needed some me time. To be honest, all the thoughts of death brought my mood to a screeching halt. As I write this, I want to be at home with my husband and give him a hug.

After dinner, I went to the pharmacy across the street from the hotel to pick up a few items. While I was shopping, a lady bumped into me and kept walking. She never apologized or acknowledged me. As I prepared to berate her in front of anyone within earshot, I followed her towards the ice cream cooler and stopped a few feet away, "Laura?"

Laura turned to the right and stared at me through the glass door like I had caught her stealing ice cream. "Joe?"

"Of course, it's Joe. Who else would it be, Ed? How did you not recognize me?"

"I can't believe you're here," she continued laughing.

I wasn't letting her off the hook, "Is this what you do on your layovers? Stalk ice cream?"

Laura continued laughing as another flight attendant walked over to investigate the commotion, "Tammy, this is Flight Attendant Joe. He's the one I'm writing a television show with."

"I'm the one she doesn't acknowledge in an Orlando CVS." We're meeting for breakfast in the morning before I have to fly to New York. I hope she remembers my face in a crowded restaurant.

I almost forgot I had a dream when I was in Mexico City. I was at a Madonna concert, and the usher brought me backstage, but the show had ended. And I don't know how this all relates, but next, I was on my knees blowing a fat Mexican guy.

Listen, I don't ask for these dreams, they come to me.

Saturday
MCO—JFK—MCO

The hotel guest service employee called my room at four A.M. to inquire why I wasn't taking the van to the airport. I told her to eat shit and die, hung up, and immediately called crew scheduling and informed them how inappropriate it was for the hotel to disturb my layover rest. In all my years, I've never had a hotel question my whereabouts. The last time I checked, I didn't work for the hotel. All they should care about is getting paid for the room, not keeping track of flight attendants. If the hotel interrupts a pilot's rest, the pilot can call in fatigue. We don't have that opportunity; we're expected to work no matter who interrupts our rest.

I ended my rant with the scheduler, "if the hotel employee has a question about a flight attendant, they should be contacting you, not waking me up for no reason at four in the morning."

The scheduler agreed with me and apologized, but it was too late. I was awake. I texted Laura, canceled our breakfast date, and then tossed and turned for a few hours. I must have fallen back asleep because my alarm jarred me awake at noon. The airport shuttle van picked me up on time, which was a shocker, and at the airport, I made my way to the flight attendant lounge to meet up with Ronald and Frank.

The two of them were exhausted after working a Philadelphia turn, and their facial expression should have warned me. I walked up with a smile, "Good afternoon, gentlemen. How are we doing?"

Ronald rolled his eyes, "Look at this bitch, sashaying up here all refreshed and glowing." Then he clicked his tongue, and we all laughed.

While we walked to the gate, Frank detailed their morning and how tiresome the Philadelphia flights had been. Completely ignorant and self-absorbed, I responded, "That sucks, but I completely understand. The hotel woke me up at four this morning, and I had a hard time falling back to sleep."

The two of them would have kicked me down the jet bridge and flung me down onto the tarmac if they hadn't needed me to work the flight back to JFK.

Frank said, "At least you were able to go back to sleep, Joe."

Roland added, "Bitch. Don't try me today with your, 'the hotel woke me up,' nonsense."

We were delayed twenty minutes leaving Orlando and then circled around JFK for the weather to clear before we landed at 6:15 P.M. The gate agent opened the airplane door, and an employee from Drug and Alcohol was standing on the jet bridge carrying a clipboard and a smile.

She stepped on the airplane and told Ronald, "We're doing a random drug test on all three of you today."

How fucking random is that?

Three flight attendants, on the same flight, on their way back from Mexico City all get randomly drug tested? That's not the definition of a random drug test, that's the definition of we' re-afraid-the-flight-attendants-snorted-cocaine-in-Mexico-City drug test. I panicked because I was on my way to Florida and didn't want to miss the flight.

Without hiding my frustration, I said, "I hope we can get this done quickly. My flight is in forty-five minutes."

She smiled, "Yes, It won't take long."

We walked to the drug and alcohol office, and I was tested first. I'll give the urine collector credit, I was in and out within ten minutes. I power walked to the gate to find out the flight to Orlando was delayed. I had rushed for nothing, which is typical in the airline industry. I exhaled deeply while the gate agent handed me my boarding pass.

I asked, "Do you know why we're delayed?"

She answered, "The pilots timed out. We're waiting on new ones."

I expected this to take hours, but by the time I returned from changing out of my uniform in the restroom, the gate agents began boarding. As I settled into my seat, the first officer picked up the interphone and announced, "Hello, everyone. We were supposed to be on our way home two hours ago, but we just found out we're operating this flight. It's gonna take us a few minutes to get everything done. Trust me, we'd rather be going home right now, too."

I quickly removed my crew ID and placed it in my tote bag under the seat in front of me.

At eight, the captain came over the intercom and stated we had a departure time of nine P.M. I had a tantrum and texted Matt, Adam, and Mike to whine about how situations never go my way.

Matt responded: *It's not the job's fault.*

Adam texted: *chill out*

Mike replied: *I'm sorry.*

My frustration stemmed from not following my original plan. I'm in St. Petersburg, visiting Mike for a few nights, and I had planned on taking the Tampa flight, but the car rentals were expensive in Tampa, and the flight was later. To save a few dollars, and what I thought was time, I changed my agenda and flew to Orlando, rented a car, and drove to St. Petersburg. I landed in Orlando, drove to Mike's house, and pulled into the driveway at the same time the Tampa flight landed. It all worked out, but I could have saved myself unnecessary frustration if I'd have taken the Tampa flight and spent a few extra dollars.

Why is it so hard for me to stay calm in these situations? Why do I go from zero to 10,000 and fall apart when nothing terrible happened? Why do I send emotional text messages to people making myself look like a lunatic? I have no idea, but I'm desperate to find answers to these questions. Not only for my mental health but the mental health of my loved ones. I find joy in giving advice to friends who need it, but I struggle to follow my own counsel. Sometimes I feel like I have it all figured out, that the next time there's drama or challenges in my life, I'll be able to handle the circumstances like a professional self-help author. And I do, but not enough. Only after the fact does everything become clear and I realize that I did not handle the situation well.

When you know better, you are supposed to do better. When will I learn that?

PAIRING 023: I'M JUST HERE FOR THE LAYOVERS

Tuesday
JFK—BGI

I'm flying with Dante and Julio, two flamboyant queens, and Simone who seemed bothered that we were traveling to Barbados. My excitement was palpable, I bounced up and down the aisle like Tigger. Simone stared at me like she was going for a pap smear.

Dante, the lead flight attendant, tried tricking me into swapping out of my recent Mexico City trip for a double Newark. Who the fuck tries trading two nights in Newark for a long Mexico City layover? He resorted to shady tactics in an attempt to fool me into swapping trips. Instead of sending me an email asking me to switch, he sent an unsolicited swap request on our scheduling software, hoping that I'd click on the accept button by mistake. That's the behavior of junior flight attendants attempting to fool senior flight attendants who have better trips, but I'm onto their shenanigans. I hit the deny button without reading the request.

I'm not trying to sound bitchy, but Julio talks too much and doesn't shut up. He's on constant send. I know that sounds weird coming from me, but trust me, if I'm calling you out for talking too much you need to take a breath and close your mouth.

During boarding, a couple, Mr & Mrs. Crab, walked on the airplane, and Mrs. Crab had a pissy attitude. I'm one of the mid-cabin flight attendants, so I was positioned in the exit row while they boarded.

Mrs. Crab immediately went off, "Where's my TV? I hope I have a TV."

I smiled, "This is an exit row. Your television is in the armrest."

"It is? That's strange."

I felt joy informing her, "And because you're in the exit row, the television has to stay secured during taxi, take off, and landing." Mrs. Crab ignored me and continued complaining about the exit row, which was absurd; the exit row has more space than most New York City apartments.

The complaining didn't end there. Mrs. Crab bemoaned that their row was too far back on the airplane. I held my tongue, wanting to remind her that she was a privileged white woman boarding a plane for Barbados. I kept one eye on her and her husband while greeting other passengers as they strolled down the aisle.

She snapped at her husband, but it was targeted at me, "How is this an upgraded seat? We're all the way in the back." To put it in context, they were seated in row nineteen, and there are thirty-four rows on the airplane.

Mr. Crab did his best at calming her down. At that point, I couldn't stand listening to the whining and offered my professional flight attendant assistance, "How may I help you?"

Mr. Crab looked up at me and smiled. "We're on our honeymoon."

"Congratulations."

Then she ruined our moment, "We're supposed to be on the earlier flight, but our flight from Boston canceled this morning, and now we've missed half the day of our honeymoon." With that, she began crying hysterically.

I juggled acknowledging the boarding passengers with managing the emotional basket case in 19B. She cried as if she'd gotten divorced instead of married. Mr. Crab stared at me and shrugged his shoulders. I wanted to offer to delay the flight and give him a running start so he could get an annulment. Hell, I'd blow a slide and help him escape. Mr. Crab is from Boston, which means he's hot, but his choice of spouse showed he was as dumb as someone wearing a MAGA hat. If she can't handle a speed bump in her honeymoon plans, how will she ever survive him cheating on her with her best friend?

I tried calming her down, but she was in full hysterics. If I didn't know better, I'd think the airplane was crashing into the fucking ocean.

With a soft voice and a few winks at her hot Bostonian husband, I soothed the lunatic down by offering her free wine, which cheered her up faster than a free upgrade.

Wednesday
Barbados

Barbados is like going to Heaven but not having to die and spend hours convincing St. Peter to let you in. My room has a hot tub on the patio; I may never leave this island. Do they take American refugees? When the front desk clerk placed the room keys on the counter, I noticed one said ocean view and snatched up that key quicker than Madonna adopts kids from Africa. After Julio, I'm the second senior person on the trip, and I have no problems letting the junior people have undesirable accommodations. I've had my share of shitty rooms.

Besides the fantastic hot tub, my patio overlooks the fabulous resort pool with views of the beach and crystal blue ocean. The hotel offers free snorkeling gear for guests, so I decided to face my fear of ocean creatures this morning and snorkeled around the man-made reef about a hundred feet from shore. I shouldn't say I snorkeled, I waded three feet into the water, saw a fish, and ran back on land where humans belong. I beached myself on the sand for fifteen minutes listening to the palm trees sway in the breeze but felt it was a waste of time. I went up to my room, changed into a new floral button-down shirt, and caught the bus to Bridgetown. It wasn't an actual bus, but a jitney, which is a small privately owned vehicle—in this case, a short bus—that transports people around the island. I missed two jitneys before I realized no big busses were stopping.

After the third jitney pulled up, the driver's window was rolled down, and I asked, "Does this go downtown?"

He yelled, "Get in."

A passenger opened the door, and I climbed into the overcrowded jitney. It reminded me of jumping into a stranger's van on a deserted highway. A stranger with no candy who drives a van that smells like fish and humidity.

Bridgetown has no Rihanna museum, which is disappointing. I did the next best thing, I listened to her music while window shopping and dodging traffic on roads that haven't been maintained since 1865. Barbados is rich with history—George Washington caught smallpox while living on the island—but each historic location reminded me of the horrors that took place here. Almost every exhibit came with a placard telling tourists that slaves had been sold on that spot hundreds of years ago. Downtown Bridgetown was basically a slave-selling outlet mall. I hiked back to the hotel along the beach thinking about the slave industry and all the other terrible things people have done on this planet.

After drinking the free hotel cocktail, I attempted snorkeling again. I swam out further than I had in the morning, but not so far that I deserve any accolades. An infant on their back would have floated farther. Trust me, I tried my hardest. I paddled with my flippers and pushed through the waves with confidence. I fought the urge to retreat while anticipating losing an arm or a leg to a shark. I might as well confess, I couldn't live without all my limbs. I'm a wimp, and I'm not ashamed to admit it. I've read articles about veterans returning home from war with missing limbs, and they're blessed to be alive. Those are special people. It takes an exceptional person to fight for their country, but it takes a superhero to return home with missing body parts.

I kept swimming in the direction of the reef, which was still considerably far away. I figured one hundred feet of water separated me from the ocean floor. I began treading water for a moment and started looking back to see how far I had swum when my feet touched the sandy bottom.

I was in five feet of water.

Standing there embarrassed, I pulled off my mask, looked straight ahead, and came face-to-face with an enormous turtle.

I screamed as if the turtle attacked me. It disappeared and swam away, possibly thinking, *Stupid human. I'm trying to give him a moment, and he screams like Madonna took the stage.*

How the hell would a turtle know about Madonna? They travel far; I'm positive turtles know about everything.

As I walked back to my room, I met up with the other three flight attendants at the pool. Dante was trashed, and it was four P.M. That's better than him being trashed at ten P.M. when our report is at 3:30 A.M. He splashed around the pool like a fool, and I kept thinking, *if he drowns tonight, we'll score another night in Barbados.*

I hope he doesn't drown, but another night in Barbados is another night in Barbados.

The three of them invited me to dinner, but I declined and went for a solo dinner at a bar a few blocks from the hotel. The service was terrible. This place gave zero fucks, and I assume it's been like that for decades because no matter how bad the service was, the patrons continued to pour into the seats.

Back at my room, I stripped naked and enjoyed the hot tub. It felt naughty being exposed on my patio, but also exhilarated, like I had a secret that nobody else in the hotel knew. It was karaoke night at the pool, and while other hotel guests were singing off-key about ten feet below my patio, my balls were floating in hot water. At 8:30 P.M., I crawled out of the hot tub, threw on gym shorts, and climbed into bed. The walls thumped with the sound of a female guest belting out an unpleasant rendition of "Eye of the Tiger." I called the hotel operator, and she connected me to the front desk clerk, who informed me that karaoke ended at nine P.M.

Currently, it's 9:15 P.M. and the awful screeching continues with a man attempting to sing "Total Eclipse of the Heart." It's fair to say I'd prefer swimming with that turtle than listening to this shit. I don't believe Dante drowned, so I need to be up in six hours to fly back to JFK.

I'm wearing my noise-canceling headphones, which should help me fall asleep.

If I miss my alarm, I'm blaming it on Bonnie Tyler.

Thursday
BGI—JFK

At three A.M., I woke to silence and a dry mouth. I reached for my water bottle, but it was empty. I refused to drink from the bathroom sink. I may have put stranger's genitals in my mouth before, but hell if I'm putting foreign water down my throat. It's not Mexico, but I don't trust Flint, Michigan's water, so I'm not taking any chances in Barbados. In the hotel lobby, I asked the front desk clerk for water. She pulled out a plastic cup, walked over to the bar, filled it from the tap, and handed it back to me. I thanked her, but when she turned around, I poured it out in the trash can and walked outside to catch the shuttle to the airport.

When we landed at JFK, an employee from Drug and Alcohol took Dante away to test him. I'll check next week to see if he still has a work email address. I know twenty-somethings bounce back quickly from a night of binge drinking, but Dante was beyond wasted last night. I'd expect his blood type was dark rum.

I zipped through the terminal and ran to another airline to catch my commute. I handed the gate agent cookies, and she gave me a boarding pass with a window seat in the last row. Disappointment set in because I knew there were first class seats available and I didn't want to be stuck in the $49.99 section of the airplane. Listen, I know that I expect my passengers to sit down, fasten their seat belts, and eat their fucking nuts, but I'm talking about my needs right now. My knees locked up, and I started to sweat. I'd have cried, but the flight attendant wasn't around to have pity on me. I refuse to waste decent tears without spectators. As standby passengers, we aren't supposed to expect special treatment, but goddamn it, I wanted a first-class seat.

Before the aircraft door closed, the purser walked to the back and greeted me with a smile, "We received confirmation from your airline to move you to the front of the airplane."

I jumped over the lady in the aisle and practically trampled the purser. He directed me to my seat and handed me a glass of pre-departure champagne. After departure, I downed a few glasses of red wine while eating my braised ribs with polenta and watching *Beauty and The Beast.*

I'm heading west on this 767 and stricken with guilt for how often I complain about this job. I've been remarkably childish. People would do anything to be a flight attendant, and here I've been whining and being ungrateful. My job is a vacation, not a burden. Don't get me wrong, it has its challenges, but all and all, it's a great gig. Yesterday, I was in Barbados for free, and today I'm flying across the country in first class for free. Transferring from LAX to JFK is the best career decision I've made. I sensed myself slipping to the point of frustration where I contemplated quitting. I don't hate my job, I hated my circumstances. I love being a flight attendant; I needed a change of scenery to remind myself that I'm fortunate.

When it was dessert time, I couldn't decide from the two options. The flight attendant said, "I'll bring you both," and a few minutes later, she placed a chocolate sundae and the cheese board on my tray table.

That's the way to end a trip back from Barbados.

THE END

The Deplaning Process

Congratulations! You made it to the end.

That wasn't as bad as you thought. A few of you may not have heeded my warning, made it halfway through the book, and quickly wrote a one-star review online.

I can't win them all.

Take a breath. It's over. You survived the cranky flight attendant and his dirty mouth. Perhaps you learned something you didn't know about the airline industry. Maybe you think I'm a horrible person. Maybe you'll never fly in an airplane again.

I doubt that, but words are powerful.

This is where I'd generally acknowledge everyone who helped make this book a reality, but I'm not doing that. The last time I wrote a book (I'm sure you've already purchased all my other books. If not, I'll keep this brief so you can start getting caught up), I listed people by name. There were a lot of names, and out of all those names, I spelled three wrong.

I was quickly reprimanded by the individuals whose names I misspelled. This time around, nobody is receiving an acknowledgment. I'm not trying to memorize how to spell fifty last names, I can barely finish a complete sentence.

I acknowledge everyone who helped bring this book to life. My family, my friends, my co-workers, strangers I've met along the way, and a special shout out to my husband, Matt, for reading this book before anyone else and giving me his honest opinion.

Wait, one last detail before I go. For privacy concerns, most names and destinations were modified in this book.

THE PAGE WHERE JOE THOMAS BRAGS ABOUT HIMSELF

Joe Thomas is an author, blogger, flight attendant, and creator of the shockingly popular blog *Flight Attendant Joe*. He resides in the San Francisco Bay Area with his husband, Matt, and their two extremely needy cats, Tucker and Harvey.